Italian Cinema

P. ADAMS SITNEY

Vital Crises in Italian Cinema

ICONOGRAPHY, STYLISTICS, POLITICS

University of Texas Press, Austin

Learning Resources
Centre

13737929

Requests for permission to reproduce material from this work should be sent
to Permissions, University of Texas Press, Box 7819, Austin, TX 78713-7819.

∞ The paper used in this publication meets the minimum requirements of
American National Standard for Information Sciences—Permanence of Paper
for Printed Library Materials, ANSI Z39.48-1984.

Library of Congress Cataloging-in-Publication Data

Sitney, P. Adams.
    Vital crises in Italian cinema : iconography, stylistics, politics
/ P. Adams Sitney. — 1st ed.
        p.   cm.
    Includes bibliographical references and index.
    ISBN 0-292-77687-X (alk. paper). — ISBN 0-292-77688-8 (pbk. :
alk. paper)
    1. Motion pictures—Italy—History.   I. Title.
PN1993.5.I88S57   1995
791.43'0945—dc20   94-26979

To Blake, Sky, Augusta, and Miranda
and in memory of Margie

così me si cambiaro in maggior feste
li fiori e le faville, sì ch'io vidi
ambo le corti del ciel manifeste

PARADISO 30

Contents

Preface

This book is quite different in subject and origins from my other writings on film history, for it is neither polemical nor centered on my lifelong association with the American avant-garde cinema and its artists. It is the product of a passion and of the scholarship animated by that passion.

The three crucial films I discuss in the chapter called "Annus Mirabilis" had been fundamental in my formation as a teenage *cinéphile*. So that when I first traveled to Italy, in 1963 as the director of an exposition of American avant-garde films, it was with great anticipation and inevitable disappointment that I glimpsed aspects of that great moment—or "vital crisis," to adapt Pasolini's phrase—as it was waning. Yet it was only as the director of a second such exposition, while visiting Italy several times in 1967 and 1968, that I began to learn the language (which I never mastered) and study the history of that fecund period, realizing that it could not be understood without reference to the florescence of Italian cinema in the years immediately following the Second World War.

My fascination with those phases of Italian film history would not have resulted in a book had I not moved from my positions as Librarian of Anthology Film Archives and Assistant Professor of Cinema Studies at New York University, where I taught mainly avant-garde film or film theory, to Princeton University in 1980, where I had responsibility for the full range of film history. Of the many seminars and courses I presented in my first years there, none so excited me as a course in Italian films attended by four or five loyal and energetic students. Later I had the advantage of coteaching a version of that course with the Renaissance scholar David Quint, who both encouraged me in my work on Italian film and influenced my approach to the subject.

The opportunity of giving an NEH Summer Seminar for College Teachers (which included three native Italians) provided a range of challenges, confirmations, and readjustments of my historical and cinematic interpretations and helped me focus this book on the two phases of its historical span.

I have translated from Italian the titles of films not distributed in English, and I have left the distributed English titles even when inaccurately translated, such as *The Gospel according to St. Matthew*, where Pasolini had deliberately excluded the honorific "Saint." In some rare cases the films were distributed with untranslated titles, such as *La dolce vita* and *L'avventura*. I have not translated them.

In researching and writing this book I have incurred many debts. Joanna Hitchcock enthusiastically encouraged me to submit the manuscript to the University of Texas Press when she assumed its directorship. Georges Borchardt, my agent, and especially Cindy Klein, who patiently handles my account within his agency, have been as usual of great moral and material support. In Italy Guido Aristarco, Lino Miccichè, Adriano Aprà, Dr. Guido Cincotti (of Cineteca nazionale), and above all, Gian Piero Brunetta have been generously helpful to me for years. Much of my viewing and reviewing of films took place at the Cinémathèque Royale de Belgique, often in the company of my beloved friend Jacques Ledoux. Since his death, his generous successors have continued to assist me. My repeated visits to Brussels would not have been possible without the hospitality of my friends Marcel and Gisele Croës. The Princeton University Committee on Research in the Humanities and Social Sciences gave me two grants to visit archives and libraries in Italy and to rent films.

Four anonymous readers submitted reports on two phases of this manuscript to the University of Texas Press. I greatly benefited from each of them, even one that I judged fundamentally hostile to my project. Bob Fullilove, my copy editor, suggested dozens of changes which I incorporated. Gaetana Marrone-Puglia, my colleague at Princeton, carefully went over the manuscript correcting numerous errors and malapropisms in Italian and many a detail. William Weaver graciously gave me his time and expertise, improving my translations virtually every week he came to Princeton in the winter and spring of 1994. If errors survive in the book, they are surely of my own concoction.

Just before I was to hand the edited manuscript in to the publisher, my wife, Marjorie Keller, suddenly died. She would have helped me with editorial suggestions on its final touches just as she had at each of its stages since its inception. For twenty years so much of our life together was quickened by our love of Italy that her spirit sustained the writing of this book, and her death has made the last cosmetic changes very slow and difficult.

It is useless to delude oneself about it: neorealism was not a regeneration; it was only a vital crisis, however excessively optimistic and enthusiastic at the beginning. . . . [I]t is the price for a lack of mature thought, of a complete reorganization of the culture.

—PIER PAOLO PASOLINI, "NOTE ON *LE NOTTI* [*DI CABIRIA*]"

Cinematic neorealism anticipated all the Italian literary neorealism of the Postwar period and the early Fifties; the neodecadent and neoformalist films of Fellini and Antonioni anticipated the renaissance of the Italian neo-avantgarde. . . . All this takes part in the general movement of recuperation, by bourgeois culture, of the terrain lost in the battle with Marxism and its possible revolution.

—PIER PAOLO PASOLINI, "THE 'CINEMA OF POETRY' "

Vital Crises in Italian Cinema

CHAPTER I

Introduction

Twice in the half century since the Second World War, Italian cinema has preeminently commanded international attention. The first period immediately followed the war and lasted, with diminishing intensity, throughout the forties. The second began in the late fifties, acquired its maximum momentum in the early sixties, and started to wane by 1964. The term *neorealism,* despite eluding definition, has stuck to the most powerful films of the first period. There is no comparable blanket term for the films of the later group, although they are all associated with the Italian "economic miracle," the enormous success of industrialization and productivity that transformed much of Italy in the late fifties.

In both periods the cinema reflected what Pier Paolo Pasolini called a "vital crisis" in Italian culture. Pasolini used the phrase to describe the contradictions of neorealism:

It is useless to delude oneself about it: neorealism was not a regeneration; it was only a vital crisis, however excessively optimistic and enthusiastic at the beginning. Thus poetic action outran thought, formal renewal preceded the reorganization of the culture through its vitality (let's not forget the year '45!). Now the sudden withering of neorealism is the necessary fate of an improvised, although necessary, superstructure: it is the price for a lack of mature thought, of a complete reorganization of the culture.[1]

Pasolini uses the noun *crisi* to denote either an outburst or a symptom of abiding cultural turmoil as well as to mean the climax of the contradictions exacerbated by the fall of Fascism. He wrote the previously quoted passage in 1957, when he was thirty-five years old, in an essay accompanying the published script of Fellini's *Le notti di Cabiria*; it was his first essay on a cinematic topic. As a Marxist who had come to maturity during the reign, unbroken since 1945, of the Christian Democratic party (DC), he had learned to see through the rhetoric of Italian rebirth and to analyze the native artistic achievements of his time as manifestations of long-established currents in the national tradition recurring in new combinations. For example, in the same essay, he wrote of *Roma, città aperta* (*Open City*) as "the fictional enlargement of Pascolian language, which was actually a dilation of the self, and an enlargement of the uniquely lexical world; one recovers a populist romanticism, in the mode of De Amicis if you will, which had been preserved in the cultural strata the nationalist rhetoric had buried and tamped down; one even recovered a linguistic elitism, hermetic or decadent in the classical spirit: prefabricated poetry, lyricism projected *a priori* on reality." Thus he saw the new look of Rossellini's film as the cinematic instantiation of stylistic modes current in Italian literature in the late nineteenth and early twentieth centuries.

For Pasolini, the crisis was "vital" insofar as it invigorated powerful films and literary works by redistributing and focusing energies latent in the tradition. Thus, I understand Pasolini to be saying that the events of 1945 were not the radical reformation of the Italian government and rejuvenation of culture that the Christian Democrats would claim them to have been. Rather, they were superficial changes ("improvised superstructure") made to ensure the continuity of power by Italian capitalists working together with the Catholic church, the politicians of the Right, and the U.S. State Department. The remarkable films and novels that coincided with this "crisis," and were crudely subsumed under the banner of neorealism, refracted with "vitality" a tangled nexus of optimistic and critical interpretations of those contemporary events in the formal and rhetorical modes of earlier Italian artistic styles.

By contrast, I believe that, in 1957, when Pasolini published this short analysis of neorealism, he would not have thought of the art or politics of Italy as manifesting "a vital crisis." Fellini's *Le notti di Cabiria* (*The Nights of Cabiria*), for which Pasolini had been a consultant and script collaborator because of his familiarity with the language of prostitutes and pimps, was the last reverberation of neorealist iconography. By 1957 it was also clear that the efforts of the parties of the Left to challenge the DC's conservatism had failed: Khrushchev's revelations about Stalinist terror and the Soviet repressions of revolts in Poland and Hungary the previous year brought the Italian Communist party (PCI) into political and moral disarray. Yet Pasolini could not have known that as he was writing about the culture of 1945 and immediately after, the Italian cinema was on the verge of a dramatic reinvigoration, of which Fellini's next film, *La dolce vita*, would be both the first sign and a major stimulus.

Naturally all the belligerent nations participating in the Second World War experienced a cultural crisis in its wake. It took at least three decades for Germany to begin to recover the prestige it had formerly enjoyed as a producer of films before the rise of Hitler. The major achievements of the French, British, and American cinemas in the late forties tended to remain consistent with the level and quality of production during and preceding the war. But in postwar Italy the cinema experienced, more intensely than that of any of the other belligerents, a critical transformation. Furthermore, the cultural crisis had more extensive ramifications in the cinema than in any other art. One tangible factor in the changes in Italy (and Germany) was the destruction or dismantling of studios and laboratories. Bound up with this crisis, the economic basis of film production was radically constricted and widely confused. The first postwar films of the key directors—Roberto Rossellini, Luchino Visconti, and Vittorio De Sica—were in large measure financed by the filmmakers themselves, out of pocket, on credit, and with whatever investment they could muster.

Moreover, the chronicles of the period describe interlocking circles of collaborators. One group, closely associated with the Communist Resistance, knew each other from working on *Cinema,* the progressive journal of Vittorio Mussolini, the Duce's son. They included Visconti, Michelangelo Antonioni, Gianni Puccini and his brother Massimo Mida (Puccini), Pietro Ingrao, Mario Alicata, and Giuseppe De Santis. From a different orientation Rossellini, who had made some explicitly Fascist films (on which Antonioni, Mida, and De Santis worked with him), was associated with Federico Fellini. De Sica, a stage and film actor since the end of the First World War, had great popularity as a matinée idol throughout the thirties. He began to direct films in 1942; his wartime films included *I bambini ci guardano* (*The Children Are Watching Us*), from a script by Cesare Zavattini, whom he met during a mid-1930s production in which he starred.

The interrelationship of these figures is extensive and complex, as indeed that of directors, writers, and actors is in any national cinema. For instance, the leftist screenwriter Sergio Amidei worked with Puccini on an unrealized project of Visconti's in the late thirties; he wrote the scripts for Rossellini's *Roma, città aperta* and *Paisà* (*Paisan*) with Fellini and others, De Sica's *Sciuscià* (*Shoeshine*) with Zavattini and others, and dropped out of *Ladri di biciclette* (*The Bicycle Thief*) after the initial stages. Technicians and actors, too, circulated through different camps: Massimo Girotti had the lead in a wartime film of Rossellini's and then in Visconti's 1943 *Ossessione,* where the director wanted to cast him with Anna Magnani, but turned to Clara Calamai when Magnani was unavailable. Rossellini, in turn, wanted Calamai for *Roma, città aperta* but ended up with Magnani.

Thus, none of the major filmmakers worked in isolation. The rapidly changing social conditions of the newly constituted democratic state contributed to a unified sense of mission. But at the same time the internal struggle between the political factions that had survived the Resistance movement and the perpetual covert friction between the social, political, and religious institutions inherited from the Fascist state and the fledgling new order generated an atmosphere of radical uncertainty in which the different filmmakers assumed often mutually contradictory positions on the nature of the society Italy was becoming or should become. Furthermore, these positions, even as reflected in successive films by one director, were liable to shift and readjust. In the three chapters I devote to that period, I shall attempt to distinguish among the aesthetic and moral positions of Rossellini, Visconti, and De Sica (and Zavattini) as articulated in the first films they made following the war. Although the Italian cinema, in its strongest instances, has been a director's cinema, the collaboration of De Sica as director and Zavattini as screenwriter requires an exceptional status in this book.

Much of the best film scholarship on this subject in Italy as well as in America and Great Britain has emphasized the continuity between the Italian cinema before and after the war, in a laudable effort at demythologizing the neorealist revolution. If I seem to run against that current here, it is not that I contest that thesis; rather, it is because my emphasis is ultimately more aesthetic than sociological. I come to this project, interrupting a long involvement with modernism and avant-garde cinema, from a meditation on what makes a number of major Italian films so powerful and original. Whatever the continuities between the Italian cinema of the thirties and that of the late forties, there were no films of the prewar period (except Visconti's *Ossessione* and De Sica's *I bambini ci guardano*) on the order of the masterpieces of the later epoch.

When I think about how *Roma, città aperta* (1945), *Paisà* (1946), *Sciuscià* (1946), *La terra trema* (1947), *Ladri di biciclette* (*The Bicycle Thief*, 1948) and *Miracolo a Milano* (*Miracle in Milan*, 1951) must have looked, and indeed continue to look, against the comparative background of the best American films of their years, their striking originality seems even more impressive—1945: *They Were Expendable, Spellbound;* 1946: *The Best Years of Our Lives, The Big Sleep, My Darling Clementine;* 1947: *The Lady from Shanghai, The Naked City, They Live By Night;* 1948: *Rope, Letter from an Unknown Woman, Force of Evil, The Treasure of Sierra Madre, Fort Apache;* 1951: *Strangers on a Train, An American in Paris, A Place in the Sun.* I cite American films in particular because they dominated the Italian screens of the period and were standards of polish and professionalism for both filmmakers and sophisticated viewers. The best British and French films exhibited a parallel degree of studio finish: The Powell-Pressberger films of those years were *I Know Where I'm Going* (1945), *A Matter of Life and Death* (1946), *Black Narcissus* (1947), *The Red Shoes* (1948), and *The Tales of Hoffmann* (1951), while Bresson employed a rich studio texture in *Les Dames du Bois de Boulogne* (*The Ladies of Bois du Boulogne*, 1945) that he would later eschew, and Cocteau used a comparable professional veneer in *La Belle et la bête* (*Beauty and the Beast*, 1946). But even if we compare the few French films that anticipated the theme and form of some of the films I shall discuss, the enduring achievement of the Italians is supported by the comparison. I am thinking of Clément's Resistance film, *La Bataille du rail* (*The Battle of the Railroad*, 1945), and Rouquier's documentary-like examination of farm life, *Farrébique* (1947), both distinguished films, but of a lesser intensity than *Roma, città aperta* or *La terra trema.* Similarly, Cavalcanti's remarkable British omnibus film, *Dead of Night* (1945), is a venerable precursor to the diversity of *Paisà*, which, nevertheless, helps us to appreciate the extraordinary intellectual unity of Rossellini's film. In short, the uniqueness of the Italian works, vis-à-vis other relevant cinemas, lies in their stylistic organization of elements of apparent rawness, their emotional intensity, and their focus on current political and social problems.

The international situation was quite different when the release of *La dolce vita* (1959) initiated the renewed preeminence of Italian filmmaking. The previous year the French *nouvelle vague* had announced itself with *A bout de souffle* (*Breathless*), *Hiroshima, mon amour* (*Hiroshima, My Love*), *Les Quatres Cents coups* (*The 400 Blows*), and *Les Cousins* (*The Cousins*). Throughout the early sixties, myths of rejuvenation—generally the fusion of a few original films with a great outpouring of polemical optimism from new journals—surrounded the cinemas of Great Britain, Poland, and Sweden, as well as the New American Cinema. All were driven by a shared sense of liberating changes in the norms of narrative and technique. Furthermore, the European film festivals of the previous decade had exposed filmgoers to the cinemas of Asia and Latin America, while an international network of film museums nurtured a serious interest in film history. Perhaps the largest single factor in the international transformation of cinematic style and the concomitant interest in film form had been the success of television; it captured a large segment of the film audience by usurping as many of cinema's functions as it could; filmmakers and producers responded in part by exploring options unavailable to television. One such response was the limited exploration of narrative complexities previously restricted to literature and avant-garde cinema.

How was the Italian situation different from that of the rest of the Western world at the end of the 1950s? Gian Piero Brunetta pointed out that the principal figures of 1960 had been the protagonists of the postwar transformation. The leading money-makers among Italian productions that year were films by Fellini, Visconti, De Sica—*La ciociara* (*Two Women*)—and by Luigi Comencini—*Tutti a casa* (*Everybody Home!*). Rossellini had made his Resistance drama, *Il generale Delle Rovere*, (*General Delle Rovere*), the year before and was "now, after a decade of silence, unexpectedly 'reborn' and ready to lead the Italian cinema to recovery."[2] Antonioni's name must be included with those above as another figure from the postwar development coming to maturity in the early sixties, although his films did not achieve the economic success of some of his colleagues. But it was also a time when a new generation of filmmakers were commanding attention by the ambitiousness of their initial efforts. That generation included Pasolini, Rosi, Olmi, Bertolucci, and the Tavianis, all of whom made their first feature films between 1958 and 1962.

The social and political situation was once again animated by grave anxiety and strange optimistic signs: after fifteen years of DC dominance gradually moving to the Right, there were both persistent rumors of a military coup d'état and signs of an imminent inclusion of the moderate Left in the government. The election of a new pope, John XXIII, in 1958 brought a surprising shift of style to the papacy and hopes of radical changes in the Catholic church. But the most significant factor in Italian life was the unprecedented strength of the economy, especially in the industrial zone, which brought with it a massive shift of the population from the country to the cities, from the South to the North.

Thus, in the period I have designated as the second "vital crisis" all of the long-stagnant institutions of Italian public life were experiencing significant transformations. Amid hiccups of right-wing extremism, the DC was shifting toward a rapprochement with the non-Communist Left; the Church had initiated its historic readjustment to the twentieth century; the agrarian South provided cheap labor (along with major social problems) for the industrial North. As membership in the PCI dramatically declined, electoral support somewhat increased: intellectuals and youth in general voted Communist in protest against the DC, but they asserted a new critical independence.

I cannot offer a formula for predicting patterns of strength or vitality in national cinemas. Certainly political crises and economic booms do not of themselves incubate moments of cinematic magnificence. West Germany experienced an even more dramatic reorganization of political institutions and an equally powerful revival of its economy during the years of my study of Italian films, but its cinema did not flourish until the seventies, after a decade of building preliminary institutions and polemical positions. But there, as in Italy, a concentration of talent stimulated by a new mode of economic support enabled such a florescence to occur. In Italy at the end of the Second World War poverty and the destruction of the studios inspired a variant on production that entailed minimal salaries or none at all and work with nonprofessionals. Rossellini, Visconti, and De Sica more or less financed their first postwar films themselves. Even when industrial production recommenced, the most ambitious films were made on reduced budgets, some radically so. Conversely, after 1959 the enormous success of La dolce vita encouraged investment in films out of the entertainment mainstream made by the veterans of the postwar cinema, while a new generation of filmmakers benefited from the growth of small production companies financed by the profits of the economic boom. In fact, Fellini himself started such a company to support newcomers. Yet another factor in the intensification of achievement within a national cinema is stimulation brought on by the consciousness of a collective historical project; mutual rivalries and a shared pool of distinguished cinematographers, editors, and composers reinforce the vitality of these periods.

I shall read six films from the first period and nine from the second in sometimes microscopic detail. My first task will be to provide American readers with topical and contextual material hitherto scattered or unavailable. Secondly, I shall try to take account of the genesis of each of the films I discuss. In a few cases that entails a comparison to their literary sources, but none of the films except *Miracolo a Milano* are, strictly speaking, literary adaptations—*La terra trema* has a complex relationship to Verga's *I Malavoglia* (*The House by the Medlar Tree*), as is well known and widely discussed, while the relationship of *Ladri di biciclette* is so tenuous to Bartolini's novella that very little has yet been written about it. For the most part, I want to call at least passing attention to analogous works of fiction, or other relevant texts that situate the films in Italian literary history, for the two half decades which are the epicenters of my book have been periods of remarkable literary activity as well. Often the most impressive novels of the period evidence very similar themes and refract the same historical issues as the films.

In 1967 Italo Calvino surveyed his literary production during these periods in this way:

> In the years 1945–50 the aim was to write novels for a shelf that was essentially political, or historical-political, to address a reader principally interested in the culture of politics and in contemporary history but whose literary "needs" (or deficiencies) it also seemed eager to fulfill. Set up this way, the operation was bound to fail. . . .
>
> In literature the writer is now aware of a bookshelf on which pride of place is held by the disciplines capable of breaking down the fact of literature into its primary elements and motivations, the disciplines of analysis and philosophy. . . . Literature must presuppose a public that is more cultured, and *more cultured than the writer himself.*[3]

Often the major films of the sixties also presuppose a very sophisticated viewer, aware of a wide range of Italian culture and of the monuments of

Italian cinema from the postwar period. In such films, baroque allusions to Dante can overlap references to *Miracolo a Milano* in a single episode.

Whenever possible I have been guided by critical discussions from the given period in linking writers and filmmakers or highlighting debates cogent to both arts. I also make liberal use of contemporary reviews from both popular and specialized intellectual journals to understand the ways in which these films were perceived by their sophisticated contemporaries. This is more than mere antiquarian scholarship, because cinema was regarded as especially integral to Italian high culture at both these periods. Thus Cesare Pavese could name De Sica as the chief "narrator" of postwar Italy; or Umberto Eco would later cite Antonioni as an exemplar of "the open work."

The films on which I concentrate are, for the most part, the canonical works of postwar Italian cinema that have already attracted the greatest amount of commentary. These are the films which have sustained my enthusiasm over many years of teaching and reviewing; they are of such magnitude that critics continually return to explore their complexities and resonances. In the course of writing this book I have come to focus on three interrelated aspects of them: the ways in which they refer, directly or obliquely, to the social and political issues of the moment of their creation, their relationship to contemporary currents in Italian literature, and their elaboration of a traditional iconography to which they actively contribute.

In order that I might dwell on individual films at length, some decisions of exclusion were necessary. The first, and most essential, was to limit my investigation to the two primary periods, thereby excluding the major wartime productions and the films of most of the fifties. But even here I had to make something of an exception, for I felt a discussion of *Miracolo a Milano* was necessary to my understanding of De Sica and Zavattini and to the iconographical theme of this book as a whole. I have furthermore confined my study to films depicting contemporary Italy. Thus, Visconti's *Il gattopardo (The Leopard)*, Rossellini's *Francesco, giullare di Dio (The Little Flowers of St. Francis)*, and Pasolini's *Il Vangelo secondo Matteo (The Gospel according to St. Matthew)*, for example, fall outside the historical schema, while Rossellini's *Germania, anno zero (Germany, Year Zero)* or Rosi's *I magliari (The Fabric Scamers)* take place outside its geography. Yet the distinction is not so rigid that Rosi's *Salvatore Giuliano* is omitted, for I take its historical reconstructions to be functions of its examination of a contemporary political scandal.

Some of the background information I present on the contexts and production of individual films reiterates what can be found in the general histories of Italian cinema. In this regard we have been particularly lucky in having Peter Bondanella's *Italian Cinema* and Mira Liehm's *Passion and Defiance* in the past decade. But books of their comprehensive scope cannot hope to include the detail I devote to fewer than twenty films. Other facts I shall bring to bear in my readings may sometimes be found in such critical studies as Millicent Marcus's *Italian Film in the Light of Neorealism* or in such studies of individual filmmakers as Peter Brunette's *Roberto Rossellini*, Peter Bondanella's work on Fellini, Naomi Greene's *Pier Paolo Pasolini*, Seymour Chapman's *Antonioni; or, The Surface of the World*, or Sam Rodhie's *Antonioni*, to name a few of the most useful recent books on this unusually well explored terrain.

Fine as the English language scholarship on Italian cinema has been, it owes a great deal to the work done in Italy that is perhaps the richest lode of film studies in the world today. Gian Piero Brunetta's two-volume *Storia del cinema italiano* seems to me the most impressive work of film history of my generation. Lino Miccichè's *Visconti e il neorealismo* and Gianni Rondolino's massive volumes *Visconti* and *Rossellini* are models of research and criticism. They are backed by an outpouring of annotated scripts, writings by filmmakers, monographs, and the proceedings of scholarly conferences that has distinguished Italian film publication for decades. Naturally, much of the background and contextual material I present can be traced to these books or to the Italian sources we share. Yet I hope I have made some contribution to that growing area of research.

Reading Pasolini and seeing his first films shaped my understanding of Italian film history. His application of the stylistic studies of Leo Spitzer to cinema, his recognition of continuity between filmic iconography and that of the history of painting (which he studied under Roberto Longhi), and his locating a context for ambitious cinema in contemporary literary phenomena anticipated and has influenced all my scholarship for at least twenty years; that is to say, Pasolini's critical and theoretical work had left its traces on my writing about non-Italian subjects long before I came to work on this book.

To introduce both my subject and my mode of analysis, I shall now turn to a film that Pasolini made a few years after the closure of the second period of my study. As an elegy to the great achievements of Italian cinema between 1945 and 1964, it offers a number of valuable insights into the works I shall look at in detail and into their historical contexts. I shall conclude my book with another film that falls on the far border of my chosen period, Michelangelo Antonioni's *Il deserto rosso* (1964). The advantage of time, and of Pasolini's historical consciousness, makes his *Uccellacci e uccellini* (1966) the more appropriate introductory topic: it surveys the confluence of Christian and Resistance iconography, plays with the questions of dialect and a national language, and illustrates the ways in which cinematic effects can be used for political allegory. These issues will be particularly significant in my first three chapters, which analyze works by Rossellini, Visconti, and De Sica and Zavattini. On the other hand, Antonioni intuited and exemplified a change in the political relevance of Italian cinema in *Il deserto rosso* (*The Red Desert*), but he did not make that change the theme of his work. Certainly, the parameters of that change were not as clear to him in 1964 as they were to Pasolini in 1966. In fact, in his theoretical and critical writings of the time he was making *Uccellacci e uccellini* (*Hawks and Sparrows*), Pasolini cited Antonioni's film as a central example of a new style, as I shall show in the Conclusion. By framing my broadly chronological analyses between these two films, I hope to delineate the stylistic and iconographical similarities and differences of the major films of the two "vital crises."

Throughout this book I stress the iconography of Italian cinema. That is to say, I concentrate on the meaningful images and image-types that tend to recur in the films I discuss. By far the largest pool of such iconographic images have their sources in the painterly tradition of Italy. The conventional visual code of the Church prescribed the representation of Christ and the narrative events of the Gospels, distinguished the saints by metonymic signs (often the instruments of their martyrdom), and symbolized virtues and vices. The churches, civic buildings, monuments, and the decorations of even the humblest homes in Italy continue to employ versions of this code. Italian poetry, especially Dante and the Renaissance epics, accumulates a vast treasury of iconographic images. Thus iconographical representation so permeates Italian life that it is not surprising to find it central to the native cinema.

One of the postwar Italian cinema's primary gestures of opposition to the Church has been in reimagining and parodying its icons. Rossellini, De Sica, and Pasolini, the three filmmakers among those I discuss who were the most ambivalent about the Church, tend to use its iconography most explicitly. For example, there seems to be a critical consensus that the shot of the dying Communist in *Roma, città aperta,* with his head bloodied and arms outstretched, invokes Christ on the Cross. A more controversial attribution would be to see in the sign "Partigiano" attached to the floating corpse of *Paisà* a variation on the cryptogram "INRI" attached to the Cross. The magical dove of *Miracolo a Milano* is a version of the Holy Ghost, while the brand name of the bicycle in *Ladri di biciclette,* "Fides," identifies it as a symbolical instrument, much as the labels in medieval paintings identify symbols. (In a later film, *Umberto D,* De Sica uses the convention of Fides, the dog, as a similar element in his allegorical pattern.)

Visconti, Antonioni, and Rosi have less use for Christian iconography. Yet Visconti concentrates on formal family portraits as vehicles of a nearly sacred aura, while Antonioni emphasizes the uncanniness of images and sights that have lost their conventional significance, creating a void which he fills with psychoanalytical meaning. It is symptomatic of the iconographic tendency in Italian films that when Visconti encountered what appears to have been a technical problem in showing a television set in operation in *Rocco e i suoi fratelli (Rocco and His Brothers),* he substituted the projection of a series of iconic images from the Renaissance for the cathode scan. Rosi drew on the often sensational photojournalism of the Giuliano affair as an iconographical fund.

It has been argued that the cinema itself is essentially iconographic. In fact, I understand that to be the point of Stanley Cavell's discussion in "Types; Cycles as Genres" in *The World Viewed.* Although Cavell dwells on the iconography of character types—the Villain, the Dandy, the Woman, the Military Man, and so on—one could see the props and settings of genre films as iconographic signs: the vampire film displays stakes, coffins, fangs; the Western uses the saloon, the brothel, the bank, even the barber shop as iconographic loci, as well as the horse, the stagecoach, and the pistol. Even the running shoes, microwave oven, German automobile, and framed museum poster can be seen as iconographic indications of Yuppie life in contemporary American films. In short, the designer who coordinates sets, props, and costumes might as well be called the iconographer. Such was certainly Visconti's role in his meticulous attention to details, especially in his re-creations of nineteenth-century scenes.

Perhaps iconography becomes a critical issue only when we are in danger of forgetting the meaning of the images. Over the thirty to fifty years since the films I discuss here were made, some of the topical and traditional associations of their images have begun to fade. This loss is vastly magnified by the distant optic of American criticism. Therefore, the best writers on this cinema have been the Italians themselves, and in America the elucidations of the professors of Italian language and literature have led the film specialists.

Finally, the interlocking of iconographical meanings constitutes an allegory. So it is a consequence of my focus on iconic images that I tend to read many of the films allegorically. Yet, although only *Miracolo a Milano* and *Uccellacci e uccellini* could be called allegories in the strict sense of the term, this tendency of mine is often abetted by structural coordinates of the films: the paratactic, episodic organization of *Paisà* or *La dolce vita* and the emblematic protagonists and simplified narratives of the De Sica, Pasolini, and Olmi films I have selected lend themselves to such interpretations, just as the narrative complexity and individualized psychology of some of the better Hollywood films from the same periods (e.g., *The Lady from Shanghai* or *Psycho*) resist them. Even when one compares a rather complex narrative film such as *La terra trema* to its novelistic source, Verga's *I Malavoglia*, it is evident that the adaptation and linearization of the narrative serves its transformation into a political allegory, roughly on the model of the Soviet films of the revolutionary period, when the iconic and allegorical mode predominated.

The causes for the allegorical disposition of Italian films from these periods of "vital crisis" are twofold. On the one hand, the allegorical and the iconic traditions are intertwined; the national poetic and fine arts education of the filmmakers, and of their audience, predisposed them to that mode. Then the consciousness, on the other hand, that they were not merely making entertainment but articulating the contradictions and agonies of national life in momentous times gave added weight to allegory's emphasis on spiritual and moral meaning.

Angus Fletcher, meditating on Walter Benjamin's conjunction of allegory and mourning, writes: "Allegory is always in conflict with itself, as it attempts to 'mourn' for some lost central governing moment which can never be entirely collected, but cannot (in allegory) be fully given over to oblivion."[4] To a remarkable degree the films on which I concentrate mourn the loss or the impossibility of an imaginary Italy where, in the concluding words of *Miracolo a Milano*, "*buon giorno* really means *buon giorno*"—that is to say, a nation of peasant values, Christian humility, meaningful labor, communal fraternity, and above all, the idealized nuclear family. When one or more of these elements are preserved in a film, it is to underline the loss of another—as, for example, the loving nuclear family in *Ladri di biciclette* makes the loss of meaningful work more poignant. In Antonioni's *L'eclisse* (*Eclipse*), where all of these ideals are characteristically absent, the heroine defines her painful freedom as a lack of "nostalgia for marriage."

I understand Pasolini to be mourning such a loss when he writes of neorealism's rhetoric as "the price for a lack of mature thought, of a complete reorganization of the culture." The truth that no other major cinema in the Western world emerges out of a complete reorganization of the culture hardly matters, because elsewhere that lack has not been a haunting problem.

Uccellacci e uccellini

It is often the case that filmmakers are the most insightful historians and critics of their métier. But there are very few individual films that demonstrate this as effectively as *Uccellacci e uccellini*, Pasolini's last black-and-white film, an elegiac essay on the sociology and iconography of neorealism. Therefore, I shall begin my scrutiny of films from the end point of the historical span I have selected, using as my introduction what I can interpret of Pasolini's embedded insights into Italian cinema from the end of the war to the death, in 1964, of Palmiro Togliatti, who headed the Italian Communist party since the fall of Mussolini. While cataloguing the stylistic achievements of the Italian cinema of the fifties, *Uccellacci e uccellini* pointed to the historical changes which made that cinema no longer viable. From the very opening the eccentricity of the film—its allegorical status— announces itself: the credits are sung, in comic rhymes, on the sound track in a style reminiscent of Brecht and Weill. This, too, was an elegiac gesture, since, as the talking crow in the film announces, the author admits: "The era of Rossellini and Brecht is over." For Pasolini this film was a palinode both to his vain hope of revitalizing cinematic neorealism and to his didactic communism.

Since Pasolini was the first to recognize, at least implicitly, that neorealism was fundamentally a system of iconography, let us begin by identifying the "intrinsic content" of the opening shots:[5] an aging man and an adolescent walk along a long flat road. The widescreen ratio and the compositional centrality of the road emphasize its virtual infinity and its isolation in the flat landscape. A quotation from Mao gives that road a figurative status. I mention the screen ratio at the start because even this element will become thematic later in the film, when the author intercuts newsreel footage of an "older," more nearly square ratio. It is not long before we learn that these figures are father and son. As picaresque figures they are the heirs of Chaplin and Coogan, from *The Kid,* and as Italians they echo obliquely "the bicycle thief," Ricci, and his son, Bruno, who prowled the streets of Rome in De Sica's film of 1948. As in *The Kid* in 1921, the father is played by a well-known comedian, Totò, the star of dozens of films since 1936. In fact, no other Italian actor could as convincingly and automatically represent the continuity of the national cinema as Totò. Like Coogan, and the principal of *Ladri di biciclette,* the son is an amateur: Ninetto Davoli, whom Pasolini had used for a minor role in *Il Vangelo secondo Matteo* (1964) and whom he would employ repeatedly throughout his career. Of course, the presence of the unrecognized actor is as central to the stylistics of Rossellini, Visconti, and De Sica in their postwar films as the icon of the child on the threshold of manhood.

Looking at Totò, in particular at his hat, an Italian would recognize a Neapolitan. As do all lonely roads in Italy, the road on which we find them distantly situates them "Nel mezzo del cammin" on a Dantean journey. But Totò's emphatic delimitation of the destination of their trip as "laggiù" ("down there") concretizes the universal allusion. Much of the road is desolate, without a single car, because they walk along sections of the *autostrada* (highway) under construction. They are its first and last pedestrians. The very construction of the highway, which will make travel between Italian cities a matter of speedy efficiency and which points to the possession of cars by all classes of Italian society, is the first iconographic sign of the transformation of the landscape of Italian films of the previous twenty years.

Totò speaks of the phases of the moon and passes on to his son the traditional lore of the best conditions for fishing. Eventually we shall learn of the transformation of the moon, from lore to the mythos of modern science; but before that, they are joined by a talking crow, who seems to know that such lore is meaningless to the young man, who is about to leave the family farm to work as a Fiat laborer. This, too, is a sign of the changes in Italy since the era of Rossellini and Brecht. For most of the film, the triune presence of the father, son, and bird constitutes a twisted variant on the most traditional of iconographies, that of the Holy Trinity. In *Mi-*

racolo a Milano (1951) De Sica had gently mocked Catholic theology by making a magical dove the agent of his Totò's powers. The blackness of Pasolini's bird, as a negation of the pure white of the Santo Spirito, yet imbedded within the Trinitarian schema, reflects the tension between the Marxist doctrines the crow spouts and the political position of the postwar Church, which Rossellini, among others, sought to reconcile in his films between 1945 and 1954. The allegorical progress of the whole film reflects a historical and quasi-dialectical dissolution of the uneasy relationship between the PCI and the Church. As Pasolini sees it, they have both outgrown and outlived the positions they represented in the two decades since the Liberation.

A rich poetic tradition links the dove as a symbol for the Paraclete to secular romanticism. In his magisterial philological study, *Classical and Christian Ideas of World Harmony: Prolegomena to an Interpretation of the Word "Stimmung"* (1944–1945/1963), and more summarily in "*Explication de Texte* Applied to Walt Whitman's Poem 'Out of the Cradle Endlessly Rocking' " (1949), Leo Spitzer had written on the phases of the symbol's transformation. Doubtless Pasolini was familiar with Spitzer's abstruse work. By the mid-1950s Spitzer's work had a tremendous vogue in Italy.[6] In René Wellek's estimation the translation of two collections of his essays, in 1954 and 1959, "all but founded a Spitzer cult in Italy." The filmmaker made frequent references to Spitzer's writings in his own essays, and in addition, I shall show in my Conclusion how the philologist's study of Verga (*Belfagor*, 1956) strongly influenced Pasolini's film theory.

Of course, the fusion of stylistics and philology with special attention to Romance dialects and neologisms, which characterizes all of Spitzer's work, would have appealed to a writer who began his career with a study of his native Friulian. It would be an exaggeration, but not a flagrant error, to say that Spitzer's book on "*Stimmung*" is the source of *Uccellacci e uccellini*. There he writes of the "Christian poetics of kaleidoscopic transformations of symbols," and touches on an issue central to the aesthetics of the film: "Synesthetic apperception always bears witness to the idea of world harmony . . . : all senses converge into one harmonious feeling."[7] There is an intimate connection between the imagery of the film and the principle of synchronization, which I shall eventually unpack here.

Just as Pasolini uses the iconography of neorealism to declare the death of neorealism, he turns Spitzer's scholarship into an elegy. The final scenes of the film, shot just out of sight of Rome's airport, suggest that the spiritual authority birds had once symbolized cannot be sustained in a landscape in which the passenger airplane is taken for granted. A correlative exists in the very "comedy" of historical representation in cinema, which I must treat in detail when I discuss the bracketed story of the catechism of the birds, again invoking Spitzer's book.

Even before Totò and Ninetto encounter the professorial crow, two episodes occur which deserve our attention. Taking the second first, we find an extension of the bird theme. Father and son have wandered into a suburban town, still in part under construction, for working-class families, where even the streets are named as if they were headlines to local-color articles of the cheap tabloid journalism practiced by the protagonist of Fellini's *La dolce vita*. Totò joins a crowd of rubberneckers standing before a house in which some unspecified lurid "tragedy" has occurred. Ninetto slips away from this group to see a beautiful young girl, dressed as an angel ("for the Feast of the Daughters of Mary"). Viewers familiar with *Il Vangelo secondo Matteo* will immediately recognize her as the actress who played the Angel of the Holy Spirit in that film, even though she wore no wings then. Ninetto greets her with the jest "You look like an airplane," innocently anticipating the final manifestation of the avian motif in the film. This encounter culminates in one of the film's most hauntingly beautiful sequences in which the girl-angel "ascends" by appearing in successively higher windows of a house under construction, making an obscene gesture from the highest, and Ninetto seems to fly as he runs and leaps back in slow motion to where his father shares in the public vigil for bodies now moved into an ambulance. The scenario makes explicit the symbolical connection between the white costume of the angel and the suits and sheets of the ambulance squad.

Throughout the film the reflection on the Italian cinema of the previous two decades coincides with a thematization of the principles of filmmaking as such, especially the relationship of sound to picture. From the socially determined ritual of silence before the scene of private "tragedy," recalling the chorus of rubberneckers who gathered around the Steiner's apartment in *La dolce vita* as soon as the police arrived on the scene of the suicide and murders, the film moves fluidly to a suppression of the sound track (described in the script as "a silence of dreams") and eventually to the replacement of speech by music. Pasolini takes pains to illustrate the independence of the visual and sound tracks, suggesting that the synchronization typical of sound narratives is merely a special case which has become a dominating convention. The major works of Rossellini, Visconti, and De Sica always employed dramatic music to underline emotional moments and to inculcate suspense. The self-consciousness of Pasolini's use of music—here as in his earlier films—can even be correlated to Spitzer's discussion of the Christian ideology of "harmony."[8]

The earlier scene, which I momentarily passed over, illustrates another dimension of Spitzer's argument: dance as "a means of proclaiming, by imitation, the harmony of the world."[9] Father and son had stopped into an isolated bus station to have a drink at the bar. There Ninetto slipped away—as he was to do in the subsequent scene—from his father, who was making a series of comically seductive grimaces at the woman behind the bar. Ninetto left in order to watch, first, and then to join the group of young men practicing a dance step as they waited for the bus. A jukebox provided the music. This episode foregrounds the "languages" of body and facial gestures in cinematic iconography.

As a writer who has turned filmmaker, Pasolini was intensely conscious of the complementary function of gesture to speech in the filmic image. Both of his principal actors are notable for their bodily presences. Totò's gestural vocabulary is a burlesque of socially conditioned poses of authority, humility, piety, and coquettishness. Ninetto plays against this system (as the comic teams of silent cinema often did, e.g., Laurel and Hardy), both imitating it and retaining a large measure of spontaneity, as though *his* gestural exuberance had not yet congealed into a rigid codification. Later, the parable of the hawks and sparrows, which occupies the center of the film, will underline the fact that body as well as voice constitute a linguistic system. When we come to focus on that episode, we shall see just how important Ninetto's spontaneity is for Totò's deciphering of one of the avian languages.

In this respect one would like to know more about Pasolini's reaction to Rossellini's bald inscription of exaggerated homosexual gesturing in *Roma, città aperta,* where the director had not scrupled to marshal a popular aversion to sexual deviation to reinforce his representation of Nazi evil. From the implicit testimony of Pasolini's subsequent films, we might say without overstepping the limits of credibility that this too is a factor in the declaration, "The age of Rossellini and Brecht is finished."

Enter the talking crow. The preparatory episodes have made us aware of the independence of the picture and sound. So the illusion of a bird that speaks Emilian Italian is a "natural" consequence of the process of filmmaking, and especially of the Italian preference for postproduction dubbing of all voices. I shall cite a long passage from Spitzer's condensation of the *Stimmung* book in his essay on Whitman:

> The thirteenth-century Spanish poet Gonzalo de Berceo goes so far as to portray learned birds that serve as preachers of religious orthodoxy. Church fathers and prophets of the Old Testament, Augustine, Saint Gregory, and Isaiah, are presented as nightingales in an earthly paradise competing under the dictation of the Virgin Mary. A one-man concert is Saint Francis' famous canticle: "Altissimo, onnipotente, bon signore,/ tue so le laude, la gloria e l'onore e onne benedizione." This minstrel of God, feeling that one human being alone would not be worthy of praising the Lord, brings into his poem all creatures which may testify with him to the greatness of the Creator:
>
>> "Messer lo frate Sole" (the Lord my brother Sun), my brother the wind, my sister the water, my sister the earth—and my sister Death.
>
> According to legend, the last stanza was added by Saint Francis on the day of his death. The Saint does not mention his brother the bird, but we remember the painting of Giotto in which Francis is depicted as preaching to the birds.[10]

Spitzer's bird catalogue goes on to include Eichendorf, Baudelaire, Arnold, Shelley, and Keats. When we note that Pasolini first published a synopsis of this section of the film as "Le Corbeau" in the Communist journal *Vie nuove,* we must add Poe and his French apologists.

The orthodoxy that Pasolini's crow preaches is political rather than religious. He identifies himself as a citizen of "Ideology, living in its capital, the City of the Future, on via Carlo Marx at number one thousand and not another thousand." Ultimately Pasolini cut most of the crow's long speeches from the film and, in a last-minute decision, made him the narrator of the episode of the "hawks and sparrows."

Originally the film was to have had three parts. Pasolini entirely discarded the first, in which Totò was the director and animal trainer of the "Grand Cirque de France" visiting Rome, and Ninetto was his assistant. In this episode Totò tries to train an eagle to talk and to become a television announcer. Although he fails, the scenario indicates that Pasolini filmed a scene in which Totò listens in French to the aspirations of his trained crocodile (to be a scholar in Brussels), his chimpanzee (a hairdresser in Lille), his python (a clothing designer in Paris), his hyena (a Roman journalist), and his camel (a professor of European culture "from Marx to Levi-Strauss" in Ghana). In the course of his efforts to educate the eagle, which include reading aloud passages from Pascal and Rimbaud, Totò himself becomes birdlike and, in the final shots, flies away, above Rome's Aquiline hill. The catechism of the birds was to have been the second autonomous episode, and the encounter with the talking crow the third.

The final construction of the film adds irony to the charming parable of a mission to the birds, for the preaching crow becomes the narrator of an illustration of the failure of preaching and sets in motion his own destruction. Furthermore, the filmmaker carefully located the long interior story at the point in the episodic adventures of Totò and Ninetto where it would most effectively underline the incidents before and after it. This organizational decision permitted him to remove some of the crow's didactic reflections on his experiences with the "pilgrims."

The entire Franciscan episode is, of course, an homage to the Rossellini film Pasolini loved best, *Francesco, giullare di Dio* (1950). In his own revisionist version, Saint Francis commissions Totò to learn the languages of hawks and sparrows so that he can evangelize the birds. Brother Cicillo's (Totò's) triumphant mastery of the hawks' language reverses, cinematographically, the simple technique which made the crow seem to speak Italian: the filmmaker synchronized the chirping of birds with the movements of the actor's lips. With equal brilliance, he "translated" the catechismic indoctrination through questions and answers, edited in shot-countershot, by subtitling the film in Italian at this point. The fun continues when the haughty hawks rush to the premature and heretical conclusion that they are gods and when, later, the hungry sparrows interpret the "good news" of God's salvation as the promise of immediate mullet, and so find it hard to understand Brother Cicillo's Franciscan doctrine of holy abstinence.

However, before Brother Cicillo can proceed from the instruction of the hawks to that of the sparrows, he must abandon the notion that all birds communicate by speech. Only an inspiration can bring him to this insight, but his spiritual exercises are hampered by the commercialization of the site of his initial "miracle." This comic interlude is a parody of the grimmer exploitation of a Marian vision in Fellini's *La dolce vita*.

Once the entrepreneurs are routed, Brother Cicillo repeats his efforts at learning the birds' language. His initial failure is even more frustrating than it had been with the hawks until an accidental sight provides him with the clue he needs. Brother Ninetto, bored with the continual prayer and meditation which has been producing no results, begs and wins permission to play hopscotch. As Cicillo notices his rigidly prescribed hopping within the confines of the game, he suddenly realizes that the sparrows communicate through their hopping motions, not by their chirps. This time he grotesquely hops around, intercut with the hopping of the little birds, as the Italian subtitles tell us what they are "saying."

Thus, the two different "languages" of the birds correspond to the distinction between verbal and imagistic sign systems in Pasolini's published essays on the cinema. In fact, the entire quest of Brother Cicillo to master the discourse of the birds matches Pasolini's vision of the filmmaker in search of and establishing the languages of *im-segni* (image-signs) in his most famous essay in film theory, "The 'Cinema of Poetry'" (which he published, appropriately, as a preface to the script of *Uccellacci e uccellini*).

The most radical revision of Rossellini's portrait of the early Franciscans in Pasolini's film is their failure, for although Brother Cicillo manages to break the codes of both species of birds, and evangelizes them within the limits of their experience, he despairs over the instinctual killing of sparrows by hawks even after his preaching. Francis himself, in the most ironic quotation of the film, urges Cicillo and Ninetto to continue their good work, promising a time when a man will come instituting justice. The words of this future man often strike listeners unaware of the quotation as dicta from Marx or Lenin. Pasolini counted on this mistake and relished it.[11] They are, in fact, from a speech of Pope Paul VI to the United Nations. Rossellini's early films fused elements of Roman Catholicism and the Left and glimpsed optimistically a postwar union of these forces in Italian politics and morality. In *Uccellacci e uccellini* Pasolini looks back, after the Second Vatican Council, from the perspective of a lapsed Catholic at the historical naiveté of Rossellini's hopes. By the time that the Catholic church came to speak with the rhetoric of Marxism, the economic, moral, and social conditions of Italy were different in ways that could hardly have been imagined in the late forties. The quotation from the then new pope was another signal of the end of the era of Rossellini and Brecht, and the conditions which made the postwar films of Rossellini, Visconti, and De Sica viable.

In his theoretical writings Pasolini repeatedly pointed to the dangers implied by the emergence of a new national "language," inflected by technocratic and managerial jargon, which was effacing the regional and class differences of the older range of Italian speech habits without ameliorating the social problems they had reflected. In one of the eliminated dialogues the crow seems to be speaking of Pasolini himself when he fails to convince the pilgrims of the danger of a homogenized language:

> They got together some statistics and found this rule, that "those who speak the same way consume the same way," thus everyone talking the same way will dress alike, will go around in cars all alike and so on. . . . I know a man who weeps for this, who says this means the end of mankind and who says that if the workers do not take back in their fists the red banners, then nothing can be done . . . because they are the only ones who can give some soul to things.[12]

The spirits of Rossellini and Brecht permeate the whole film but are particularly evident in the fable of the hawks and sparrows and the episode following it. Pasolini's application of Brechtian ideas is formal rather than iconographical: he underscores the allegorical dimension of his film with ironical title cards, subtitles, a mime within the film, and the repeated variations on the independence of sound and image. The first incident the crow witnesses pays homage to the Florentine episode of *Paisà* (which film may have been one model for the overall episodic structure of the film). Rossellini, probably driven by budget constrictions, had evoked the terror of the battle between the Resistance and the Fascists of Florence almost entirely with the offscreen sounds of sporadic gunfire: the protagonists of the episode scramble through the emptied Uffizi Gallery and across deserted piazzas in their effort to reach a part of the city that had been cut off by the fighting. In his parody Pasolini hyperbolically couples the familiar sounds of a Hollywood-style war film—aerial strafing, machine-gun fire, and so on—with images of Totò and Ninetto ducking imaginary bullets.

The scene begins with a play on the notions of privacy and property, when the pair temporarily enter someone's "private property" to relieve themselves in the hedges. As they talk to each other, as if in the adjacent stalls of a lavatory, they describe how they experience a pseudo-

Leopardian moment of aloneness with the visible morning moon. But even that invocation of Italian romanticism is complicated by Totò's allusion to Yury Gagarin and his (invisible) orbiting between earth and moon. The Soviet scientific achievement, and the anticipation of an eventual moon landing, are yet other signs of the transformation of traditional iconography.

The sudden arrival of the property owner with a gun initiates a belligerent state of affairs which Totò cannot smooth over. Within minutes it escalates into the Brechtian parody of a war film. The script calls for a speech from the crow on nonviolent opposition, which Pasolini cut from the film. Instead he put this section just after the parable, a modern "flower of Saint Francis," in the crow's voice. By shifting the construction of the film around, he made what had initially been the second section into a demonstration of paradoxes of pacifism, which made the brief discourse on Gandhi superfluous.

After the conclusion of the "private property" episode, the trio of father, son, and bird encounter a Fellinian troupe of actors, the "Spettacoli volanti" (The Flying Shows). The Spettacoli volanti demonstrate the language of gesture and historical iconography with the mime "How Rome Ruined the World." Before departing in their rickety Cadillac, they sell Totò an ointment for his sore feet, which turns out to be contraceptive jelly. The father of eighteen children, including Ninetto, he is barely capable of understanding the function of this chemical "salve," which is yet another element in the transformation of modern Italy in Pasolini's catalogue.

The relationship of music to filmic images merges thematically in the subsequent interrelated episodes. Totò descends on an impoverished family, apparently his tenants, and threatens them with eviction for failure to pay their rent. Then he himself is humiliated by the "Ingegnere," apparently his landlord, when he cannot pay him. The former scene is accompanied by pseudo-Chinese music, which reinforces the absurd image of the starving mother boiling a bird's nest for her husband's meal. This comic allusion to the exploitation and misunderstanding of the Third World helps to clarify the strange road markers seen in other parts of the film noting the kilometers to Istanbul and Cuba. Rather than indicate spatial distances they point to the fact that the changes in the European economy had led to the replacement of southern Italians by Turks as the exploited alien work force of Germany and industrial Europe and that the success of Marxism in Latin America had disturbed the centrality of Moscow for the Italian left.

In opposition to the "Chinese" poverty stands the affluence of the Ingegnere, who is hosting the Convegno dei Dentisti Dantisti in his home. The Dantean Dentists take their name from a hackneyed Italian joke. In Pasolini's variation it marks the superficiality of those who continue to assert the primacy of Florentine pronunciation as "correct" Italian. We should keep in mind at this time that Pasolini had written poems in his native Friulian and edited an anthology of poems in dialect. To underline the scene's allusion to Steiner's grotesque intellectual salon in *La dolce vita,* the butler greeting Ninetto and Totò at the door parodies the gesture of Mrs. Steiner. The dentists themselves are played by prominent Italian intellectuals and, typically, are found gossiping about an English intellectual who had written "Bloody Underpants at Scotland Yard." After a private interview with the Ingegnere, the protagonists pass the intellectuals again. But this time Professor Baldini stands before his rapt admirers waving his arms as if he were a conductor and they were his orchestra. Off-screen, the music of Wagner seems to emerge from his silent direction. This playful manipulation of the independence of image and sound tracks has a historical pedigree in the postwar Italian cinema: in *Miracolo a Milano* one of the magical tricks the character Totò plays on the attacking police is to turn their orders into grand opera: a dubbed sound track allows the substitution of song for speech.

Within the interview another transformation of natural sounds puts the roars of lions in the mouths of the host's German shepherds, suggesting that Totò and Ninetto are the sacrificial victims in the Coliseum and connecting this scene with the mime of the Spettacoli volanti. Yet Naomi Greene rightly stresses that by "accepting the system as it stands, they are links in a chain of oppressed and oppressor" and that, in fact, Pasolini felt "that the humble people were destroyed, turned into 'horrible petit-bourgeois' by the merciless growth of media and consumer capitalism."[13]

Not the lessons of the crow but the harshness of the Ingegnere effects Ninetto's immature political education. He tells his father that the crow is a good Christian after all, and declares that as soon as the first strike begins in the factory where he is about to go to work, he will invade the Ingegnere's villa and kill all his dogs. Totò joins him in miming and making the noise of a submachine gun. But just as they are enacting this audiovisual fantasy, Pasolini intercuts portions of a newsreel. The change of screen ratio is startling. He cuts back to Ninetto and Totò to reinforce the illusion that they have suddenly encountered a massive crowd in a solemn ceremony before we see enough of it to realize that it is Palmiro Togliatti's funeral.

The longish documentary interlude, accompanied by Bach's *Saint John's Passion,* concentrates on the masses of both stoic and tearful supporters of the longtime leader of the PCI. Their gestures reflect in symbolical form the contractions within Italian life: they raise the clenched fist of Party solidarity or make the sign of the Cross as the funeral procession passes. In the script Pasolini described this material poetically:

> Our story gets lost this way; it almost cancels itself, in these sequences of images, in this immense funeral like a war or a universal judgment.

> Three, four, five minutes: a story within the story. But a story made of documentary reality and of mysterious poetry: politics and death, united in a solemn, serious, endless violence.[14]

However, the careful placing of this documentary within the story raises the issue of a different mode of violence. Ninetto's fantasy of a purely symbolical act of terrorism runs counter to Togliatti's politics. It forecasts the future orgy of terrorism in which youths of Ninetto's age, who did not experience Fascism or the Resistance, would repudiate the PCI. The funereal gestures of the crowd at Togliatti's funeral echo the mime "How Rome Ruined the World." For there we saw a woman, who played the role of a primitive Christian, praying and making the sign of the Cross, when Nero, crowned with laurel like the Dentisti Dantisti, and holding a lyre, condemned her with the gesture of turning his thumb down. The association of the Ingegnere's dogs with lions completed the allusion and carried the theme into the episode that separated the Spettacoli volanti from Togliatti's funeral.

In the final encounter on the road, the moon becomes flesh in the person of the prostitute Luna. Wittily, Pasolini situated her on the highway between Rome and its airport, thereby acknowledging the transformation of prostitution from the legalized houses, which can be seen in *Ladri di biciclette,* to the streets near the Aquedotto Felice, where cars are liable to pass (as in *Le notti di Cabiria, Accattone,* and *Mamma Roma*), to this imaginary location for men on the way to and from the airport. As an element of the iconography of modern Italian cinema, the prostitute's presence near the airport confirms the inscription of her iconographic status into the future-oriented landscape of the Italian economic miracle.

First Totò, and then Ninetto fake a sudden attack of dysentery in order to dive into the field and crawl to her. This erotic farce calls to mind the old, and dying, Italian custom of fathers taking their adolescent sons to a brothel, where they both could find relief from the repressions of the traditional erotic code. The airplanes and the weather balloons in the background of this episode mark the final transformation of the bird motif. It was not the actual achievement of human flight but the economic accessibility of airplane travel to the Italian population at large that marked the desanctification of the winged creature.

In the final moments of the film Totò dramatizes this desanctification and dialectical subsuming of the bird, by grabbing and cooking the crow. As they disappear down the road in the final shot, Totò and Ninetto are just where they began, but they have consumed (and presumably will defecate) Togliattian communism and have interiorized the iconography of the modern Italian cinema.

Of course, Pasolini's emphasis on Togliatti's funeral falsely pinpoints a moment in Italian cultural history to stand for a transformation that had been taking place through most of the early sixties. But he was not alone among Italian filmmakers in recognizing its symbolical power. Vittorio Taviani called the iconography of Togliatti's funeral "the common patrimony of a certain moment." At first he and his brother, Paolo, were "disconcerted" by the release of *Uccellacci e uccellini,* because they were editing *Sovversivi (Subversives)* at the time.[15] Their film intercut the stories of six Communists, each facing personal crises, on the day of the funeral of the longtime Party leader. The Tavianis had wanted Pasolini himself to play one of them, the filmmaker Ludovico, but he felt the role was too close to his life to accept it. Pier Marco De Santi pointed out that when the fictional Ludovico, in *Sovversivi,* attends Togliatti's funeral his eye falls on Cesare Zavattini:

> A closeup frames him in profile, against a black background. Black glasses, black pullover, with imposing baldness, the father of neorealism is the only artist we see, in the whole film beside the coffin of one of the "fathers" of

Italian communism. Thus, the death of Togliatti signals, in a way, the death of neorealism, or vice versa.[16]

One might also say that the very fact that an image of a living film artist could be used iconographically more than anything else represents the closure of the period of cinematographic history described in this book.

Thus, Togliatti's return to Italy in 1945 from his long Soviet exile and his death on 21 August 1964 neatly frames the two historical high points of Italian cinema that are the foci of this book. Iconographically, in Pasolini's film the image of Togliatti stands for Italy from the Resistance and Liberation through the economic miracle. This entails the memory of his absolute and heroic struggle against Fascism, the guarded optimism he had during the first National Committee of Liberation (CLN) governments, the electoral defeat of 1948 (coupled with an unsuccessful assassination attempt which further heroicized his stature), and his long and difficult opposition to De Gasperi and his successors, as the nation grew progressively richer. The very gestures of the mourners reflect the parallelism between Catholic faith and Party solidarity that animates many of the finest films of this period. This is particularly true of Rossellini's first two postwar films.

CHAPTER 2

Rossellini's Resistance

Less than two weeks after the Allied invasion of Sicily and the bombing of Rome, the essentially Fascist Gran Consiglio gave a vote of no confidence to Mussolini. The next morning, 25 July 1943, he was arrested by the newly appointed government of General Badoglio and imprisoned on the island of Ponza, from which the Germans rescued him in September, just a few days after Badoglio reached an agreement with the Allies for Italy to become a cobelligerent on their side. The Germans used Mussolini to set up the Fascist Republic of Salò in northern Italy, while General Kesselring occupied most of the peninsula with German troops deployed as far south as Naples to face the Allies.

These events generated a coaliton of long-standing anti-Fascists, young patriots who would resist the occupation of Italy, and figures from all sides of the political arena who saw the time had come for a transformed nation. Their National Committee of Liberation included brigades of Communists, Socialists (PSI), and the Action party (Partito d'Azione, a radicalized movement for liberal democracy led by Ferruccio Parri, who would later serve as the first postwar prime minister from June to November 1945), cooperating with right-wing Liberals and the Catholics of the newly formed Christian Democratic party.

Most of the central leaders of the parties of the CLN took central posts in the Badoglio government. These same men of the Resistance remained the dominant figures of Italian political life, even after the United

Front government splintered at the end of 1945 under pressure from both Churchill and Truman and the DC (along with the minor parties of the Center and Right) took firm hold of the new republic and held it for twenty years. Palmiro Togliatti returned from his exile in Moscow in March 1944 to lead the Communist party. Pietro Nenni, the Socialist leader, continued to be his chief opposition on the Left. Vatican librarian, Alcide De Gasperi, led the DC and would remain prime minister from the fall of Parri until 1953. The paradigmatic example of the continuing legacy of the Resistance and of Italian political longevity would have to be Giulio Andreotti, who is prime minister as I write, and who filled that position in 1972–1973 and 1978–1979. He was a leader of the DC youth movement during the Resistance and reappeared in the 1950s as the undersecretary of entertainment who tried to suppress the exportation of neorealist films as damaging to the international image of Italy.

The success of the CLN was met with extreme and bloody reprisals by the Germans and the Fascists of Salò. Perhaps as many as a third of the more than one hundred thousand Resistance fighters died in the conflict. Thousands more were wounded and tortured. Even after the Germans were driven out of Italy, many more Italians died as the partisans attempted to settle scores with collaborators and Fascists.

The major literary representations of the occupation and the Resistance did not appear until 1947 (Elio Vittorini's *Uomini e no* [1945] is the exception): Italo Calvino's *Il sentiero dei nidi di ragno* (*The Path to the Nest of Spiders*, 1947), Cesare Pavese's *La casa in collina* (*The House on the Hill*, 1947) and *La luna e i falò* (*The Moon and the Bonfires*, 1950), and Renata Viganò's *L'Agnese va a morire* (*Agnese Goes to Die*, 1949).

Yet in 1945 and 1946 at least seven feature films depicted the Resistance movement and the Liberation. In the order of their release they were: *Roma, città aperta* (directed by Roberto Rossellini), *Due lettere anonime* (*Two Anonymous Letters*, Mario Camerini), *O' sole mio* (Giacomo Gentilomo), *Un giorno nella vita* (*A Day in the Life*, Alessandro Blasetti), *Paisà* (Roberto Rossellini), *Il sole sorge ancora* (*The Sun Rises Again*, Aldo Vergano), *Pian delle stelle* (*Level of the Stars*, Giorgio Ferroni), and *Vivere in pace* (*To Live in Peace*, Luigi Zampa). Of these only the two Rossellini films have attained a canonical status in Italian and international film history.

Roma, città aperta

Roma, città aperta was not only the first film after the war to represent the crecent Italian past; it was, unlike all the Resistance films in its wake, a great commercial success as well. Nearly all sides of the political spectrum acclaimed it. In *Il Popolo,* the Christian Democratic organ, Carlo Trabucco wrote:

> Of the two parts, the first, in which no single protagonist dominates the action, but Rome, the whole city, which lives and trembles, suffers and conspires, resists and exalts itself, this first part is truly choral and is representative of the whole population whose hidden and unknown merits have been well recorded with an objectivity lacking in rhetoric.[1]

In the Communist daily *L'Unità,* Umberto Barbaro extolled the film, as Alberto Moravia did in *La Nuova Europa.* The former recognized Eugen Dollmann in the figure of Hartmann, the SS Standartenführer, and Pietro Caruso in the unnamed Italian police chief. Moravia, like Trabucco, identified the figure of Don Morosini, a priest executed for helping the Resistance, behind the fictional Don Pietro. The professional journal *Star* even named the two elderly women who appear in the opening sequence, the inhabitants of the house where the Communist Manfredi had been hiding, as Signora Riccieri and her maid Nannina at Piazza di Spagna 51, where the Communist leaders Alicata and Ingrao proofread the galleys of *L'Unità* and Palmiro Togliatti stayed as soon as he returned to Rome. Barbaro echoed Trabucco's expression "priva di retorica" in his praise of the film's re-creation of recent history:

> The life of a working-class tenement and their unanimous feeling of hatred toward the nazi-fascisti, the abominable house in the Via Tasso [where the Gestapo tortured those suspected of aiding the Resistance] with all of its filthy and wretched undercurrents, the backstage of corruption and treachery, the squalor of the city streets in the nights of curfew and arrests, the tortures, the crimes, the ghastly figures of Caruso and Dollmann, all this is remembered with an objectivity *lacking in rhetoric* and with an implicit political judgment, that is judicious and fair, so that the film undoubtedly deserves the praise of all honest men.[2]

The lack of rhetoric, praised in the film, had been lavished on the reviews.

The concept of "coralità," first used by Trabucco, has subsequently become a commonplace in the criticism of the film.[3] It was also used by Alberto Vecchietti in his dissenting review three days later in the Socialist newspaper *Avanti!* In one of the most critical treatments of the film, Vecchietti focused on a taunt in the film delivered by the Gestapo chief Bergmann to his victim, Manfredi, that his capitalist allies in the anti-Fascist movement will soon be his enemies.

> From this sentence come the most serious criticisms to be leveled against Rossellini's film. A revolutionary, considered in the absolute sense, had every reason to seize the opportunity of ridding the country of its so-called authorities, turning them over en masse to the invader. An enlightened response dictated it. A response that honestly would have clarified the new spirit which, promoted by the ethos of the Committee of Liberation, animated that revolutionary at that moment. However, the protagonist of the film remains silent. And together with him the film is silent about many other problems, which it no less vividly raises nevertheless. Therefore, are we confronted with a choral film (the drama of the historic city once again invaded by barbarians)? Or a Catholic film (would everything have a special meaning under the great shadow and the great light that Saint Peter's casts over Rome)? Or, on the other hand, does it particularly try to express the spontaneous spirit of the people working under oppression (for this is what the children make one think of with their heroism)? In other words, it does not seem to us that the film knows how to develop its theme . . .[4]

The most interesting American response to *Roma, città aperta* was refracted through the perspective of political partisanship. The novelist James T. Farrell, writing as he regularly did in the Trotskyist monthly *The New International,* argued that Manfredi is a "Stalinist functionary" inflated to heroic status:

> This is precisely the kind of myth the Stalinists want people to swallow. Furthermore, Manfredi is thus established as the major hero of *Open City.* The priest is subordinated to him. While it is true, therefore, that the film embodies a content of collaborationism between the Communist Party and

the Church, this content has a special as well as a general feature, and it is with this special feature that this analysis is concerned. Omissions that establish the Stalinist myth give credence in turn to Catholic myths. The Church as represented by Don Pietro is presented in a benevolent light only.[5]

By stressing Manfredi's personal heroism and leaving his ideas in obscurity,

> [a]rt is given a practical function. This function is not performed by a simple and obtuse didactic emphasis, but rather with the aid of tendentious characterization, tendentious organization of plot, a tendentiousness in details. This tendentiousness serves, further, the purpose of distorting and concealing the politics of a political movie.[6]

Today, forty-five years after Farrell's review, Rossellini seems to have been anything but a calculating propagandist for the PCI. In fact, he was the DC representative for the film workers in the CLN. I quoted from Farrell's vigorous misreading of the film in part because it focuses so intently on its political message, but even more so because it elicited a highly sophisticated response from the art historian Meyer Schapiro, which in many ways prefigures my analysis of the film and to a degree the critical method of this book at large.

I shall quote from Schapiro's response at length:

> [The] collaboration with the Church constitutes, in my opinion, a basic theme of the film. It is carried through in many details and even assumes the pattern of a familiar Christian legend. In the conclusion, always vital for the effect of a film or play, the two martyrs, Pietro and Manfredi, recall the martyrdoms of Peter and Paul in Rome. Like Paul, Manfredi is the energetic, uncompromising apostle, who engaged in world propaganda for the new religion; like Paul he began as a persecutor of the church, and like Paul he dies under another name, a more Christian one than his original one. The priest, Pietro, has made out for him a fake passport as Giovanni Episcopo (Bishop), and it is under this suggestive name (borne also by a character of d'Annunzio) that the Gestapo register his martyr's death. I may be permitted in this context to carry the mythical pattern further and observe that just as Saint Peter was crucified upside down, so the priest Pietro is shot from behind. . . .

. . . The sacraments appear as flexible instruments at the disposal of human wants, rather than as magical rites administered under fixed conditions. The priest hears Pina's confession while she accompanies him on the street when he is on a mission of the Resistance, as one human being with another. The rite of extreme unction is acted out as a ruse to deceive the Gestapo and to save Romoletto whose bomb might be discovered by the enemy searching the house. . . . The audience is given the feeling that the church is tolerant, human, warm, adaptable, superior to dogma and rite. . . .

. . . The religious woman, Pina, the real heroine, is not only a believer, but conforms to the church teaching about manners and dress. If she has been living in sin, that is because of the unsettled war conditions; she is about to be married in the church. Opposed to her is the mistress of the Communist Manfredi and ultimately his betrayer through a German spy, Ingrid. The latter, a sinister figure, resembles in her features and action the cruel females of Beardsley and the literature of the 1890s, the vampire or Salome of that period. She is a Lesbian and a hater of men. Her political role issues from a psychological deformity. . . . Similarly, her Gestapo chief is a homosexual animated by a cold vanity and sadism. . . . The polarity: German-Italian, is stronger, more decisive than the differences among Italians.

. . . There were many who sincerely believed that the unity of the Resistance would be maintained after the war, even if under CP leadership. In the film the preponderance of Pina and the priest, humanely, dramatically and artistically, is such that I supposed at first that the whole was the work of men closer to the people and the priest, somewhat in Silone's sense, than to Stalinism, although certain touches suggested a Stalinist hand.[7]

Schapiro recognized, as no Italian critic of the time seems to have done, the degree to which the Italian cinema, at least as exemplified by *Roma, città aperta*, reflects and recasts the iconographic tradition of Renaissance art. Perhaps those associations were so obvious that the native critics did not count them worthy of mention, or perhaps they were so deeply and universally interiorized that they went without conscious notice. Throughout this book I shall examine the iconographic dimensions of some major Italian films, fusing that critical perspective to a discussion of topical and historical keys, such as the Italian critics pointed out.

A discussion of the topical allusion can lead to a clarification of political nuances, the lack of which misled Farrell and to some extent Schapiro. For example, before *Roma, città aperta* had been conceived, that is, as early as the summer of 1944, filmmaker Giuseppe De Santis prepared a script for a film to be entitled *G.A.P.* (the acronym of the Gruppi di Azione Patriottica, the small urban bands of the CLN) with the collaboration of a number of Communist partisans, including Antonello Trombadori, Franco Calamandrei, and Gianni Puccini. One of the episodes would have depicted the death of Maria Teresa Gullace, a pregnant woman with five children, who was killed by a German soldier in front of the barracks where her husband had been rounded up and was awaiting deportation to a work camp; before a large crowd of women, she had approached a window of the barracks and had thrown her husband a packet of food.[8] For this, she was killed. The GAP made an immediate reprisal: two Fascist guards were shot at the barracks, and three trucks were blown up.[9] Furthermore, according to Maria Michi, who played Marina Mari (Manfredi's mistress who ultimately betrays him for drugs), the scriptwriter Sergio Amidei was responsible for the film's narrative, which he adapted from the experiences told to him by Communist partisans, including Togliatti and Celeste Negarville.[10]

Yet *Roma, città aperta* had its genesis in another political direction: Rossellini had been commissioned to make a documentary about Don Giuseppe Morosini, a former military chaplain who came to Rome in July 1943. Working for the partisan band "Mosconi," he stole plans of the German deployment at Monte Cassino and smuggled them to the Allies. After he was denounced for a reward and arrested, he worked with political prisoners and Jews in the Regina Coeli jail until his execution at Forte Bravella just outside of Rome on 4 March 1944. Rossellini incorporated a detail of the execution in his film: either from insufficient bullets or because the firing squad deliberately missed, he was not shot until a Fascist official put two bullets in his head.[11]

When De Santis abandoned *G.A.P.*, he went to work with Mario Serandrei on the documentary *Giorni di gloria (Days of Glory)*, which was released a month after *Roma, città aperta,* in the fall of 1945. In essence Rossellini took over aspects of his fictional re-creation of the Resistance, while De Santis and his Communist collaborators concentrated their efforts on a film of fact that recorded the trial and executions of Pietro Caruso and Piero Koch, the head of the Pensione Jaccarino torture chamber, and re-created through montage the most dramatic GAP action in Rome—

the explosion of a bomb in the Via Rasella which killed thirty-three Germans. In retaliation the SS shot 335 prisoners, half of them Jews, and sealed the bodies in a cave on the Via Ardeatine. Luchino Visconti, who had been among Koch's victims, both testified against him and directed the shooting of the trial. Director Marcello Pagliero constructed the montage of the Ardeatine Caves massacre. This same Pagliero played the Communist Manfredi in Rossellini's film.

Rossellini combined what he "inherited" from De Santis's project with the Don Morosini commission. Just as he retained enough of the story of Gullace in the character of Pina to keep the topical allusion pertinent, he based the figure of Manfredi on that of a known Resistance hero. Roy Armes records that the model was Celeste Negarville.[12] Negarville was a Communist from Turin, who was arrested in Bologna in 1927 and condemned to twelve years in prison for political crimes. But in 1934 he was released in an amnesty celebrating ten years of Fascist rule. He slipped into France and ran the Paris office of the PCI for a year before going to Moscow to serve in the presidium of the International of Young Communists. Between 1938 and 1943 he settled in France. He got back into Italy in January 1943 and was elected the PCI representative to the military command of the CLN. By the time Rossellini made *Roma, città aperta*, Negarville was the editor of *L'Unità* and the undersecretary of state in Parri's cabinet.[13]

Rossellini and Amidei kept close enough to Negarville's story to make it recognizable, but they gave it a melodramatic twist. When Bergmann and the unnamed figure for Caruso disclose the biography of Manfredi, a pseudonym for Luigi Ferrara (Negarville's underground code name was Gino Ferri), they date his birth and arrest in Bologna a year later, in each case, than Negarville's; but more significantly, the pardon becomes an escape, and in the film he is caught and tortured to death by Bergmann's henchmen.

Roma, città aperta was a low-budget production, the timely expression of a historical moment in which studio polish could not have been purchased even if Rossellini and his associates were not struggling for the barest means of completing the film. Furthermore, it is a commonplace of criticism that these impoverished means lent the film a look of authenticity. Without disputing these truths, I want to elaborate how a series of very bold directorial strokes enhanced the power of this quite straightforward, even simple film.[14] The first was sound. The entire film had to be synchronized after the shooting was completed. This permitted Rossellini to develop a "realistic" approach to dialogue: the Italians spoke their native language, while the Germans, when speaking to each other, spoke theirs. Yet the consequences of this choice were both structural and political. To understand that as such, we must see the uniqueness of the representation of Germans in this film and comprehend the political motivation behind that uniqueness.

The film effectively propagandizes for Italian unity at a time when many felt the necessity of a purge of all those who had cooperated with the Fascists. But Rossellini's Germans monopolize villainy. The Italian Fascist sergeant looks the other way when hungry women raid a bakery;[15] later, he abets the priest Don Pietro in his cover-up of the children's Resistance group when the Germans raid the apartment house where Pina and Francesco have been hiding Manfredi. A comic type of the well-intentioned but feeble policeman, the sergeant represents the Fascist police as the object of amusement rather than revenge. The police commissioner, the closest collaborator with the German SS, has no ingratiating features. Still, the overweight, balding bureaucrat becomes a figure of pathos when he silently endures Bergmann's scorn for Italians. We see him only in Bergmann's company, where he plays the foil to foreground his counterpart's maliciousness, conducting offscreen the research that reveals Manfredi's real identity.

By concentrating all of the evil in the Germans, Rossellini discovers a safely distant scapegoat that could play no role in the political situation of 1945. One index of his realism is the incorporation of German language. This alienates them from the Italian viewer, who had to read the subtitles to know what they were saying, as if "behind their backs."

To further alienate the Gestapo, he portrayed the two most visible figures as stereotyped homosexuals. Rossellini cast Harry Fiest, a ballet dancer, as Bergmann, directing his gestures to suggest a "stage queen." The cries and the blood of his tortured victims offend him aesthetically; the monotonous repetition of such torture, he calls "boring." Although we never see him displaying sexual desire, his elegant, butch agent, Ingrid, seems a parody of Marlene Dietrich in an explicitly lesbian role. She repeatedly caresses Marina, Manfredi's girlfriend, whom she seduces with drugs and furs. It is suggested that she had been the original source of Marina's now hopeless addiction.

A third German, the heterosexual, aristocratic officer, Hartmann, acknowledges in his cups the failure of the idea of the master race. Even he cannot calmly execute Don Pietro in the final scene of the film. But here we see him outdoors in the harsher light which the filmmaker has implicitly portioned off as the theater of reality. Although an Italian finished off the execution of the historical Morosini and an Italian betrayed him to the Gestapo for seventy thousand lire, the fictional representation reimagines these events to stress the Germanization of evil in the film.

For the most part, we encounter the Germans indoors, in interrogation headquarters, where the music of a piano cannot cover up the cries of prisoners' screams. It is the remarkable achievement of Rossellini's film to disguise this melodramatic morality drama and political allegory as realism. One of the conditions for our acceptance of the stagey German behavior is their difference from the Italians.

Sounds and suggestive shots of instruments and burners effectively concentrate the scenes of torture. The cries which can be heard in Bergmann's office through opening doors whenever his aide enters or leaves heighten the cruelty of his hyperstylized mannerisms and suggest, because they leave so much to our imagination, an arena of pain surrounding the cramped theater of Nazi posturing. Thus the economic limitations of a makeshift soundstage (where the headquarters was constructed), and the inadequacy of sound mixing, forced Rossellini into a situation where his invention triumphed: the well-timed punctuation of torture sounds distracts us from the trite cinematic conventions of the headquarters dialogues, but more profoundly, they create a context in which the very staginess of the German scenes can be absorbed into a rhetoric of realism.

The myth that Italian neorealist cinema originated with the making of *Roma, città aperta* ultimately testifies to the power if not the uniqueness of Roberto Rossellini's film, since in stylistic and even political terms it continues the prewar work of Rossellini and other Italian filmmakers, as Brunette elaborates in his study on the filmmaker and James Hay argues more generally in *Popular Film Culture in Fascist Italy*. Its production benefited from a near accident of exquisite timing: as the first serious film from liberated Italy, it attracted international attention as a morality drama of the purging of Fascism. Rossellini's apparent ambivalence about the political options for a renewed Italian state may actually have strengthened the film by taking it out of the sphere of the conflicting ideologies of the Italian liberation movement. In the domain of electoral politics a homologous ambivalence, taking the form of a desire for an utterly new political framework, manifested itself in the brief success of the Action party; that is not to say that *Roma, città aperta* directly reflects the platform of the Action party, but merely that both the film and the party were charged with the energy of an optimistic vision of a Center-Left consensus that would steer clear of the threats both of revolution and of a return to a modified form of Fascism.

Naturally, the auditory inventiveness does not function exclusively in portraying the Germans. The band of children who imitate Resistance fighters speak Roman dialect. The Resistance song they whistle at the end of the film, witnessing Don Pietro's execution, in a field on the outskirts of the city, balances the German song heard at the very opening of the film when soldiers march at dawn through the Piazza di Spagna searching for Manfredi. His presence is introduced by another sound: the illegal BBC news on the radio in the apartment where he hides. The auditory richness of the film is underlined by the effective if conventional score of Renzo Rossellini, the director's brother.

Angela Dalle Vacche, who argues in *The Body in the Mirror* that a dialectic of opera and commedia dell'arte animates the image of the body in major Italian cinema, identifies Rossellini's work with the latter:

> In contrast to the marble heroes of fascist cinema, the body in Rossellini's neorealism is the human organism inhabited by the antithesis of sheer biology, the soul, as if a Christian spirituality had developed next to a pagan attachment to the earth. In representing the impact of official history on daily life and anonymous people, neorealism adopted the microscopic scale of the commedia dell'arte and turned away from the monumental setting of opera.[16]

The dialectic between opera and commedia dell'arte actually operates within the film in contrasting the heroic fates of the protagonists with what Dalle Vacche calls "daily life and anonymous people." The heritage of commedia dell'arte is exemplified in the second brilliantly simple ploy Rossellini used: representing the Italians as comic figures. Rossellini avoided the caricature latent in an opposition of evil Germans and benign Italians, by deflecting the axis of polarity to humorless and ultimately ineffective Germans against funny and good-humored Italians whose bumbling heroism succeeds.

The old ladies who harbored Manfredi, panicking and crossing themselves when the Nazis arrive, the bedridden grandfather in Pina's house who is fixed on the idea of eating wedding cake, the gently hypocritical sexton who receives stolen bread, and the sergeant I've already mentioned provide a comic chorus. Closer to the emotional center of the film is the youthful gang of Resistance-minded boys under the leadership of the crippled Romoletto. These boys can blow up a German truck, but they are afraid to face their parents for coming home late. Finally, at the very core of the film there are two splendid comedians, the clown Aldo Fabrizi who plays Don Pietro, and Anna Magnani, a film actress better known as a cabaret performer, whose Pina is one of the great performances in modern Italian cinema. Don Pietro, stock comedy's sissy priest in his daily activities, shows unlimited bravery when needed. But first we see him awkwardly playing soccer with his schoolboys, taking a shot off the head accidentally. His is a mixture of an inept fat man and a sexual naive: when he has to make a pickup of money for the Resistance, he reports to a knickknack shop. As he waits he notices a statue of Saint Rocco placed on a counter so that his eyes seem to peer at the bust of a naked Venus. Don Pietro chastely turns the Venus statue around, only to realize he has exposed the buttocks of the goddess to the plaster saint.

His comic performance par excellence occurs when he rushes to Pina's apartment building, under the guise of performing an extreme unction, to cover up Romoletto's guns. First he makes a Chaplinesque save of a grenade which he had knocked off the table by catching a rifle with his cassock. The timing is exquisite and pure slapstick, including a bug-eyed catch of the bomb. Then, to top this, he has to knock out the old grandfather with a pan because the old man, misunderstanding the emergency, won't play dead. As a finishing touch he revived him with a comically heavy dousing of holy water from his aspergillum.

Pina is an earthy, pugnacious, loud Roman woman of the proletariat who will melt instantly into a figure of maternal and uxorious generosity when a Resistance fighter or a priest approaches. Just as quickly she can harden scornfully toward a Fascist or erupt with slaps when her son comes home late. Rather than projecting an instability of character in this way, she suggests a center of self-confidence with such a wealth of love and justice that the viewer identifies with her gestures and recognizes their appropriateness. Even the German soldier, a Teutonic troglodyte of cartoon dimensions who paws her when the apartment is emptied for inspection, acquiesces to her moral authority.

The romantic leads in this film, Manfredi and Marina, the beautiful friend of Pina's inane sister, do not come from the stock of comedy, but they play diminished roles. Pina and Don Pietro dominate the film. Pina's fiancé, Francesco, whose name reflects his gentleness, is not a comedian either, but he is fully drawn into the high-spirited world of Pina's family, where he plays the peacemaker and father figure to her son by a now deceased father.

The humorlessness, perversity, and even lugubriousness of the Germans—the chief torturer resembles a Hollywood version of Frankenstein's monster—set off in relief the comic spectrum of Romans. Propagandistically, the comic vision, insofar as it emphasizes the humanistic ground of a tendency to error and solicits our tolerance of it, deflates the evil of native Fascism, as if the goodness of a Pina and a Don Pietro could redeem the weakness of the comic Fascists. The difference in tone between the representation of Italians and Germans prevents that comically induced good will from encompassing all the figures of the film and thus diluting and confusing the political message.

While Rossellini uses comic figures and comic skits, his film is by no means a comedy. This can be seen most clearly in his use of irony, which is consistently tragic. At the very climax of the film's most comic moment—the priest's clever diffusion of the raid on the apartment—Pina is murdered. Her death is triply ironical. In the first place, none of the suffering depicted in *Roma, città aperta* need have occurred. The title names a place, Roma, and a time, the period of the German occupation of the city after General Kesselring concurred with the Vatican that the city would not be a battleground; the open city would be abandoned by the Germans as soon as the American troops arrived. All of Bergmann's efforts were in the name of a lost cause, as he admits in the film. Secondly, the imitation Resistance of Romoletto's gang drew the attention of the Gestapo to the apartment house. Their bombing of a truck played no strategic function; it was an undisciplined act, without the sanction of the highly organized Resistance movement. Finally and most important, had Pina not recklessly chased after Francesco as he was carted away on a truck, she would not have died, and she would have been able to celebrate her wedding to him that day; for the organized Resistance succeeded in ambushing the prisoner trucks in the very next scene, freeing all those rounded up. Of course, she could not have known this. Instead she ran after the departing truck, only to be shot in the middle of the street before the eyes of her neighbors, the priest, and her son. The scene is the most dramatic montage of the film, intercutting shots of the moving truck, the running woman, and the witnesses. In a very reduced way it is the Odessa Steps of *Roma, città aperta.*

Even this melodramatic scene was inspired by a comic incident that occurred during the shooting of the film, according to scenarist Sergio Amidei. After a night's shooting, Magnani had an argument with a male friend. He ran to a film production truck, which took off as she chased him down the street bellowing obscene curses. Magnani's temperamental explosion, the material of comedy, became something very different when translated in the film.

Nothing prepares us for Pina's sudden death. After it, all comedy ends. The last act of the film describes the deaths of Manfredi and Don Pietro at the hands of the Gestapo. A further irony spares Francesco once again. Marcello, Pina's son, detains him for a moment to give him a scarf as a memento of his mother. During that time the Gestapo pick up Don Pietro and Manfredi. Francesco would have been with them had not the intervention occurred. The film encourages, in this way, a Catholic audience to see this scene as the quasi-miraculous work of a "mother in heaven," both saving her fiancé and providing a stepfather for her son.

Meyer Schapiro's insightful article points to the functions of the sacraments in the film. He might have pressed that argument further: in this subtle transformation of ritual the seven sacraments not only become "flexible instruments at the disposal of human wants," but assume a new political meaning as well. Here the marriage of Francesco and Pina is a union of Communism and Catholicism, nurtured by the trials of war, but also cut off by its violence. The film points optimistically to a period of national renewal and social justice (without reprisals against those who were seduced by Fascism) which is best summarized by the speech of Francesco to Pina as he consoled her after a spat with her sister: "We shouldn't be afraid now or in the future. Because we're in the right. . . . Maybe the way is hard, it may take a long time, but we'll see a better world! And our kids will see it!" The film ends with an image of the group of boys who have imitated the Resistance turning back toward the center of Rome from the outlying field where Don Pietro was shot. The city to which they return is dominated by the image of St. Peter's dome.

All seven sacraments undergo a transformation into their political counterparts. Pina is pregnant from her premarital relationship with Francesco; her fetus dies with her unbaptized. Yet the plot turns around the "baptism" of a newspaper, *L'Unità,* the underground organ of the Communist Resistance; Marcello tells Don Pietro that he repeatedly misses school because "the way things are" makes catechism a waste of time; instead he prepares for his "confirmation" by imitating the fighters in Romoletto's gang; Pina tries to make a confession before her wedding, but pressing political duties keep Don Pietro from hearing it; later he will let Manfredi die reassured that "you did not talk" when the Gestapo tried to torture a confession from him; Pina and Francesco never have their church wedding, but the exchange of the scarf assures the continuation of her "family." Finally, even Holy Orders has its place in this film: Bergmann does not want to make a martyr of Manfredi, so he orders that he be buried under his pseudonym Giovanni Episcopo. That name, like many in the Resistance, was a literary allusion, in this case to a fictional creation of D'Annunzio. But *episcopo* is the Italian word for "bishop"; so, in the end, the atheist hero is ordained and elevated. Just before his death the camera frames his bloody torso with arms outstretched beyond the edges of the frame to suggest the image of Jesus crucified.

Don Pietro gave a fake extreme unction to the grandfather, after knocking him out; shortly afterward, he performs the actual rite for Pina. In fact the one communion mass we see is her funeral, but the eucharistic celebration is dispersed throughout the film—in her offering food to Manfredi when he arrives, in the populist riot over bread, and in the slaughter of black-market sheep for a restaurant where Resistance fighters gather safely.

In the early criticism of *Roma, città aperta* the accusation of rhetoricity was a serious aesthetic condemnation. I have already quoted two positive reviews of the film, from opposed political positions, extolling the film for its freedom from rhetoric. In the independent journal *Il Tempo*, Fabrizio Sarazan praised the first part of the film at the expense of the whole: "Rossellini had fallen into a rhetoric of Gran Guignol that neither gives pleasure nor follows the pure and fixed laws of poetic transformation."[17] Even within the film itself the issue of rhetoric arises. Its implications unfold the most subtle of Rossellini's insights into the complexities of the political present. Bergmann had told Manfredi, "You Italians, whatever party you belong to, are all addicted to rhetoric. But I'm quite sure that you will see things my way before dawn." Of course, he means that Manfredi's statement that he hopes he is up to the standard of other Resistance fighters who were tortured without confessing is without foundation, and that after a night of torture he will confess. The film proves

Bergmann was wrong in his conviction that he could bend Manfredi, but it does not refute the accusation of the national addiction to rhetoric. Through the character of Pina, Rossellini acknowledges the emotionalism of the Italian character. When she and Francesco cry out to each other after his arrest, they are engulfed in an operatic moment that will cost Pina her life. The film hints through that scene that the emotionalism which had hitherto been seen as a redeeming national characteristic is also a danger for the construction of a postwar society in Italy. When we recall that in 1945 many observers anticipated an armed revolution in Italy, the warning against the tragic consequences of melodramatic action is pertinent. Rossellini's film propagandizes for a broad popular consensus, encompassing both the Left and the Church, predicated on an unquestioned valorization of the nuclear family, heterosexuality, and the goodwill of Italians. By melodramatically interweaving versions of the histories of Gullace, Negarville, and the children's Resistance groups with the biography of Don Morosini, he emphasized the centrality of Catholic charity to that imaginary consensus.

Paisà

Roma, città aperta was a great success both in Italy and abroad. No other film associated with the concept of "neorealism" would ever repeat that success. Rossellini was the first Italian artist (excepting musicians) of his generation to have a success in America. His artistic recognition had the immediate effect of making the financing of his next film a little easier. Rod Geiger approached him to produce his next film, claiming grandiose connections with Hollywood actors. Sergio Amidei produced an outline (*soggetto*) for an episodic film about American and Italian cooperation in the liberation of Italy which would take advantage of this scheme for co-production. However, I believe, there is a more profound issue at stake in the philoamericanism of *Paisà*. The literature of the United States had a large influence on Italian writers and artists throughout the Fascist period. In part, because of the large numbers of Italians who emigrated, they felt especial kinship for America. More significantly, American writing, and its translation and publication in Italy, came to take on an aura of intellectual resistance.[18] Elio Vittorini's voluminous anthology, *Americana*, over a thousand pages of stories translated by Pavese, Montale, Moravia, Vittorini himself, and others, had been temporarily suppressed and then released during the war. The flat, lean style of writers like Hemingway, Saroyan, Caldwell, Lardner, and Anderson appealed to a generation of Italian writers trying to escape the rhetorical flourishes and elegant belletrism of D'Annunzio. Furthermore, the regional differences apparent in the century covered by *Americana*—it included Poe, Hawthorne, Melville, Twain, Harte, O. Henry, Norris, Cather, Stein, Fitzgerald, Faulkner, and Steinbeck, among others—had cultural and political relevance for Italy. The Italian nation had been the result of a mid-nineteenth-century bourgeois revolution, which sought to build national unity by standardizing a language otherwise marked by dialectical diversity. Fascism further stressed the unity and homogeneity of the peninsula and its islands. Thus, the cultural diffuseness of America, the representation of poverty, crime, and injustice in its literature, and varieties of pared-down declarative prose were all factors in the nearly cultic interest in American writing. The best Italian writing of the forties was written in the "American style": Pavese's novels, Levi's *Christo si è fermato a Eboli* (*Christ Stopped at Eboli*), Vittorini's *Conversazione in Sicilia* (*Conversation in Sicily*), and Calvino's *Il sentiero dei nidi di ragno* (*The Path to the Nest of Spiders*).

Rossellini's *Paisà* is the cinematic counterpart to the Americanism of that writing. Two Italian critics, writing some months before and immediately after its premiere at the 1946 Venice film festival, compared its style to that of Hemingway.[19] André Bazin intuited the literary influence succinctly: "The Naples episode . . . is an excellent Saroyan story. Another makes us think of Hemingway, yet another (the first) of Faulkner. I am not merely referring to the tone or the subject, but in a profound way to the style."[20] Indeed, both the form and the style of the film are radically different from Rossellini's earlier work. The cool, clinical direction avoiding melodrama, the cinematography distinguished by long takes and attention to landscape and cityscape in its extensive use of exterior shooting, the employment of amateurs and nonactors for the Italian roles and of unknown Americans with modest stage experience—all combined to give the film a look and a tone that encouraged the literary rather than a filmic comparison.

Paisà is a film about the unity and diversity (as Peter Brunette has argued) of Italy itself, as seen through American eyes and told in a series of six stories which reflect the "American style" as it was perceived in Italy. Writing of Vittorini's *Americana* in 1943, Giaime Pintor described the style as one "in which the earth materials are still fresh, which owes its freshness to the presence of new objects: new machines, new houses, new human relations." In *Paisà* the new machines are merely jeeps, airplanes, and guns; the houses are the old buildings of Italy, when they are not in ruins; but there is such a freshness in the representation of simple acts of survival, and of the terrain newly charged with danger or transformed by destruction, that Bazin claimed the film was made up of "image facts" rather than shots and Robert Warshow observed that "here the qualities of the men and the nature of their situation are inseparably contained in the particulars of their physical presence."[21] Above all, the newness that *Paisà* depicts is largely that of human relations. In the first half of the film the American soldiers regularly fail to understand or misinterpret the Italians they encounter, but their errors highlight the Italians' courage and strength. The Americans of the second half of the film lack the arrogance and obtuseness of the soldiers portrayed earlier; they are sympathetic witnesses who often share the natives' bravery. Rossellini's morality drama anatomizes these "new relations" at the delicate historical moment when the optimism of the Liberation and the Resistance was beginning to wane, giving the film "a vaguely elegiac tone," according to Umberto Barbaro. Weighing the costs of the Liberation, *Paisà* suggests the different options and pitfalls for a new Italy in each episode. I shall take pains to distinguish the distinct admonitory moments at the risk of distorting the moral economy of the film; for Rossellini made a vigorous and successful effort to downplay the parabolic force of each episode (except the fifth) in emphasizing its autonomy and integrity as a realistic vignette. Nevertheless, the film repeatedly delivers its message in the form of a memorial and a warning. It reminds its viewers that the price of liberation was enormous suffering, and it warns them not to forget the moral lessons of the Resistance and the first unity government. The shift of tone between Rossellini's first two postwar films parallels the different representations of the Resistance in Italo Calvino's first two books, *Il sentiero dei nidi di ragno* (1947) and *Ultimo viene il corvo* (*The Crow Comes Last*, 1949). JoAnn Cannon interpreted the altered tonality in Calvino's writing thus: "the failure of the liberation movement to bring permanent change to Italian society was a bitter pill for Calvino and his generation."[22]

I understand *Paisà* to be an expression of the historical crisis described by Carlo Levi in *L'orologio* (*The Watch*, 1950): the failure of the Parri government and De Gasperi's gradual weeding out of the parties of the Left from the Council of Ministers exacerbated party and class conflicts and renewed the possibility of civil war. Rather than focus on the pressing social issues of the moment—land distribution, border realignment, runaway inflation, unemployment—which would have been manifestly visible in his passage through Italy, Rossellini invoked the even greater suffering of the recent past while symbolically supporting the DC's common cause with American interests. Regardless, the film reviewers of the Communist and Socialist press were as enthusiastic about *Paisà* as they had been for Rossellini's previous film.

The return of the Americans, many of those in the film of Italian origin, reversed the pattern of immigration as well as that of the geographical unification of the previous century. Whereas Garibaldi's movement began in the North and secured most of the peninsula before sweeping through Sicily and moving northward to Rome, the American troops moved from Sicily north. The film follows this historical pattern as far as Rome and projects it farther north with stories of the Italian Resistance in Florence and the Po Valley. The six episodes of the film recapitulate and extend that directional sweep. In fact, according to the original plan—called first *Left Behind,* then *Seven from the U.S.* (both titles in English)—there was to be a seventh episode and the film would have concluded with British agents advising partisans in the Valle d'Aosta. In that case, the striking visual effectiveness of the movement from the verticality of the opening scenes in Sicily to the flatness of the Po Valley which ends the film may be fortuitous or an afterthought.[23]

As the film progresses, the military presence of the American army diminishes. Only the first episode depicts armed conflict between Americans and Germans. The fourth and sixth center on the Italian Resistance, the fifth on the experience of military chaplains; but this episode, which could have occurred anywhere in Italy, was actually filmed in the south and fictionally located in Romagna for the sake of the geographical structure of the film. Three of the episodes are ostensibly tragic love stories between Italians and Americans: the first in Sicily, the third in Rome, the fourth in Florence.

The script went through so many revisions and so much was left to improvisation that it is difficult to account for the film's many felicitous symmetries and internal correspondences. There may even have been an iconographic strategy, corresponding to the subtle inscription of the seven sacraments in *Roma, città aperta,* to cast the whole film as a *pretella* of martyrs and saints of the Resistance and Liberation performing versions of the seven Corporal Acts of Mercy. In orthodox terms these acts are feeding the hungry, giving drink to the thirsty, clothing the naked, taking in strangers, tending the sick, visiting or freeing prisoners, and burying the dead. Six of the seven can be said to occur in the final, thoroughly improvised episode alone; the exception would be clothing the naked, which is ironically represented in the Neapolitan episode. Spread through the film we find also the extraordinary care of strangers in the Sicilian story, giving drink to the thirsty in Rome, care for the sick at the center of the Florentine episode, and feeding the hungry in the Romagna monastery. In the opening and closing episodes the performance of these acts costs the life of, first, an Italian woman and, later, an American man. One would be stretching the scope of the Corporal Acts of Mercy beyond credence to construe the implicit argument on behalf of a humane treatment of captured Resistance fighters in the final story as "visiting prisoners." However, in the jumble of plans and scenarios there was an excluded episode called "The Prisoner," wherein "a deaf and dumb Italian rescues and keeps hidden, at the cost of his life, an American pilot, shot down a few days before the landing at Anzio."

The initial episode is an elaborate mesh of misunderstandings: the Sicilians think the Americans are Germans at first; the soldiers speak of the landscape and its ruins in terms of horror films (*Frankenstein,* witches) and ironically compare them to luxury hotel rooms. The focus of this section is Carmela, played by an illiterate nonactress, who offers to guide the soldiers through a mined lava basin. Her generous gesture is all the more significant in Sicily because she jeopardizes her standing in her town by leaving unescorted with the soldiers. In traditional Sicilian families young women were not to be left alone with men until they married. The fact that these are strangers compounds the violation. An old woman and a man—probably a figure of the previous Fascist authority structure—try in vain to stop her. In offering to help the soldiers, she did not realize that she would be left alone with one of them while the others scouted the neighborhood.

Left alone, "Joe from Jersey" and Carmela have a primitive conversation, each in their own language, with only partial comprehension of the other's sense, in a remarkable sequence shot. During a lull of gunfire they see shooting stars, and manage to find the terms for them in their own languages, although their communication breaks down immediately when she hears "home" as "come" ("what?"). By her disappointed reaction to a photograph he shows her, he understands that she takes his sister for his wife and her child for his. In clearing up this confusion, he inadvertently alerts the Germans of their presence by illuminating the photographs with his cigarette lighter. From the distance he is shot.

The chain of errors and misinterpretations does not end with Joe's death. The Germans interpret the ruins as a pirates' castle. One of them acknowledges that he could be romantic in such a spot ["hier könnte ich romantisch werden"]. However, it is soon clear that the Germans intend to rape Carmela. (The surviving scenario fragment makes the rape explicit.) With Joe's rifle she kills one of them. That shot in turn alerts the Americans who left Joe and Carmela, but they mistake the sound for German fire. When they find his body, they assume "that dirty little eyetie" killed him. The episode ends by showing Carmela's shattered body at the foot of a cliff.

The ambiguities of the narrative result from the elliptical style. Naturally, the evidence of the scene will reinforce the rigid Sicilian code, "proving" that young women who go off alone with soldiers will be raped, even killed, by them. By her version of that same code, she committed herself to Joe and executed the vendetta for his death. Without knowing the details of Carmela's end, we know more of the drama than the Americans, Germans, or Sicilians could surmise. Placed in the beginning of a film that was said to be constructed from incidents known to the collaborators on the scenario—Klaus Mann, Fellini, Pagliero, Hayes, and Amidei, as well as the uncredited writers Renzo Avanzo (who may have supplied the idea for the sixth episode), and Vasco Pratolini, the Florentine novelist who worked on the fourth—the Sicilian story alerts us that a fictional imagination has intervened; these events could not have been known by anyone who lived to tell about it; all that remained were three bodies: a shot American, a shot German, and a mangled Italian.

Only the Americans accepted at face value the assistance of Carmela. The older Sicilians could not see a reason for her leaving the church where they had taken refuge, even though she was seeking traces of her lost family; the Germans thought she was awaiting a lover in the ruins. One dimension of the American "liberation" was her opportunity to reject the oppressive code for women in her native region. As a film for Italians, studying the recent past for guidance in the imminent future of a newly united Italy, *Paisà* defends her heroism and challenges the rigid Sicilian sexual code.

If the fictional status of the first story is announced by the death of the participants, a reenactment of one of the most noted instances of Cervantes's Don Quixote's madness identifies the iconographical type of the Neapolitan episode which follows. In the first section of this two-part story, the streets and bombed-out lots of Naples represent the destructiveness of the war. Amid a clamor of fire-eaters and peddlers, the streetwise urchin, Pasquale, first sells a drunken black soldier to a man who will roll him for his clothes, then cheats the man of his purchase by shouting that the Military Police are coming. To keep his prize, Pasquale drags the soldier, Joe, into a puppet show, where he attacks a puppet as if it were a person. Whereas the Knight of La Mancha destroyed the puppets of Maese Pedro because he thought he saw Moors attacking a knight, Joe seems to be defending the black Moor against the Christians. After he is driven out of the puppet theater, Joe's delusions continue as he imagines he is on a ship and an airplane. As he narrates his triumphal fantasy of a tickertape parade in New York City, he suddenly realizes a moment of truth: he does not really want to return home, to his southern shack. Complementarily Pasquale speaks honestly when he warns him not to go to sleep, for if he does he will steal his shoes. If Joe is a Quixote, his fantasies derive not from romances of chivalry but from American popular mythology, including the movies. At this moment, the pathetically practical boy becomes his Sancho Panza.

We do well not to forget that Joe is a product of segregated America and, as we soon learn, an MP in the segregated army. Joe's term for Pasquale, "Paisan," exemplifies the natural migration of language from the expressions of Italian American soldiers to a generalized nickname for all Italians. Yet, in the second half of this story the term comes to have a richer meaning when applied to the bond between the soldier and the waif. Now sober, Joe catches Pasquale rifling a military supply truck, but he does not recognize him until he finds his own harmonica on the boy. He forces him to take him to his "home," in the hope of recovering his shoes, but when he sees the massive squalor of the shantytown within a cave where Pasquale lives, he is stupefied. Eventually Joe communicates that he wants to see the boy's mother and father, only to be told that they were killed in the bombing. Joe then departs speechless.

The two-part narrative, marking a gap of three days, allows for a reversal of the idea of victimage. In the first part, the American soldier is the victim of the collectivity of Neapolitan urchins and hustlers; then, in the second part, Pasquale emerges as a victim of the American invasion. There is a pathos in the parallelism of the black MP (whose authority would be exclusively over black soldiers) who gets uncontrollably drunk when he is off duty and the street con cheating his own countrymen by shouting that the MPs are coming. They implicitly make common cause in the abysmal poverty that eradicates the idea of a home for each of them. Brunette reads the cave image as a descent into hell. I take it rather as an extension of the Cervantean allusion; for shortly before fighting with Maese Pedro's puppets, Quixote had entered the Cave of Montesinos, the site of the most elaborate of his phantasmagoric delusions. Rossellini inverted the sequence and reversed the dramatic meaning of his model: saving the most powerful image for the finale of the episode, he reminds his viewers of the horrors of postwar devastation which are so appalling as to rouse his Quixote from his delusions.

A flashback signals the fictional structure of the Roman story, the third in the film. After a documentary montage of the Allied liberation of Rome, the title "Six Months Later" introduces a bar for American soldiers and Italian prostitutes. When the MPs break up the club, Francesca, a prostitute, ducks into a movie theater to avoid arrest. Offscreen we hear the voice of an Italian newsreel commentator describing the Allied bombings in the North. Thus the hitherto objective voice which had introduced all the parts of *Paisà* linking them in a historical schema and boosting their authenticity fuses with a fictive moment in the story which, more than any other in the film, dwells on the tension between cinematographic realism and the inscription of present time. The newsreel voice both reminds us that at that time (now past) the war was still being waged in the North and reduces the newsreel mode to an iconographic status. But more than this, it is the unexpected occurrence of a flashback in this episode which marks the fictive temporality of the Roman story.

When Francesca drags Fred, a drunken soldier, to her room anticipating, as she tells the landlady, an easy job because he will soon fall asleep, his conversation dissolves into a flashback in which he encounters the very same Francesca before she was driven into prostitution. She recognizes herself in the story, although he does not.

For the audience of 1946 this episode might be said to dramatize the rapid dissolution of liberation optimism and its replacement by the sordid economy of the Occupation. In this sense, the entire film is a reminder of the recent past, a plea for the continuation of the spirit of the Resistance during the dismal days of the first De Gasperi government, which systematically dismantled the political force of the CLN.

In the second half of *Paisà* the Committees of National Liberation in Northern Italy (CLNAI) take precedence over the American army. The Florentine (fourth) and Po Valley (sixth) stories are separated by a comic episode, supposedly located in the middle of Communist-dominated Romagna (actually shot in the South), about religious tolerance. The two Resistance dramas rely less on the peculiarities of character than the first three; instead, they suggest the collective heroism of the Resistance fighters.

The fourth episode brilliantly evokes the battle for Florence by a dramatic reduction of visual information and an emphasis on sound. Rossellini's strikingly original and effective mode of representation may well have been a function of the limited funds for his film. Restaging a battle was out of the question economically and aesthetically. So he evoked the ominous "invisibility" of the final stages of the guerrilla battle between the partisans and the Nazi-Fascisti through shots of uncannily empty public squares, suggesting De Chirico's paintings, with the persistent sound of gunfire. It was this junction of empty images and battle sounds that Pasolini parodied in the "private property" episode of *Uccellacci e uccellini*.

The strange fusion of familiarity and strangeness gives this episode its strength. The very barrenness of the Uffizi Gallery, and the view of a virtually empty Piazza della Signoria, with only a German motorcycle and a few soldiers, set the scene for the brilliantly effective and unforgetable images to follow: partisans ferrying a wagon with water by ropes across the street to avoid sniper fire, and the summary execution of three terrified Fascists in the street. Against the backdrop of these images Harriet's tragic love affair seems trivial.

The story is minimal. Harriet, an American nurse doing volunteer work for wounded Resistance fighters, has heard that her lover, the CLNAI leader "Lupo," has been wounded. She desperately wants to cross the city to find him. In this she is abetted by the painter, Massimo, who wants to find his wife and children. When they reach the scene of fighting on the other side of the Arno, she learns, accidentally, that Lupo is dead.

The historical monuments of Florence are important in this episode. We learn that the Ponte Vecchio is the only bridge that has survived the German demolition. Massimo and Harriet sneak past the Germans by crawling through the empty Uffizi Gallery. Early in the episode, Rossellini mocks the British soldiers (whose high command was eager to disarm the leftist forces of the CLNAI) by portraying them as tourists who try to identify the sights of the city from their strategic position near the Pitti Palace with binoculars. This hostility toward the British army is in marked contrast to the sympathy toward Americans.

Throughout the episode the sound of scattered gunfire of varying degrees of intensity supports the illusion of the partisans' guerrilla war. When Massimo and Harriet pass over the rooftop of a retired Italian major, who saw service in the First World War, he identifies through his binoculars the weapons which we only hear on the sound track. In the midst of the fighting he, too, is merely a military tourist, the equivalent of the British officers at the Pitti Palace.

The Florentine episode ends with the death of an unknown partisan cradled by Harriet. It is an antidramatic substitution for the conventional melodrama which otherwise might have given her a final scene with Lupo. This partisan was shot by the Fascists while Massimo was crossing a street. He narrowly escaped, but Rossellini does not give us his reunion with his family either. The final words of the dying partisan are addressed to the dead leader, Lupo: "Ora non mi farai più cicchetti, Lupo, che stiamo per essere uguali [You won't scold me any more, Lupo, now that we're in the same boat]." Instead of the return of Massimo to his family or Harriet to her lover, we hear of the grim democracy of death, as Harriet learns indirectly of the death of the lover she risked her life to find. This sets the scene for the even harsher final episode, but it is postponed by a comic interlude.

The visit of three army chaplains—an Italian-American Roman Catholic priest, a Protestant, and a Jew—to a monastery purported to be in Romagna diffuses the painful history of the partisan movement, while introducing a religious theme that will become significant in Rossellini's films of the 1950s. Fellini has been credited with the origination and development of this story of the hysterical reaction of the naive monks to the presence of a Jew in their midst. They fast and pray for his conversion, failing to understand why the priest has spent so many wartime months with him without even attempting his conversion. The ostensible message of the episode is the success of American religious pluralism. The filmmaker emphasizes both the camaraderie and sincerity of the chaplains and the quaint superstitious folly of the monks. As such it is another version of the pluralism inherent in the allegiance of Catholic humanists and atheistic Communists in *Roma, città aperta*.[24] Yet, it is just because the Americans come off so well that Rossellini can insert, in the final speech of the Catholic chaplain, an encomium to the "pure faith" of the monks. He covertly warns his Italian audience of the loss of what he takes to be most important in the Catholic tradition. The modernization of the postwar Church, which Rossellini anticipated twenty years before it occurred, would risk the loss of "umiltà, semplicità e pura fede" in an effort to sustain political relevance and power. In both *Francesco, giullare di Dio* (1950) and *Viaggio in Italia* (*Voyage to Italy*, 1953) he locates the continuing importance of Catholicism in its primitive faith in prayer and miracles.

The sixth and final section of *Paisà* is its finest; it is the most sustained achievement of Rossellini's art and a triumph of the neorealist style. Devoid of plot or suspense, the episode derives its strength from the power of its images. The first and most important is that of a dead CLNAI fighter floating down the Po with the sign "partigiano," fixed in the life preserver into which the corpse has been stuffed, as a vicious warning from the Nazis of the fate of resisters.

The slow-paced editing follows the downstream movement of the body as it is observed by Italian peasants, thus establishing the centrality of symbolical representation in this culminating episode. When the partisans recover the body and bury it, they reverse the function of the admonitory sign by using it as a cross and legend to mark the grave. Throughout this finale the filmmaker dwells on the imagery of death.

The three Americans in this episode represent the OSS, Italian-speaking soldiers working with the CLNAI behind German lines. They have run out of ammunition and supplies at a time when the British general Alexander, fearing the ad hoc Communist republics set up by the CLNAI, has ordered the partisans to cease fighting. Here, as in the fourth episode, one of the Americans expresses the hostility to the British position: "These people aren't fighting for the British Empire. They're fighting for their lives." Although Truman and Churchill were in agreement about the danger of the CLNAI, Rossellini focuses the hostility on the British, who were the central military presence in the North at this moment in the war.

This sixth story emphasizes the integration of Americans with the Italian Resistance. Dale, an American, explodes a mine to distract the Germans while Cigolani, a partisan, fishes the corpse out of the river. The second dominating image of the episode shows a dog and the baby of the executed family that harbored partisans and their American contacts, wandering among the slain bodies outside the house where they had found food. A rare moving camera shot expresses the subjectivity of Dale and his OSS companion as they see this scene of mass murder. Within the fabric of *Paisà* this image is the equivalent of the cave of the dispossessed in Joe's eyes. Furthermore, like Pasquale from the Neapolitan episode, this anonymous baby is one of the child witnesses of the agony of Fascism and war. Of course, he is too young to remember fully the scene of his family's death. Yet, the image of this sole survivor of the massacre—and of the sixth episode as a whole—is so strong that it suggests that the next generation of Italians will have to bear preconscious memories of this historical disaster.

Paisà moves from a story of unacknowledged and misinterpreted heroism to a divestment of heroic types. Lupo, of the Florentine episode, a man like Manfredi in *Roma, città aperta,* never appears on-screen: we learn nothing of his achievement as a Resistance hero. In the course of the film several of the stock types of neorealism appear: the independent southern woman, the good thief driven by necessity, the innocent whore, and the well-meaning priest. Most of these figures are portrayed, like Pina had been in Rossellini's earlier film, as vessels of an emotionalism that both ennobles and endangers them.

The finale, however, has no room for emotionalism nor for the character types who express it. At the very end, the narrating voice tells us: "This happened in the winter of 1944. At the beginning of spring, the war was over." In a way the effort of these partisans was in vain; the final commentary is a stoic irony. However, the film itself partially undoes that futility, keeping alive the stories of antifascism in the immediate postwar years as the aspirations for a new kind of political organization were fading, and even preserving those stories for the children of the war period.

A great deal of the film was improvised, often to great advantage if we compare the surviving scripts. The whole final episode was made up in the Po Valley when the lack of snow in the Valle d'Aosta led the filmmaker to change locales. In both the *soggetto* and the surviving scenario Carmela does not die in the opening story. The Quixotic subtext of the story of

Naples is not in the *soggetto:* there the soldier dies in the boy's company, killed by a contraband gang.

The film nearly follows the order of shooting. Rossellini filmed the Sicilian episode first, off the Amalfi coast. Then he shot the monastery story in the southern Apennines. Later he dubbed the monks' parts with Romagna accents. (In his review of the film at the Venice film festival, Francesco Callari, recognizing two of the actors' voices, found them a comic touch in an otherwise "silly and false" episode.[25]) Moving his crew north, Rossellini filmed the Florentine and Po (around Porto Tolle) stories, and then came back to Rome, where he needed studios to shoot the Roman episode. Thus, the internal cohesion of the film results from the accumulation of experience through its gradual making. The sixth and third parts, which are the most sophisticated and complex, were the last to be shot. In them, the film is most eloquent.

Despite its minimal form, the plot of the last section has a marked reference to the first episode. The partisans and the OSS have to use flares to indicate their position so that a supply plane can drop arms and food. Not only does the mission fail, but the light betrays them to the Germans, just as the cigarette lighter of "Joe from Jersey" leads to his death. More remotely, the "stella cadente" of the Sicilian story foreshadows the fallen British airplane.

The drama is secondary to the chain of images of death that give the film its closure: the floating partisan with his warning sign, the child amid corpses, a partisan resting the muzzle of his rifle under his chin to kill himself before the Nazis capture him, and finally the bound partisans being pushed to their deaths in the Po by the Germans, despite the pained protests of the Allied captives.

Throughout the film the iconography of the partisan struggle predominates over that of the vestigial Corporal Acts of Mercy. Yet, the Catholic undercurrent remains problematic. Roy Armes cited Curzio Malaparte's lurid semiautobiographical novel, *La pelle (The Skin,* 1947), to confirm the practice of Neapolitan street urchins buying and selling black GIs (unbeknownst to them) to rob them of all their clothes when drunk.[26] Perhaps more than just the shared topical reference is relevant here. Rossellini seems to share Malaparte's conviction that victims rather than victors reveal genuine Christianity. Robert Warshow, in his vigorous interpretation of the film, makes the same point, although he does not associate the moral advantage of Rossellini's victims with the Church. In fact, he finds the Catholicism the most objectional aspect of the film: [27]

> Rossellini neither requires nor dreams of victory; indeed, it is only defeat that has meaning for him—defeat is his "universal." . . . From this hopeless-ness—too inactive to be called despair—Rossellini gains his greatest virtue as an artist: the feeling for particularity. In the best parts of *Paisan*, it is al-ways the man who dies, and no idea survives him unless it is the idea of death itself.
>
> . . . .
>
> Rossellini has no intellectual defenses, and when he attempts to go beyond the passive representation of experience, he falls at once into the grossest sen-timentality and falsehood. The monastery episode . . . is so outrageously vul-gar that it must surely be the product of a calculated dishonesty, probably for political reasons. And the dishonesty is made all the plainer by the fact that a view of the Church such as no sophisticated Italian could seriously advance in his own name is here presented through the eyes of three simpleminded Americans (what little intelligence they display among them is all given to the Catholic); by this device, Rossellini tries to preserve his "neutrality." [28]

Warshow may still remain the film's finest critic, but he is wrong in his accusation of politically motivated hypocrisy. The monastery episode re-veals the filmmaker's appreciation for naive spirituality, as his *Francesco, giullare di Dio* would confirm three years after Warshow wrote his essay. Furthermore, that version of Christianity is intimately connected to the exaltation of victims that he astutely perceived at the heart of the film. Dalle Vacche recognizes this when she speaks of the "Eucharistic transub-stantiation of appearance into being" and the "transubstantiation of inte-riority into social identity" in this film.[29] Finally, Rossellini's politics can-not be distinquished from the fusion of just that religious and social vision. Rossellini told Dacia Maraini, in 1973, that he had never been a member of any political party: "I believe that it is necessary to keep alive and or-thodoxies frighten me because they make me feel dead."[30] Yet he was enough of a fellow traveler of the DC to sit as its representative on the film workers' committee of the CLN. Although his first postwar films are not expressions of the dominant political party, there was within the DC a position that corresponded to his vision of patriotic unification, tolerance, and Christian spirituality: Giuseppe Dossetti, an anticapitalist founder of the DC with CLNAI experience, began to voice a similar position at this period; his supporters promulgated his views in the Catholic-Left journal *Cronache socialia.* But it was not until the climax of the economic miracle that such views penetrated to the center of power.

In the films I shall consider in the next two chapters the topics and icons of Christian art tend to disappear, rejected by the anticlericalism of Visconti, De Sica, and Zavattini; yet in their place these directors substitute an iconography of both provincial and urban life with affinities to Rossellini's first two postwar films.

CHAPTER 3

Visconti:
The National Language,
Dialect, and the
Southern Question

Throughout the late 1940s the possibility of revolutionary change haunted the Italian republic. Its repression was the function of the Ministry of the Interior. In the Parri government of late 1945, the prime minister himself served as interior minister as well. Although the Socialist Giuseppe Romita had suppressed Communist-inspired revolts during his term as Alcide De Gasperi's first interior minister (Dec. 1945 to June 1946), the prime minister assumed the role in his second government (July 1946 to Jan. 1947) in order to keep leftist mobilization firmly under control. On 31 May 1947 De Gasperi formed the first postwar government without the participation of the far Left. Thereafter, in his subsequent six cabinets, until 1953, he left a Sicilian from his own party, Mario Scelba, in charge of the Interior Ministry.

The exclusion of the Communists and the Socialists from the government meant concessions to the parties of the far Right—Liberals, Monarchists, and Uomo Qualunque (The Common Man), an anticentrist party largely composed of ex-Fascists from the South—for their support in the Assembly. Responding to pressure from the United States, the Christian Democrats created what they called the first "government of rebirth and salvation of the country." The period of consensus government by the heirs of the CLN had ended. Actually, the consensus had been withering as the DC consolidated its power. Although the political and economic turmoil which the far Left eagerly anticipated failed to come to a climax, the Left still believed that Italy could become a socialist republic by either parliamentary or revolutionary means.

Scelba organized antiriot police to break up demonstrations during the violent campaign which led to the April 1948 elections. Janet Flanner, in her *New Yorker* letter following those elections, described Scelba's riot squad: "These half-dozen special police who filled these little open cars were uniformed and helmeted, like soldiers. All carried tommy guns in their hands. Their handsome faces were expressionless. These *celere*, like gangster police, are what the duly elected new Christian Democrat government has declared it will use against the Communists if the Communists try force. The use of force has become the world's gravest communicable disease."[1] Occasionally demonstrators were killed. During the same campaign the neo-Fascist party (MSI) was formed and the populist Uomo Qualunque movement dissolved.

In the national elections of 1946 the Christian Democrats collected 35.1 percent of the vote; the Socialists followed with 20.7 percent; and the Communists, with 18.9 percent, far outpolled any of the other five parties, each of which failed to top 1 percent. The two parties of the far Left, the Communists and the Socialists, went into the 1948 elections as a United Front hoping to match their previous tally and emerge as the dominant power in Italy. But the coincidence of four factors crippled the United Front: the Communist coup in Czechoslovakia in February 1948, a split in the Socialist party which cost them more than 7 percent of the national vote, spiritual threats from the Vatican, and formidable economic threats from Washington. De Gasperi's party won a landslide 48.5 percent of the vote; the United Front fell to 31 percent. The era of postwar unification and coalition had definitively ended. For fifteen years the Socialists would be excluded from the ensuing fifteen governments of the Center and the Right. The Communists were to be the permanent opposition until their formal dissolution in the wake of the termination of Soviet communism.

Although the Left was strongest in the industrial North, it had anticipated gains in the far South where the suppression of unions and the resistance to agricultural reformation had led to violent incidents. Sicily had unique problems at the end of the war. Mussolini's efforts to suppress the Mafia had been undone by the American occupation. Washington enlisted the help of gangsters to facilitate the invasion of the island. Subsequently the Occupation army put Sicilian mafiosi in positions of political power. Many of them initially supported the separatist movement for the independence of the island. The Italian government managed to squelch separatism in May 1946 by allowing an autonomous regional legislature, cabinet, and administration in the province, which controlled its industry, mining, and agriculture. When the first elections indicated that the parties of the Left were considerably stronger than the DC, the separatists, the Mafia, and the neo-Fascists threw their support to De Gasperi's party, doubling its power base. Part of the price of this allegiance was the reluctance of the DC governments of the forties and fifties to prosecute Mafia crimes. There were also severe repressions of Left-sponsored efforts to organize workers in unions and to occupy uncultivated land. For example, Don Calogero Vizzini, the mafia boss and mayor of Villalba, had his bodyguard shoot up a leftist meeting in 1944, but he died ten years later before the case was even brought to trial. Salvatore Giuliano, a bandit with legendary popularity, murdered a number of Communists at a May Day celebration in 1947. When he was killed in 1950, a scandal implicating Scelba in an attempt to silence the bandit ended inconclusively with the poisoning of the principal witness in prison. In a later chapter I shall discuss in detail Francesco Rosi's film about Giuliano's death and the subsequent scandal.

The Italian Communist party commissioned Luchino Visconti to make a short film on Sicilian fishermen which could be used as election propaganda. Thus *La terra trema* was conceived in anticipation of the 1948 election. By the time the shooting began in November 1947, Visconti had radically transformed the idea of the inexpensive PCI documentary into a three-part epic. Then, by the time it was shot, two months before the election, the film as we know it had taken shape. Visconti returned the initial budget (under ten thousand dollars) to the Communist party. He used his own substantial funds to underwrite the filming.

The three-part fictional epic which Visconti had quickly elaborated from the idea of a documentary on fishermen surveyed the problems of labor and collectivization on the island. The first of the three was to be the story of a fishing family that tried and failed to break from the exploitation of the wholesalers who owned the boats and fixed the prices for fish. The second episode would have described the limited success of a cooperative of sulphur miners, led by an energetic organizer who is distraught over his inability to marry and support his pregnant girlfriend. According to the schematic treatment published in 1951 in the journal of the Centro Sperimentale di Cinematografia, *Bianco e nero,* the miners' eventual revitalization of an abandoned sulphur vein, with the help of a sympathetic engineer, brings Cataldo, their leader, to see his emotional life "at last in an optimistic light."

The third and climactic episode was to have concerned land reclamation, a central issue in the PCI's program for the South. It was to have opened with a barely fictionalized version of Giuliano's May Day massacre at Portella della Ginestra. An organizer of landless farm workers, Saracino, stands up to the terrorism of the Mafia and landowners, leading a group of his comrades in the takeover of uncultivated land. This time the neighboring city gives mass support to the farmers' revolution. The solidarity of other organized fishermen, factory workers, and farmers forces the government to intervene on behalf of Saracino and his collective.

Like many of Visconti's film projects, only a fragment of the grand scheme was realized. The published treatment suggests that he had hoped to intercut the episodes, underlining the stages of entrepreneurial, collective, and class actions. The initial story of the fishermen would only have represented the negative phase of the composite, the analysis of the failure of an individualistic, entrepreneurial vision of economic melioration.

As in the two unfilmed parts, the story of the fishermen took on melodramatic dimensions when Visconti moved from the epic plan to a full-length examination of the fishing family. All of Visconti's films tend toward the operatic in the depiction of emotional and social struggles. In many of his films there is an episode explicitly evoking opera as a gorgeous delusion. Bragana's success as an amateur singer immediately precedes his death in *Ossessione; Senso* links the bourgeois revolution of Garibaldi to the Verdian self-image of the Italian ruling class. Don Salvatore, the police chief and destructive seducer of Lia in *La terra trema,* whistles and praises the music of Bellini, "the swan of Catania."

Geoffrey Nowell-Smith has made the case for seeing the whole film as an operatic structure, pointing out that in opera "words . . . are . . . generally incomprehensible. What comes over from the stage are the elements of the action, the style of the setting, the grandeur and subtlety of the music. . . . [C]haracters tend . . . to be stock types." In the film, he writes, the "action unfolds slowly, in a series of tableaux, with its choruses, solos, and duets."[2] In a text that Visconti could not have known before 1949, Antonio Gramsci had commented upon the problematic nature of the influence of opera in Italian life:

Verdi's music, or rather the libretti and plots of the plays set to music by Verdi, are responsible for a whole range of "artificial" poses in the life of the people, for ways of thinking, for a "style." . . . To many common people the baroque and the operatic appear as an extraordinarily fascinating way of feeling and acting, a means of escaping what they consider low, mean, and contemptible in their lives and education in order to enter a more select sphere of great feelings and noble passions. . . . Opera is the most pestiferous because words set to music are more easily recalled, and they become matrices in which thought takes shape out of flux.[3]

Yet *La terra trema* is the least melodramatic and the most overtly and programmatically political of Visconti's films. Several reasons may be suggested for this. In the first place, his explicit allusions to opera hint that he shared Gramsci's suspicions of the tendency toward the operatic in Italian culture, even though he could not have known Gramsci's as yet unpublished text. His highly melodramatic *Senso,* made six years later, describes the pitfalls of confusing politics and melodrama, giving a prominent place to Verdi's *Il trovatore.* However, an even more pressing limitation on the histrionic was the rigorous use of fishermen and tradesmen, instead of actors, to play all of the roles in the film. Furthermore, Visconti insisted on directly recording their voices rather than dubbing, even though he was filming in the streets and houses of Acitrezza rather than in studios.

The players worked without a script. Visconti described the dramatic situations he wished to represent. They, in turn, suggested ways in which they would react and speak in such circumstances. Amplifying and adjusting their responses, the director arrived at the dialogue of the film, which occurs entirely in Sicilian dialect, making it difficult or even impossible for many Italians to follow it. The emphasis on dialect is itself a political gesture. Again, Gramsci had addressed the problem of dialects in his extensive writings on the Italian language (also published after the film was made), arguing that "[e]very time the question of language surfaces, in one way or another, it means that a series of other problems are coming to the fore: the formation and enlargement of the governing class, the need to establish more intimate and secure relationships between the governing groups and the national-popular mass, in other words to reorganize the cultural hegemony." The appearance of "authenticity" in the dialogue of *La terra trema* is important insofar as it points to the question of language in postwar Italian politics and culture.

In *Paisà* Rossellini followed the dominant approach to this problem. His Italian nonprofessionals do not speak dialect, but rather versions of the official Florentine Italian. Apparently the accents of the dubbing voices, and minor linguistic markers, indicate regional differences, although my ear is not attuned to these nuances. *La terra trema* is the single instance of a major postwar Italian film in which the actors speak exclusively in dialect.

The rolling title which opens the film concludes with a comment on the selection of the cast and the use of dialect: "All the actors of the film were chosen from among the inhabitants of the region: fishermen, girls, day laborers, masons, fish wholesalers. These people do not know a language other than Sicilian to express rebellions, griefs, hopes. The Italian language is not the language of the poor in Sicily." The note is in Italian, as are the voices of the two commentators who repeatedly intervene on the sound track. The commentary is more than an expedient to make the film available to an audience that does not understand Sicilian. The very copresence of the dominant and the local dialects brings the issue of language and what Gramsci called "the cultural hegemony" into the film. Visconti himself alludes to the economic meaning of that hegemony when he asserts that Italian is not the language of Sicily's poor. Furthermore, he points out that the mode of histrionic representation (rebellions, griefs, hopes) coincides with the use of the dialect.

From the very start of his film, Visconti locates a problem for the neorealist cinema, insofar as neorealism was a convenient name for the emerging Italian national cinema of high seriousness. Within the national entity there are regions, especially in the South, not accessible to on-location filming without professional actors because the language of the centers of filmic production is not that of the marginalized poor. Thus, by implication, he rejects the unrealistic language of the Sicilians in Rossellini's *Paisà*.

The question of dialect plays a large role in the history of the Italian novel. Two foci of that issue were the decisions of Manzoni, a Lombardian like Visconti, and of Verga, a Sicilian, to write in the literary Florentine which nineteenth-century nationalism favored. In writing *I Malavoglia* Verga constructed a stylistic mode that would accommodate literary Italian to the rhythms, diction, idioms, and mentality of oral Sicilian. His achievement gave his novel a privileged status in Italian literary history. One of the most vital and fascinating scholarly debates in Italy in the forties and fifties concerned the definition and analysis of Verga's linguistic invention; it is directly relevant to Visconti's project insofar as it shaped the style of the voice-over commentary. In the pioneering work of Luigi Russo (especially the 1941 chapter on language appended to his 1919 book) the "choral" nature of the narrative language, which suggests the popular mentality of the community of Acitrezza and allows for subtle transitions into the thoughts and linguistic habits of the protagonists, has been linked to "free indirect discourse." In free indirect discourse the omniscient and neutral narrating voice uses the language peculiar to a character or a group of characters to reveal the perspective or thought of that character or group without the direct quotation of thought or speech. Giacomo Devoto (1954) and Leo Spitzer (1956) made significant contributions to this discussion, as I have indicated in the Introduction.

The situation of *I Malavoglia* commands our attention because Visconti loosely adapted the novel in organizing the plot of the fishing episode of his three-part film. *La terra trema,* as released, is an adaptation of Verga's book without formal acknowledgment, in its titles, of the borrowing. The intertextual relationship was never disguised or hidden, however. In the late thirties, even before making *Ossessione,* Visconti had adapted Verga in his scenarios for *Jeli il pastore* (*Jeli the Shepherd*) and *L'amante di Gramigna* (*The Lover of Gramigna*), the latter of which was stopped by the state film censor before it entered production in 1941. At that time he had also purchased an option to film *I Malavoglia,* but turned to *Ossessione* instead.

In the 10 October 1941 issue of *Cinema,* Mario Alicata and Giuseppe De Santis, who were collaborating on scripts with Visconti at that time, coauthored "Truth and Poetry: Verga and Italian Cinema," a brief call for realism as "the true and eternal measure of every narrative significance." They cite the need for Italian cinema to "redeem itself from the easy suggestions of a moribund bourgeois state" through the stimulus of Verga's "revolutionary art inspired by, and acting, in turn, as inspiration to a humanity which hopes and suffers."

The opposition of "a moribund bourgeois state" to "revolutionary art" in this essay suggests that more than the tradition of Verga's *verismo* was at stake in this nearly encoded polemic by two clandestine Communist activists. Verga's confrontation with poverty and economic exploitation gave his name a symbolical significance for the writers and filmmakers around the magazine, *Cinema,* in the last years of Fascist rule.

The "revolutionary" force of an adaptation of Verga would have dwindled after the Liberation. Yet Visconti's vision of Sicilian life had been so deeply mediated by his work on Verga that he continued to organize his plot around *I Malavoglia* when he came to make his first film in Sicily. More than that, Verga's great novel and the theoretical issue of its synthetic language play dialectical roles in the meaning of *La terra trema:* rather than being an adaptation of *I Malavoglia,* the film reinterprets the novel's theme and plot in terms of the problems of De Gasperi's Italy; it suggests to literate Italians that very little has changed in Sicily since the novel was published in 1881; and furthermore, that the DC, as the direct heir of Fascism, is committed to a policy of violently resisting any change in order to maintain the oppressive class system in the South.[4]

The filmmaker retained enough of *I Malavoglia* to make its intertextuality obvious. The Malavoglia family becomes the Valastros with minor changes: the central figure remains 'Ntoni; Verga's nucleus of grandfather (Padron 'Ntoni), mother (Maruzza la Longa), a dead father (Bastiano), 'Ntoni, two younger brothers (Luca and Alessi), and two younger sisters (Mena and Lia) expands a little to become 'Ntoni and his three brothers ('Cola, 'Vanni, and Alfio), three sisters (Mara, Lucia, and Lia), and a baby. Mara's frustrated love for the mason, Nicola, and Lucia's seduction by the policeman, Don Salvatore, repeat the romances of Mena with Alfio Mosca and Lia with Don Michele, including numerous borrowings of dialogue. The loss of the family house to creditors, 'Ntoni's fall into drunkenness and idleness, and the grandfather's removal to a charity hospital come from Verga. Whereas in Verga the second brother Luca dies in the Garibaldian sea battle at Lissa against Austria, 'Cola disappears as a Mafia recruit. But the death of the mother in a cholera epidemic has no counterpart in the film.[5]

The crucial differences concern the representation of the other inhabitants of Acitrezza and the economic vicissitudes of the family. From the fascinating array of townspeople—gossips, swindlers, reactionaries, republicans, girls competing for husbands—Visconti selected only the men whom the sisters attract and Nedda, 'Ntoni's girlfriend, who stands for a series of romances in the novel without duplicating any of them. He invented, in turn, a few wholesalers who conspire to fix prices and suppress the rebellion of fishermen led by 'Ntoni. The recasting of the town population indicates that life in Acitrezza has become more oppressive since Verga imagined it: the rigid economic and sexual codes of behavior prescribed for women have remained fixed, but the consolidation of a class that controls capital has worsened the lot of fishermen. In Nowell-Smith's words, "Basically what Visconti has done is to rewrite Verga in the light of Marx." The following synopsis of the plot can clarify that act of revision, which is no longer an issue of language or characterization but of political allegory. I shall return to the examination of language, particularly the use of free indirect discourse in the voice-over, after examining the allegorical, rhythmical, and iconographical aspects of the film.

The political allegory entails a major revision of Verga's economics. His Malavoglia family suffered because they were cheated by an unscrupulous businessman who sold them a cargo of rotten forage and demanded payment when their boat was nearly destroyed by a storm in which the cargo was lost. A severe code of family honor bound them to that debt. After they lost their home to the cheat and after 'Ntoni's effort to make a living on the mainland failed—driving him to alcoholism, smuggling, and the attempted murder of his sister's seducer—the rest of the family's savings were lost in a vain attempt to keep him out of jail. In the end the youngest brother, Alessi, married his childhood love, accepted economic responsibility for her many siblings, and eventually repurchased the house by the medlar tree through his dogged work as a laborer.

Visconti's story of the Valastros deemphasizes the dire fatalism of Verga's severe vision. Young 'Ntoni's experience as a sailor in the Fascist navy of a world beyond Sicily contributes to his feeling of injustice at the exploitation of fishing families like his own who work the boats of the wholesalers and who must abide by their prices for the fish they catch, leaving them without enough income to afford adequate food. Against the conventional fatalism of his grandfather—a character out of Verga without reconstruction—he organizes a revolt of the fishermen which ends in their arrest. The wholesalers decide to drop the charges in order to defuse the rebellion and keep Communist organizers out of Acitrezza. Their ploy isolates 'Ntoni. Rather than pursue a tactic of organizing the fishermen, he proposes mortgaging the house by the medlar tree in order to buy an independent boat and salting the fish they catch for sale when the prices are high in nearby Catania.

Visconti neatly lays out the stages in which an individualistic response to class oppression emerges and fails. The wholesalers, because they are organized for their mutual benefit, are able to defeat the initial, furious response of the fishermen even though an irrational desire for primitive revenge and the redressing of wounded pride causes dissension within their small circle. The filmmaker emphasizes this resolution of internal dissension through the only scene that he films within the home of the senior wholesaler. Elsewhere in the film at least one of the Valastros is on the scene.

'Ntoni can raise enough money to start his enterprise, but not enough to continue its operation without risking the sea on days the wholesalers find too perilous. Nor can he underwrite the cost of repairing his one damaged vessel. The wholesalers strategically maintain a cooperative, but one family of fishermen can only resort to individual, and therefore highly precarious, sallies aimed at self-sufficiency. In the overall tryptic scheme of the film, the episode of the sea would have represented the panel of the failure of an antiquated fantasy of entrepreneurial emancipation, crudely corresponding to the ideology of the Christian Democrats and their rightist allies.

Thus, when the Valastros' crew benefits from an unprecedented catch of anchovies, the salting constitutes an occasion of false euphoria. But since the salting itself represents an investment against future profits, the family cannot afford to wait out the storm which ultimately wrecks their boat and nearly kills the crew. The maintenance of a boat entails the continual hiring of day laborers, despite the size of the family; daily expenses of feeding the family and keeping up a boat thereby absorb nearly all of the Valastros' profits. The individual lacks the capital required to compete with the wholesalers' cooperative, to make up for the loss of days on a threatening sea, and to put aside stores for future sale.

Verga's storm had been an ironical manifestation of harsh fate; Visconti's becomes a factor in a high-risk investment. Whereas Verga vividly described the experience of the chaotic waters, the filmmaker only shows the Valastro women keeping vigil on the tempest-swept rocks of the harbor, itself one of the film's most powerful images, and the arrival of the wrecked vessel after it had been given up for lost. Similarly, 'Ntoni's failure has a more strictly economic tone in the film than in the novel. He becomes a drunk when he can find no work on other boats, but he does not try emigration or smuggling like his literary ancestor, nor does he turn to violence. The wholesalers seize the opportunity to take advantage of the destitute family, fixing a low price for their salted anchovies. In the end 'Ntoni and his young brother Alfio have to enlist as crewmen on a boat of the cooperative for poor wages, in a humiliating scene in which the wholesalers publicly mock them.

The hint of a political education compensates for the disaster of the experiment at self-improvement. There is no Alessi in the film to rebuy the house and initiate a new cycle of suffering. At the nadir of the family's fortunes, while the town is celebrating the christening of a new fleet of boats for the cooperative, 'Ntoni encounters some men repairing the boat he once owned. A little girl speaks kindly to him, telling him she would help him if she could. Apparently she is a child of the family that now owns his boat. This undramatic expression of sympathy occasions the protagonist's conversion. He tells her, and himself: "Some day they'll all realize I was right! Then it'll be a blessing for everybody to lose everything like I did! We have to learn to stick up for each other, to stick together. Then we can go forward."

The little girl, called Rosa in the script, instantiates the iconographic emblem of the child as a figure for the future of Italy found in nearly all the major neorealist films. In the subsequent scene of humiliation at the Cyclops Cooperative office, 'Ntoni's young brothers 'Vanni and Alfio perform the same symbolical function. Unlike Verga's Alessi they are hardly individualized figures, but deliberately undefined agents of an uncertain future.

The reduction to types which characterizes the whole film is most striking in the scene of the christening of the cooperative's new boats. The assembly of a middle and upper class in Acitrezza is particularly jarring because the film dwells so intently on the daily life of the Valastros that we do not expect them to have such neighbors. Within the economy of the narrative, this episode emphasizes 'Ntoni's alienation and prepares for his encounter with the encouraging little girl, whom he meets as he wanders away from the celebration. It is in this group scene that we see Nedda, formerly 'Ntoni's girlfriend, at the side of Lorenzo, the most vicious of the wholesalers. The class portrait is completed by the figure of an old, rather senile priest aspersing the ships as Nedda breaks the christening bottle on one of them and by an equally ancient and decrepit woman, called "our noble lady Baroness" by the wholesaler when he addresses the crowd. She sits under an umbrella wearing dark glasses and munching candy. The speaker gets a laugh from the crowd by alluding to the Valastros as "the few who are sick in the head and want to do for themselves." Thus Visconti caricatures the ritual presence of Church and aristocracy at a celebration that caps 'Ntoni's defeat with the loss of his fiancée to his class enemy.

Nowell-Smith pointed out the tension between the ideological allegory of the film's plot and the anthropological tonality of its images:

> [Visconti's] initial scenarios have an ideological clarity and purity about them which is then systematically betrayed in the final elaboration. . . . Here . . . it takes the form of abandoning a totally unworkable discipline and reshaping the film in accordance with objective demands. The documentary moment prevails over the ideological. . . . The use of images and of the cutting between them is in fact pictorial rather than narrative or conceptual. The effect aimed at, and achieved, is a form of pictorial realism which is occasionally at odds with the analytical tone of the exposition.[6]

A very slow pace, complexly composed shots in depth, and an unaccented flow of narrative give the film an epic quality. Acitrezza claims to be the site of Odysseus's encounter with the Cyclops, Polyphemus; the jagged monoliths in its harbor are said to be the stones the blinded monster hurled at the departing Ithacans. The film evokes that ancient heritage, intimating that the Valastros' mode of life recalls ancient traditions of heroic dignity despite cruel exploitation.

Visconti manages to make a number of political points subtly by the sequencing of events. For instance, the connection between the wholesalers and the police is made without any direct representation of their collusion. After we see the wholesalers agreeing to drop charges against the fishermen who fought with them and threw their scales into the sea, the policeman, Don Salvatore, appears at the window of the room where Mara and Lucia sit to say that 'Ntoni will soon be free. With impressive economy Visconti seems to be effecting a change of pace when he cuts from the self-satisfied and derisive wholesalers at the dinner table to Lucia inventing a fairy tale for her little sister, Lia. Even though the story of a prince on a white horse coming to marry a poor girl of Trezza comes virtually unaltered from Verga's depiction of the anchovy-salting session, Visconti has Lucia tell it as a fantasy about herself in the film. (The minor character, Cousin Anna, told it to children in the novel, making her daughter the heroine.) Thus, when Don Salvatore shows up at the conclusion of it, this storytelling helps define Lucia's naive romantic susceptibility, so that what seems at first merely a change of tone with the shift of scene actually becomes a tightening of the net of exploitation around the Valastros. The economic and sexual naiveté of the fairy tale encourages Lucia along a path that will end in her exploitation and degradation.

On the other hand, a number of factors contribute to the softening of the didactic strategies of parallelism, contrast, and cause and effect at work in the sequencing of episodes. The repetition of a very limited number of locations—the beach, the Valastro house, a tavern, village streets—and the length and pace of individual shots give a sense of ritual within a scarcely changing physical and moral environment that the voice-over ironically reinforces. The paratactic arrangement of scenes itself is one of the aspects of the film which suggest that an epic rather than a dramatic mode organizes its parts. Thus, some disengagement from the seductive rhythm of village life veristically rendered is required to notice the implied relationship of the police and the wholesalers in the conjunction I have just described. Similarly, the brutal series of events that follow the wreck of the boat can be seen as isolated turns of the plot or as the immediate and aggregate consequences of the loss of the Valastros' economic power. In fact, the elaboration of the collapse of the family crowds around the moment of the grandfather's removal to a hospital or poorhouse for the aged. The following events occur in succession, but without emphasized interconnections, almost as if they were merely an extension of the paratactic series I listed as occurring after the boat wreck: the representatives of the bank arrive to repossess the house; 'Cola departs at dawn for a criminal life; the grandfather collapses and Lucia's "disgrace" is suggested; 'Ntoni keeps the company of drunks. Crime, prostitution, and alcoholism figure as consequences of the system that favors the wholesalers, the bank, and the police.

There is a fundamental tension between the political allegory of the filmmaker's rewriting of I Malavoglia as a drama of Sicily on the verge of the 1948 election and the monumental nostalgia of the iconography of daily life in the Valastro family. The attention to detail and to the rhythms of village life often pushes the political schema to the background. In 1943 Visconti had written in Cinema: "The most humble gesture of a man, his face, his hesitations and his impulses, impart poetry and life to the things which surround him and to the setting in which they take place. Every other solution to the problem will always seem to me an offense against reality as it unfolds before our eyes: made by man and continuously unmade by him."[7] The unsentimental delineation of the varieties of Sicilian customs, gestures, and social interactions "imparts" an anthropological "poetry" to the film which complements its political meaning, as when the bank representatives systematically catalogue the flaws of the house by the medlar tree, poking soft spots in the walls with their umbrellas. When we see the dying grandfather stretched out on his bed, the religious cards hieratically placed on his chest iconographically delimit his passive inscription in the magical and fatalistic worldview of the least resistant victims of exploitation; the drunks dancing in the empty alleys at night, wary of the police, demonstrate the repressive control of the alienated even in their rituals of escape. The ethnographic authority which derives from the convincing depiction of village life extends to the political discourse, isolating and anatomizing the forces—"made by man and continuously unmade by him"—at work in maintaining a status quo.

The iconography of *La terra trema* is secular: the Italian photographers of the first years of the twentieth century recorded images of both the natural beauty of South Italian seascapes and the daily life of fishermen. The film recalls Arturo Cerio's moody pre–World War I images of Capri's rocky harbor and of fishermen mending their nets, or the even more directly pertinent photographs made by the painter Francesco Paolo Michetti in his 1907 examination of the tuna slaughter in and around Acitrezza. Photography itself has a crucial status in the film: the photograph of 'Ntoni in his naval uniform and the group portrait of the family are displayed honorifically beside the religious icons which decorate Sicilian Catholic homes; the former photograph becomes the symbolic focus for 'Cola's desire to leave the island, while the latter represents Mara's interiorized ideal of the family despite the losses to death and desertion.

A detailed examination of a passage from the film will indicate something of its remarkable stylistic density and rehearse some of the ways in which blocking, gesture, and the strategic placement of objects (such as the photograph of 'Ntoni) fill the gap left by the reduction of conventional histrionics and the diminution of character psychology. I have selected five minutes from the middle of the film, immediately following the Valastros' trip to Catania, but the features I shall stress can be found throughout the film. Thirteen shots describe the confirmation of the mortgage, the reaction of the neighbors, and the remarkable catch of anchovies. Seven of the shots make significant use of panning; at least ten of them organize depth of field in an impressive pictorial manner. Although there are no tracking shots in this series, the moving camera is another crucial feature of *La terra trema*'s stylistic vocabulary. Broadly described the shots are:

1. A busy alley in Acitrezza. 'Ntoni, well dressed, appears in the background and proceeds forward, greeting people. A pan to the left reveals the entrance to his house. The camera movement precedes and predicts his turn.

2. Inside the Valastro house. 'Vanni runs in announcing 'Ntoni's return a moment before he enters. The room is crowded with his mother and most of the Valastro children. As he passes through, announcing the success of his trip, the camera follows him, panning to the right until he exits through a door.

3. Another room in the house. 'Ntoni enters. In the mirror beside him we can see 'Cola, offscreen, shaving.

4. Reverse angle. 'Cola speaks to him.

5. Return to position 3, as 'Ntoni explains that he has put the money in the bank and anticipates getting married now that they are independent.

6. Same room. In the left foreground 'Ntoni and 'Cola are concluding their conversation. To the right we can see another room behind them. Through the window in that room we see a woman hanging wash in the deep background. 'Ntoni leaves 'Cola in the foreground, walks into the room behind, singing a love song, exits to the right and reappears in the depth where the woman is hanging wash, while 'Cola continues shaving in the foreground.

7. Outside. Still singing, 'Ntoni in the middle of the image at medium depth is accosted by the woman hanging wash very close to the camera at the extreme right. When another neighbor interrupts their banter, the camera swings left and tilts upward to frame a woman in the far depth on her balcony.

8. Reverse of 7, with camera close behind the woman on the balcony shooting down to 'Ntoni in depth. The camera sweeps right across roofs to center another neighbor on another balcony.

9. Reverse of the final position of 8. The camera is very low to the ground beside 'Ntoni's head as he stretches on the ground. When he turns from the second woman on the balcony to speak to a man in the far background, playing a pipe in a second-story window, the camera moves left to accommodate his shifted perspective.

10. Evening, at sea. A dense telephoto shot, with little depth of field, of the Valastro crew in their ship. 'Ntoni is in the center. They row, then lift the sail.

11. Long shot from the beach. The Valastro boat at full sail passes beyond the massive rocks. Other rocks in the foreground help us measure the depth of field.

Dissolve to 12. Dawn. An old man on a rock in the foreground, his back to us, shouts to the lights of boats in the depth. When the first boat approaches, the camera pans right to it. It is so close that we see parts of the crew as they carry anchovies on flat baskets and clinging to nets.

Dissolve to 13. Salt shop. Day. The camera moves slightly to follow the placement of a heavy bag of salt on a scale, then to the weighing, and then pans to the right and up to show Mara, on the far side of the counter behind which the camera has been placed, paying for the salt.

The first two shots of the series describe the ritualized routine of 'Ntoni's passage through the town and into his house. The sequence of greetings is characteristic of the first part of the film before 'Ntoni's marginalization—first, as a failure, then, a drunk. As he enters the house from the street, we hear a greeting to his offscreen grandfather; once he is within the house he greets his mother first, then each of the siblings. Elsewhere in the film the entrances and exits of the sons occasion a benediction from the mother. This time 'Ntoni calls "Sa binirica, nannu!" ("Bless me, Grandpa!") as he enters the courtyard.

The two opening shots set the stage for the important exchange between 'Ntoni and 'Cola in the inner room where the men of the house sleep. The voice-over which could be heard in the first two shots glossed the conversation of the third, fourth, fifth, and sixth: "A month later the mortgage was concluded and 'Ntoni returns to Trezza . . . He feels like the master of the world. He put the money in the bank and has plans for the future . . . He can even think of getting married now that the family will begin to be their own masters."[8] In the exchange with 'Cola and especially in the sequence of gestures whereby he shows his brother the bank book, 'Ntoni reveals the confusion of eros and money in his ambitions: he leans against the open door with his hands in his pockets, adjusts his beret to a rakish angle, singing a love song as he proceeds outside for banter with the neighbors. His passage from the street through the house into the garden confirms his temporary place in the social order of Acitrezza and his false confidence in his success. The three domains of family stability, marriage, and self-employment would insure prestige within his class in Acitrezza. He proudly and good-humoredly enjoys the envy his success naturally arouses. In moving into the garden he even seeks to measure that envy.

The moment catches 'Cola in a reflexive ritual of shaving; he keeps his attention on the mirror while 'Ntoni talks of marriage, but when 'Ntoni moves outside he turns to watch him. Inscribed in this elegant shot there is a hint of the difference between the two brothers which becomes thematic later in another, more intricate passage of 'Cola staring into a mirror, this time with a photograph of 'Ntoni as a sailor tucked in the corner. 'Ntoni, like Mara, sees his fate fixed to his village; but 'Cola and Lucia must escape the village at a heavy price. Within the fictive family the dilemma of the South is suggested. Twelve years later, Visconti will take up the question of the South again, from the perspective of the emigrants, in *Rocco e i suoi fratelli*.

The shot-countershot sequence in the garden (shots 7, 8, 9) is one of the most remarkable in the film. The filmmaker capitalizes on his tendency to articulate depth by organizing the image with significant material in the immediate foreground and in far depth. The inclusions of 'Ntoni and his interlocutors in the same shot delineates the social space of working-class Acitrezza; the cinematic figure which conventionally represents the exchanges of more proximate speakers suddenly expands to include the neighbors. The instantaneous reestablishment of shot-countershot after the sweeping pans introduce new characters in the conversation, without the benefit of an establishing shot of the overall space, underlines the communal forum of the interlocked gardens, while the placement of the camera so close to the head of the supine protagonist declares him the subjective center of a sphere of neighbors.

Such scenes reflect a dimension of Verga's prose style which has been the focus of considerable critical attention: the citizens of the town as a chorus responding to the central family. In shot 7 of the series the first woman congratulates 'Ntoni, "A happy man sings! Good for you!"; but the second offers a cautionary proverb, "The world is made of stairs, some go up and some go down!" and turns vituperative when he spits on her wisdom. The third has a commonplace ready to describe the incipient altercation: "Neighbors are like roof tiles! They're always pouring water on each other!" In the end the first woman calls out that 'Ntoni "laughs, sings, and spits at everybody." The grandfather shares the perspective of the "chorus," bringing it into all family discussions by arguing in proverbs. 'Ntoni, for all of his rebellion against the old ways, imitates his grandfather unwittingly when he tries to convince 'Cola that he should live out his life in Acitrezza, telling him: "The sea's salty all over the world. As soon as we're outside our rocks the current can destroy us." The chorus passively accepts the oppression of the status quo while it aggressively attacks every effort at change as either an expression of pride or a foolish contempt for received wisdom.

In cutting from the garden scene to the Valastro men at sea, the film-maker delays the establishing shot for a more dynamic transition. From the depth of the shot-countershot exchanges the image compresses into the telephoto shot of the crew rowing. We do not know where they are. The next shot, a distanced establishing shot of the now familiar harbor from the shore, informs us that they are just about to pass the massive peaks that mark the outer line of the harbor. The suddenness of the transition, the emphasis on human labor and expression before showing the grace of the ship under sail, and the use of Willi Ferrero's conventional movie music at this point give a heroic accent to this moment of setting sail which the voice-over, coming in for the first time since the first shot in the series, tells us "will remain a memorable day for the Valastros. They go for the first time to fish for themselves."

Throughout the film the voice-over carries the burden of keeping the viewer informed of details that may be missed because of the inaccessibility of the dialect. Ultimately Visconti or perhaps his distributors found this inadequate and added Italian subtitles. Subtitling, however, does not make the commentary superfluous. Along with the information it conveys, the commentary echoes and refracts the tone of Verga's narrative. The very first words "Come sempre . . ." ("As always . . .") ironically align the commentator with the tradition-bound "choral" voice. The ancestral house by the medlar tree gets mentioned before the family is named: "A house like so many others, made of old stone, and its walls have seen as many years as the fisherman's trade . . ."

Here the hyperbole has a "choral" function, as elsewhere metaphor (the wholesalers must "swallow" their anger), hypothetical formulations ("But perhaps the old men are used to submitting; if the young men would go to the pier to sell, who knows, things might turn out differently"), rhetorical questions ("So why shouldn't the fishermen try to do without the wholesalers who oppress them?"), anaphora ("There sat 'Cola and there grandfather, there 'Vanni and there Alfio . . ."), and proverbs ("Che il mare è amaro e il marianaio muore in mare" ["How bitter is the sea and the sailor who dies at sea"], the final line of the commentary which includes a play on the sounds *mar* and *mur*)—all indicate an affinity between the voice-over and the world view of those in the film.

The implication of the narrating voice in a form of free indirect discourse can be best illustrated by bringing together the interventions on a single theme. I have chosen the four which comment on the relationship of 'Ntoni to Nedda, because they are particularly rich in irony and figuration and because they are not too extensive. (1) The first accompanies the transition from the Valastro house, after the first night of fishing, to the introduction of Nedda: "If there is any relief, a moment's happiness, it's in thinking about one's girl and for one's girl. One can even give up the rest, because men are made to be caught by girls just as the fish in the sea are made for those who eat them." (2) After the great catch of anchovies, 'Ntoni visits Nedda to make a date for a stroll. The voice-over comments on the girl's hesitation: "Nedda wanted to be begged only out of coquetry, of course, because in Trezza even the things close to the heart are tied to work and wealth." (3) The day after the salting Nedda keeps her date with 'Ntoni. When it ends the voice-over poses a rhetorical question and concludes with free indirect discourse: "What does your heart say, 'Ntoni, now that you have everything you wanted? Everything you dreamed of seems near to you." (4) Finally, after the wreck of the boat and the destruction of 'Ntoni's dreams, the ironical free indirect speech underlines the pain of finding Nedda's door closed to him: "Meanwhile 'Ntoni and his younger brothers perhaps still don't realize the full extent of their misfortune . . . But 'Ntoni still has Nedda's love. Nedda will stand by him" [ellipsis in original]. When Nedda appears for the last time, as the girl or perhaps wife of one of the wholesalers, the commentator says nothing.

Inherent in the very nature of a third-person voice-over narration is a subtle distancing from the characters that voice-over describes. In bridging this distance through free indirect discourse and the repetition of proverbs, the external voice calls attention to the very gap it would cover. Miccichè describes a dialectical movement between the filmmaker's empathy and his inevitable distance from the men and women he has filmed:

> The Italian commentary certainly synthesizes the point of view—intellectually enlightened and ideologically advanced—of the author on the archetypical conditions of class struggle; but also ratifies the estrangement of the spectator and makes an abstract ethical-ideological question of the call to complicity instead of a concrete and immediate historical-political problem. . . . In fact, the evident aporia of *La terra trema*—and in certain ways the very reason for its greatness—is above all the fact that it is a represen-

tation of age-old injustice, but also a document of his own passive contemplation. As if Visconti had intended to denounce at once both the cruel established order and his own incapacity to do anything but contemplate it aesthetically: if the social order of things is determined by bourgeois "economy" the formal order of their representation is determined by bourgeois "esthetics"; even if it is called "Neorealism."[9]

In the last minutes of the film, in an episode that has no source in Verga, a bold and vivid illustration of the ghostly pertinence of a seemingly outdated text occurs in the offices of the Cyclops Company for Selling and Transporting Fish. As in a great many public and corporate buildings, a banal slogan of the Duce had been inscribed on the wall. Behind the heads of the wholesalers we read the traces of a varnished-out phrase, "Decisamente verso il popolo—Mussolini" ("Decisively toward the people"). The director seems at pains to include the reminder of the dictatorship in several of the shots of the wholesalers grossly taunting the Valastros and another hungry worker, whom they need for their new boats. Their cooperative aptly bears the name of the cannibal bully who tried to devour Odysseus and his crew. The classical allusion remains distant and tentative: the wholesalers may be gloating prematurely before the men they misuse seize power, but the writing on the wall makes it abundantly clear that there has scarcely been a cosmetic transformation of Fascism in Acitrezza.

The visual concomitant of the unblottable traces of a literary and political past that still largely defined the Sicilian reality would be the photographic family portrait of the Valastros, taken while 'Ntoni was in his navy uniform and before the sea death of his father. At the beginning of the film Lucia stares at this photograph for a long time before the camera reveals it to us in an accentuated tracking gesture. Lucia's speech introduces the viewers to the characters within the Valastro family and informs them of the father's death. A comparable tracking toward the picture accompanies 'Cola's secret farewell as he speaks to the individual figures in the group portrait, asking forgiveness from their images. When the remnants of the family must leave the house the bank has seized, the mother carries the photograph and her baby. In the end when the sons go back to the sea, Mara puts the photograph on the wall of their rented house, beside the cheap representation of the Sacred Heart of Jesus.

The photograph is an illusion of familial stability from the period of

Fascism that acquires the quasi-religious aura of an icon as its optimistic promise of continuity proves a fraud in the face of desertion, sickness, and death. Conventionally posed in a studio, in Catania (Lucia tells us), it is antipodal to the analytical gaze of the film camera and its incessantly temporal perspective. For Lucia, 'Cola, the mother, and Mara, the Valastro family is most real and powerful in that idealized form. At its most trenchant moments, Visconti's film suggests that the cliché "the sea is bitter" should be read: life in the Italy of the Christian Democrats is a bitter maintenance of the Fascist and pre-Fascist economic and social order at the tragic expense of those most easily deceived by slogans and icons.

CHAPTER 4

De Sica's and
Zavattini's
Neopopulism

Those "most easily deceived by slogans and icons" in the urban centers of Italy are the protagonists of the major collaborations of Vittorio De Sica and Cesare Zavattini in the years of the vital crisis following the war. In 1971 De Sica told Charles Samuels:

> All my films are about the search for human solidarity. In *Bicycle Thief* this solidarity occurs, but how long does it last? Twenty-four hours. One experiences moments, only moments of solidarity. . . . One needs something that lasts longer. . . . I wanted to call my films from *Shoeshine* on, "Egoism #1, #2, #3." *Umberto D* is "Egoism # 4." [1]

The first thing to note about this astonishing statement is the filmmaker's isolation of the four canonical films from the corpus of twenty-five films he had directed until then. The burden of this chapter will be to discover the relationship of the symbolic structures which reveal the conflict of "egoism" and solidarity to the historical contexts in which they are inscribed and to which they deliberately refer. I shall concentrate on the first two films in the series and more briefly discuss *Miracolo a Milano*. *Umberto D* falls outside of the historical framework of this book.

Even though he does not include it in the canonical list, De Sica's first collaboration with Zavattini illustrates the moral consequences of selfishness more blatantly than any of the four which follow it: in *I bambini ci guardano* (1942) a mother's adulterous affair and her husband's subsequent suicide are seen from her young son's perspective. By linking his so-called neorealistic work under the rubric of "Egoism," De Sica poses a curious puzzle that the interview never solves: Are we to read the protagonists of these four films as egoists or as the victims of egoists, or perhaps as both? Ultimately what does he mean by "egoism"?

Taken as a series the four films confirm the idea that the vice of "egoism," as De Sica apparently conceived it, entailed the failure to keep faith. This loss of fidelity is not so much religious as intersubjective, a lack of solidarity. Gian Piero Brunetta astutely observed: "De Sica and Zavattini are the authors who were most free from the ideological and religious conditioning"[2] of the major filmmakers of the postwar period. Let us consider schematically their four postwar collaborations in terms of "egoism" and broken faith. The horse that the two young protagonists of *Sciuscià*, Pasquale and Giuseppe, share is a pledge of faith, which the law courts throw into question; that faith is further undermined by the cruelties of prison, until the horse becomes the proximate cause of homicide. In *Ladri di biciclette* from the very start the unemployed Ricci's loss of faith exacerbates his appetite for despair and defeat, which became apparent the moment he received his long-awaited job; for then he complained to his wife that he would not be able to accept it because the bicycle he needed to execute it had been pawned. That despair turns to childish delight when she pawns their sheets to redeem it. But after it is stolen, his sudden anger at his son and, ultimately, his own attempt at theft could be said to represent progressively crippling stages of egoism. Totò, the utterly benign hero of *Miracolo a Milano,* runs to the opposite extreme: his incautious goodwill renders him unfit for worldly egoism. Finally, the despair of old age in *Umberto D,* complementing the desperation of youth in *Sciuscià,* marks the nadir of this dissection of faithlessness in human relationships. In the end, that despair turns against the very icon of faith, when the protagonist attempts to kill himself and his dog; for in the Christian iconographical tradition the dog is such a symbol.

In fact, each of these four films revolves around the acquisition and loss of a symbol of secular faith. Even though the filmmakers chose symbols with progressively more traditional and religious resonance, they seem to have done so in order to point up the social failure of religion.

Along with the state, the courts and the justice system, the political parties, and the police, institutional religion breaks faith with De Sica's and Zavattini's heroes and poses obstacles to their quests for solidarity.

The white horse of *Sciuscià* has only a marginal religious significance. The Renaissance tradition in which horses generally represented lust has no relevance whatsoever in the context of the film. The white horse, specifically, was the first of the four in Revelation. In the almost magical atmosphere of the final scene there is a trace of its apocalyptic menace when Pasquale accidentally kills Giuseppe. Significantly the brand name of the bicycle Ricci lost was "Fides," Latin for faith, as if so incongruous an object of iconographic meaning had to be labeled as in a medieval painting. The dove Lolotta gave Totò clearly traces an ironical distance from its Christian significance as a seal of faith. I shall elaborate on the parabolic meaning of the playful transformation of the icon of the Holy Ghost below. Thus, *Miracolo a Milano* marks the culmination of the iconographic exercise in this series of films.

Sciuscià

According to Paul Ginsborg:

> During both the Parri and De Gasperi governments the traditional state structure and administration inherited from Fascism was quietly being consolidated. . . . No serious critique was made of the many semi-independent special agencies created by Fascism for the purposes of social assistance or intervention in the economy. Finally, no moves were taken to alter the structure or recruiting patterns of the judiciary, even though Togliatti was Minister of Justice. . . . *Epurazione* proved a disastrous failure. The judiciary itself went untouched, and duly proceeded to discharge as many cases as it dared. . . . In 1960 it was calculated that sixty-two out of sixty-four prefects (the central government's principal representatives in the provinces) had been functionaries under Fascism. So too had all 135 police chiefs and their 139 deputies. Only five of these last had in any way contributed to the Resistance.[3]
>
> . . . .
>
> The judges who had served under Fascism kept their posts, and the Codice Rocco, the Fascist penal code, remained in force.[4]

Sciuscià exposed the void in the system of Italian justice that had not been corrected by the mere overthrow of official fascism. Pasquale and Giuseppe represent an even more optimistic and pathetically naive vision of entrepreneurial success in occupied Italy than the Valastros did a couple of years later. The horse they purchase, of course, is a romantic symbol of their friendship and the illusion of liberation and happiness opened by the new order in Italy. But it is also a vestige of the old order with its outdated fantasies of Garibaldian heroics, as its martial name, "Bersagliere,"[5] suggests; it has become so outmoded that it comes within the grasp of their meager capital. Within the economics of the film, the horse is of use only as a decoration for traditional funerals or as a tourist attraction.

Ironically, the family is one of the social institutions corrupting the idyllic friendship of the two boys. Although Pasquale, the orphan, should be the more deprived of the pair, Giuseppe suffers most, precisely because he has a family. His criminal brother tricks him and Pasquale into the scam for which they are arrested. The code of family loyalty keeps him from naming his brother as his victimizer; the lawyer his family hires, presumably an agent of organized crime, wants to throw the blame onto Pasquale to get his client a lighter sentence. In this he succeeds, but only after the prison authorities have successfully and deceptively driven a wedge between the boys. The critique of the family is carried into the prison scenes: Raffaele, Pasquale's friend who is dying of tuberculosis, suffers from his mother's neglect, and the affluent Archangeli can get money from his mother but not his father, who wants him "to pay his debt to society."

Furthermore, the film alluded to the widespread corruption of the postwar society in a number of details: An American soldier repeatedly gets a free shoeshine by saying "Tomorrow" when Giuseppe demands payment; the reformatory director returns the Roman salute (a Fascist gesture) by automatic reflex to his cook; and the police chief condones a guard's theft of food sent to the juvenile prisoners. De Sica accounted for the polemical thrust of these details thus: "That is the result of the war, whose first victims were those poor youngsters, ruined by Americans, money, the black market in cigarettes. And then we put them in jail!"[6]

The justice system itself is a mere continuation of Fascism. The public defender, Pasquale's lawyer, is nearly senile. The argument of Giuseppe's lawyer deliberately scapegoats Pasquale, who receives a sentence of two years to Giuseppe's one. But it is the judge who does the final damage. Questioning Pasquale about the horse, he inquires about the contract of

Uccellacci e uccellini:
Father and Son.
(Courtesy of the
Anthology Film
Archives.)

Ladri di biciclette:
Father and Son.
(Courtesy of the
Museum of Modern
Art, Film Stills
Archive.)

Uccellacci e uccellini:
Parodic Trinity:
Father, Son, and
Crow. (Courtesy of
the Pacific Film
Archives, Berkeley
Museum.)

Partial and Parodic Trinities

Roma, città aperta:
The torture of
Manfredi. (Courtesy
of the Museum of
Modern Art, Film
Stills Archive.)

Rocco e i suoi fratelli:
Simone about to kill
Nadia. (Courtesy of
Robert Haller.)

Paisà: The burial of
an anonymous
partisan. (Courtesy of
the Museum of
Modern Art, Film
Stills Archive.)

Signs of the Cross

Accattone:
Accattone between
two theives, just
before his death.
(Courtesy of the
Museum of
Modern Art, Film
Stills Archive.)

*Salvatore
Giuliano:* Pietà of
Giuliano's mother
mourning over
his corpse.
(Courtesy of the
Anthology Film
Archives.)

L'avventura:
The final shot of
Claudia and
Sandro, a modern-
ist pietà. (Courtesy
of Seymour
Chatman.)

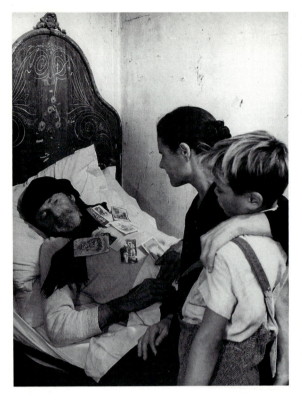

La terra trema:
Grandfather Valastro,
near death, covered
with religious images.
(Courtesy of the
Museum of Modern Art,
Film Stills Archive.)

Salvatore Giuliano:
Giuliano's corpse shown
to his family. (Courtesy
of the Museum of
Modern Art, Film Stills
Archive.)

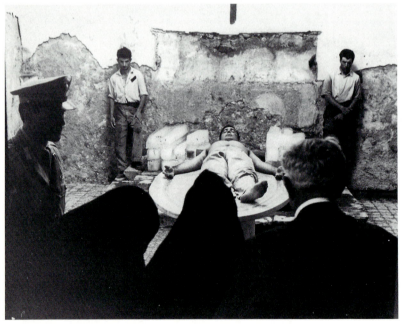

Echoes of the "Christo morto"

La terra trema:
Morning in the
Valastro house.
(Courtesy of the
Pacific Film Archives,
Berkeley Museum.)

La terra trema: 'Ntoni
visits the boat that the
Valastros once owned.
(Courtesy of the
Anthology Film
Archives.)

Salvatore Giuliano:
The occupation of
Montelepre.
(Courtesy of the
Museum of Modern
Art, Film Stills
Archive.)

Depth Compositions with Foreground, Middle, and Background Details

Roma, città aperta: Don Pietro reads the suggestive glance of Saint Rocco toward Venus. (Courtesy of the Museum of Modern Art, Film Stills Archive.)

La dolce vita: The statue of Christ carried across Rome at the beginning of the film. (Courtesy of the Museum of Modern Art, Film Stills Archive.)

Fellini and Mastroianni examine the fish that will appear at the end of *La dolce vita.* (Courtesy of the Museum of Modern Art, Film Stills Archive.)

Ironic Versions of Sacred Sites

Miracolo a Milano:
The final scene at the
Milan cathedral.
(Courtesy of Robert
Haller.)

Visconti directing
Rocco and Nadia in
Rocco e i suoi fratelli
atop the cathedral of
Milan. (Courtesy of
Robert Haller.)

L'avventura: Claudia
in the bell tower of
the cathedral of
Noto. (Courtesy of
the Museum of
Modern Art, Film
Stills Archive.)

Ironic Versions of Sacred Sites

Paisà: The American soldier challenging Neopolitan puppets—an echo of *Don Quixote.* (Courtesy of the Museum of Modern Art, Film Stills Archive.)

L'avventura: Sandro turns from the baroque painting of Roman Charity. (Courtesy of Seymour Chatman.)

Baroque Misreadings

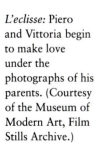

La terra trema:
'Cola studies the
family portrait
before leaving
home. (Courtesy
of the Museum of
Modern Art, Film
Stills Archive.)

L'eclisse: Piero
and Vittoria begin
to make love
under the
photographs of his
parents. (Courtesy
of the Museum of
Modern Art, Film
Stills Archive.)

Responses to the Photographic Image

Roma, città aperta: Marcello and a friend walk away from Don Pietro's execution. (Courtesy of the Museum of Modern Art, Film Stills Archive.)

Sciuscià: Pasquale and Giuseppe sleeping in the stable. (Courtesy of the Museum of Modern Art, Film Stills Archive.)

The Child as the Icon of a New Italy

La dolce vita: Marcello
and Anita in the fountain.
(Courtesy of the Pacific
Film Archives, Berkeley
Museum.)

La notte: Lidia and
Roberto at the pool.
(Courtesy of the Pacific
Film Archives, Berkeley
Museum.)

Erotic Follies

La dolce vita: The
final party at Fregole.
(Courtesy of the
Museum of Modern
Art, Film Stills
Archive.)

La notte:
Gherardini's party.
(Courtesy of the
Anthology Film
Archives.)

Il deserto rosso: The
party in the cabin.
(Courtesy of the
Museum of Modern
Art, Film Stills
Archive.)

Orgies and Carnivals

Il posto: The New Year's office party. (Courtesy of the Museum of Modern Art, Film Stills Archive.)

Olmi filming the New Year's party in *Il posto.* (Courtesy of the Anthology Film Archives.)

I fidanzati: Sicilian Carnevale. (Courtesy of the Museum of Modern Art, Film Stills Archive.)

La notte: Solo image of Valentina when Lidia and Giovanni leave her room. (Courtesy of the Anthology Film Archives.)

La notte: Dual foregrounding of Lidia and Giovanni in a nightclub. (Courtesy of the Anthology Film Archives.)

La notte: Triadic grouping of Valentina, Lidia, and Giovanni. (Courtesy of the Pacific Film Archives, Berkeley Museum.)

Antonioni's Compositions

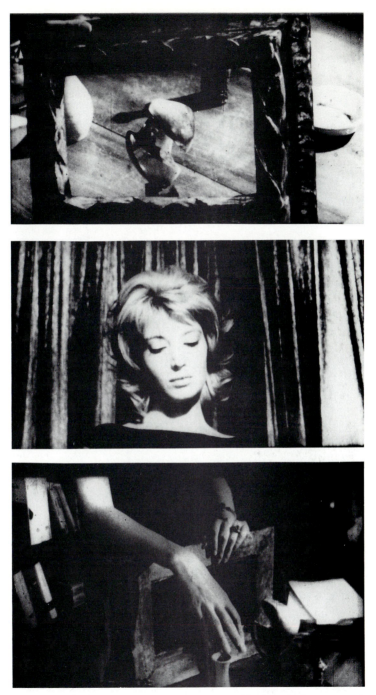

L'eclisse: Consecutive shots. Vittoria composes objects at the beginning of the film. (Courtesy of the Anthology Film Archives.)

L'eclisse: Riccardo and Vittoria before the EUR Tower.
(Courtesy of the Anthology Film Archives.)

Il deserto rosso: Corrado's seduction of Giuliana includes a visit to a radio telescope.
(Courtesy of the Museum of Modern Art, Film Stills Archive.)

Antonioni's Compositions

mutual ownership the boys have drawn up. Of course, they have none. Thus the judge introduces the concept of the horse as a capital investment and the question of contested ownership which constitutes a factor in the final tragedy. Giuseppe's lawyer quashes all discussion of the whereabouts of the horse; for, as the court correctly guesses, he expects to sell the horse for his fee.

Rhetorically, in his defense of Giuseppe, the lawyer articulates the filmmakers' condemnation of the society that criminalizes children: "Return these innocents to their homes, their families, their schools, and their jobs. This is not rhetoric, gentlemen. Because if you find them guilty, then we, all of us, are also guilty; for in pursuing our passions we have abandoned our children to themselves: they are always more and more alone." Yet he is so thoroughly corrupt that his speech indeed seems to be merely formular; for he told Giuseppe that truth is only for the confessional, when he urged him to pass the blame on to Pasquale.

The accumulation of deceptions, frauds, and misinterpretations is so thick in *Sciuscià* that it reflects the heritage of New Comedy. The characters surrounding the protagonists are the one-dimensional "humors" of that genre: the obese confidence man, the corrupt lawyer, the senile lawyer, the insensitive reformatory director. Even the other juvenile prisoners are stock types: the rich bully, the mortally afflicted peacemaker, the spy, and even an intellectual with his head always in a book. Finally, the fact that Pasquale has no parents completes the New Comedy pattern. But instead of a festive conclusion—in which the orphan would discover a previously hidden, and usually rich, parent—the film ends in melodrama, which would have been even more extreme, according to Sergio Amidei, without the behind-the-scenes intervention of a shady Vatican official[7] who persuaded the producer to disallow Pasquale's suicide after he accidentally murders Giuseppe. Thus the film reverses New Comedy's traditional staging of the triumph of the young over the old; the adult world, with its heritage of Fascism, destroys the children it could not corrupt.

The misinterpretations and deceptions driving the film also occur in the iconographical and the cinematic details. A comic moment illustrates the symbolical confusion of justice and power, in its most antiquated form, when a group of schoolchildren, companions of Pasquale and Giuseppe who have come to observe their trial, pass through the inner courtyard of the Palazzo della Giustizia. Confronted with Enrico Quattrini's "Statua della Legge," one of the children asks who the colossal female form is;

another erroneously identifies her as Queen Margherita—the mother of the king, Vittorio Emanuelle III. The iconographical mistake equates, in the eyes of those who will inherit the nation, the legal system with the controversial and moribund monarchy; for less than two months after the film premiered, Italy voted to become a republic (2 June 1946).

Bondanella:

> In all his early neorealist films, De Sica is even more conscious than Rossellini of the fact that his filmed "reality" is a product of cinematic illusion, and he takes pleasure in revealing this to the careful viewer. Inside the prison, an American documentary film . . . is screened, but it is interrupted by a freak accident as the director humorously but unmistakably rejects the view that the cinema must necessarily reflect the outside world of social reality. Earlier, the prisoners in the courtyard mimic grand opera . . . , warning the viewer of the melodramatic qualities of what will follow.[8]

The film screening leads to a fire which makes possible the escape of Giuseppe and his cellmates, and brings about the death of a tubercular boy trampled in the riot that ensues. The newsreel, *Notizie del mondo libero*, describes MacArthur's war in the Pacific. In a pathetic variation on the misidentified statue, the tubercular prisoner who misses his fishing family in Naples, now dispersed, exclaims in delight "il mare! il mare!" at seeing a shot of waves intercut between images of battleships firing their guns. His longing for a sight of the southern seascape generates his inventive misreading of the American military propaganda film. His tacit censure of the manifest violence of the film forebodes his imminent death.

A more subtle comment on the nature of cinematic illusion occurs when Pasquale "witnesses" the beating of Giuseppe. He is made to watch as his friend is dragged into an adjoining office through an open door. But he cannot see that he has been led out through a back door. His angle of vision permits him to see only the "teacher" wielding his strap. The camera reveals to the viewer that he is hitting a sandbag while another boy, a "spy" bribed into collaboration, howls as if in great pain. The synchronization of a framed image—a synecdoche of the beating—with the theatricalized howls deceives Pasquale precisely the way in which in *Roma, città aperta* the very similar framing of the torture of the Resistance hero, Manfredi, witnessed through the open door by the priest, Don Pietro, creates a powerful cinematic illusion for film viewers. If the allusion is deliberate, it would suggest a continuity between the cruelties of the Nazi occupation and the penal bureaucracy of the liberated monarchy. A less generous view of the linkage of these two scenes might suggest that De Sica alluded to, and rejected for his film, the illusionary violence that contributed to the popular success of *Roma, città aperta,* the one box-office hit of neorealism.

Bondanella suggests that there is an autocritique in the oppositional play between opera and documentary film. The recurrence of operatic allusions in *Miracolo a Milano* and *Umberto D* supports this contention. Whereas problems of melodrama come to the fore in Visconti's frequent citations of opera, in the De Sica–Zavattini films opera has a negative association with middle-class pretensions: Totò uses the magical dove to make the commander of the carabinieri attacking his shantytown sing rather than issue orders; Umberto's landlady listens to operatic recordings when she aspires to marry the owner of a cinema and evict Umberto, her long-standing tenant. In *Sciuscià* the operatic parody crucially bridges the transition from the interview with Giuseppe's mother, in which he learns that Pasquale told the authorities about his brother, and their subsequent confrontation in the exercise yard. Thus, it isolates the sentimental agon of the two boys from the assembly of juvenile prisoners.

The very conception of a film on the shoeshine boys of Rome came from a project in the journal *Film d'oggi,* in which De Sica participated with De Santis, Puccini, Amidei, and others more closely associated with the Communist Resistance than he had been. However, the producer Armando William Tamburella chose De Sica to direct a script he himself had drawn from this material. Although he rejected Tamburella's script, De Sica seized the idea for the film and brought in Zavattini for a new plot line. The subsequent scenario, written by Amidei along with the writers of *I bambini ci guardano,* novelist Cesare Giulio Viola and Adolfo Franci, inscribes class issues within the prison: the most vicious delinquent, Archangeli, is animated by an Oedipal rage against his wealthy father; and the most bathetic figure is the tubercular boy parked in the prison by his irresponsible middle-class mother.

Both the assembly of screenwriters and the emphasis on the child's perspective link *Sciuscià* to De Sica's (and Zavattini's) earlier film. The well-organized plot, with New Comedy elements, is a further indication of the continuity between his films of the Fascist period and his postwar production. The shift from middle-class to proletarian protagonists, the criticism of the system of social discipline, and the inscriptions of class difference are indices of their altered perspective after the collapse of Fascism and of the influence of their collaborators from the Left. Yet the complex of thematic issues De Sica collapsed into the category of "egoism" would be the most significant elements of continuity over this period of political change. In the light of such "egoism" the solidarity between the two protagonists proves very frail. In prison, the rival cells unwittingly conspire with the jailers to wreck that solidarity, so that the melodramatic consequence of so strong an attachment is homicide.

The casting of *Sciuscià* demonstrates the cosmetic compromises that were part of De Sica's conception of the limits of cinematic realism, even when censorship was not at stake. He based the film on his acquaintance with two Roman shoeshine boys—Scimmietta, who lived in an elevator even though he had some minimal family support, and Cappellone, an orphan whose head was deformed by rickets. By the time the film was made Cappellone was in prison for theft. According to the filmmaker, "Cappellone and Scimmietta could not be actors: they were too ugly, almost deformed."[9] Instead he found two nonprofessionals, Rinaldo Smordoni and Franco Interlenghi. According to De Sica, it was Smordoni "who seemed prodigiously talented, and being the more beautiful of the two, attracted everyone's attention; they said he would grow up to be a true actor." Actually the handsome Interlenghi eventually became a popular movie star. De Sica and Zavattini overlooked the sexual lives of their characters, even though one of the actors had pimped and Zavattini recorded in his diary the story of three shoeshine boys who "kept a girl of twelve as a mistress; they paid her fifty lire."[10] De Sica told Charles Samuels he did not develop the homoerotic implications of jealousies within the boys' prison because the idea "revolted"[11] him.

De Sica and Zavattini transformed their observations of the horse-riding passion of Cappellone and Scimmietta and of the latter's actual conviction for stealing a gas mask into the sort of Dickensian or Chaplinesque fable they both thought an effective film should be. The symbolic aura of the white horse Bersagliere—emblematic of their yearnings for freedom at the beginning of the film, a mute witness to their mutual affection as they sleep together in a hayloft the night they purchase him, proleptically appropriated to draw a hearse when they are in jail, ironically pulling a sightseeing coach for GIs past the Palazzo della Giustizia the day of the boys' trial, and witnessing their fate at the conclusion—suggests the fairy-tale world of Zavattini's fiction and the magical realm of *Miracolo a Milano*.

The artificiality of some of the sets, particularly that of the final scene (for which the filmmaker blamed the producer's economies), distances De Sica's work from the location shooting of Rossellini and Visconti. The studio sets also permit more camera movement, and even craning in the juvenile prison, than is found in the indoor scenes of *Roma, città aperta, Paisà,* or *La terra trema.*

De Sica has spoken regretfully of the commercial aspects of his film career: "All my good films, which I financed myself, made nothing. Only my bad films made money. Money has been my ruin." [12] Yet even in making his so-called good films he admitted making damaging concessions and compromises to producers and their formular conceptions of viable cinema, with the sole exception of *Umberto D.* The conclusion of *Sciuscià* was a concession to the producer's budget; De Sica wanted to shoot on location. He has also claimed that he dislikes using music to provoke emotional effects, but producers insist upon it. Alessandro Cicognini's score insistently determines the emotional tone of every scene. Yet it is evident that De Sica and Zavattini have assimilated and interiorized dramatic and narrative conventions that Rossellini and Visconti challenged in their radical incorporation of documentary strategies in *Paisà* and *La terra trema.*

De Sica put much more emphasis on preproduction than his distinguished contemporaries. That is why Cesare Zavattini's role is so important. He provided the director with a simple and effective plot, integrating the dramatic anguish of alienated victims with glimpses of the social institutions that failed to alleviate their sufferings or even made them worse. When sets were to be constructed, the filmmakers studied actual locations, such as the Porta Portese prison which provided the model for the boys' reformatory. Interlenghi recalled:

> De Sica had total patience, total and obsessive; he was able to keep explaining for hours on end precisely what he wanted to get. . . .
>
> *Sciuscià* had a perfect shooting script, a perfectly fixed, well-worked-out scenario. Only it was based on the truth. [13]

The mimetic integration of setting and gesture, resulting from the research, planning, and meticulous direction, lends a degree of verisimilitude to the blatantly sentimental narrative, characteristically provided by Zavattini— for although he is not so credited, his letters made it clear that the story line was his alone. [14]

Ladri di biciclette

Here is De Sica's description of the literary origins of *Ladri di biciclette:*

> One day Zavattini said to me: "A book by Luigi Bartolini just came out;
> read it, and use the title as the starting point." The book was *Ladri di bici-
> clette.* Bartolini granted the title and the right to adapt the idea of the book
> into a film for a certain fee. Later, when the film was finished, he would pro-
> test violently. . . .
>
> In truth the plot is radically different from that of the book (which is
> actually cheerful, colorful, and I would say picaresque). It is enough to say
> that the protagonist, the man who is robbed, isn't Bartolini but a poster
> hanger who runs around Rome desperately looking for his vehicle. There is
> another ambience, other interests adapted to my means and my aims. Why
> have we kept the title and even acquired the rights to make a free adaptation
> of the book? In due recognition of a remarkable artist whose vivid pages
> have given, even if indirectly, the inspiration for my new film. My aim, I have
> said, was to reintroduce the dramatic into quotidian situations, the marvel-
> ous in a little news item, even in the smallest news item, considered by most
> people throwaway material.[15]

Apparently Bartolini complained later that he did not get a screen
credit, and even that the filmmakers were under an obligation to make a
faithful screen version of his book. Zavattini's answer (29 June 1948) has
been published in his letters:

> In fact, there's not a single shot in the film from your book and there's not
> even anything in the scenario from it. . . . Let's see if I can refresh our memo-
> ries a little. I read your book and got excited over it. Frankly I'm tired of
> repeating left and right that I liked the book profoundly and it profoundly
> amused me. I thought and rethought about the thieves and the bicycles and
> through the most indirect and obscure ways the idea of a film for De Sica
> came to me, of the poor worker who searches in vain along with his little son
> for his vehicle. I wrote twenty pages immediately and De Sica said I had truly
> found the theme he wanted. . . . [W]e made a contract because I was pleased
> to let you know that the occasion of the long-sought scenario for De Sica had
> been presented by your book, just as recently, looking at some swimmers in

the Tiber, I got the notion out of the blue that one of them pretended to have died for some reason. I hope the swimmers won't demand screenwriting credit now. . . .

Zavattini exaggerated when he claimed that he took *nothing at all* from the novel besides its title, which, he pointed out to Bartolini, had been used even earlier for a short story by Arturo Tofanelli. There is indeed *very little* from the novella in the film. Bartolini's first-person narrator, a middle-class writer and painter who shares any number of biographical traits with the author, searches Rome for several days for his stolen bicycle, moving about on a second, less elegant bicycle he kept in his studio. One of his hunting grounds is the outdoor Porta Portese flea market which appears in the film. His encounter with an angry working-class crowd in the Via Panico, a street of bordellos, appears in the film without the political resonance of Bartolini's story in which the protagonist avoided a beating by producing his Resistance and left-wing credentials until a policeman showed up. Eventually he learned the name of the thief, but he could not recover the bicycle until a prostitute, who had formerly modeled for him, mediated with a bribe.

Bartolini's novella captures the spirit of the immediate postwar corruption as no film quite does. The pervasiveness of robbery, the hypocrisy of former Fascist supporters mouthing republican slogans, and the varieties of prostitution depicted in it may have been too controversial for the sentimentalizing strain of the cinema. Furthermore, the dearth of heroic or even generous and sympathetic gestures in the novella should have made it a very unlikely candidate for adaptation.

The cinema itself is one of the cultural forces for which Bartolini expresses his contempt in *Ladri di biciclette:* "I look upon cinematography as a vulgar art which because of its very nature will never be able to detach itself from the commonplace."[16] But even though this rejection has its counterpart in *Sciuscià*—and, in fact, in each of the four major De Sica–Zavattini collaborations following the war there is a negative or ironical reference to cinema—these allusions are not as sweeping as Bartolini's: De Sica and Zavattini refer disparagingly to the commercial industry rather than to the kind of cinema to which they aspired. In the film the protagonist finds a job as a poster hanger. On his first job he is sent out to paper billboards with advertisements for a Rita Hayworth film.

The massive domination of the American cinema in Italy was disturbing to many of the filmmakers of the period, especially those of the Left. In 1948, according to Carlo Lizzani, 54 films were made in Italy, but 874 were imported, of which 558 were from the United States. Only 13 percent of the tickets sold that year were for Italian films. At the same time Italy was surpassed only by the United States and the Soviet Union in the number of its movie houses. It was thus a very lucrative market for American exploitation. In 1949, the year following the release of *Ladri di biciclette*, a law was passed requiring the screening of Italian films in every cinema at least eighty days a year. Thus, ironically, the job for which Ricci waited so long and which was to have given him so much security reflected the then unregulated collusion of the municipal advertising machinery with the colonization of Italian filmgoing by the American industry in 1948.

The narrator of Bartolini's novella is a more ferocious "egoist" than any of De Sica's inventions. Unlike the film's passive Ricci, Bartolini's hero tirelessly heaps rancor on publishers, women, critics of his works, the poor, post-Liberation leftists, in short, everyone he encounters. The milieu of the novella is much closer to Moravia's *La noia*, written fifteen years later, than to De Sica's film, released only two years after his book. Bartolini seems blind to the character of the self-important artist he has created. He represents misanthropy as sensitivity:

> A poet such as I am needs a bicycle as he needs bread; and if bread serves to nourish him, so the bicycle represents another kind of bread, the bread of spiritual good. That spiritual good, which I have already experienced, is attained only after the city has been left at least a dozen kilometers behind, far beyond the outskirts of the suburbs. So I have a great need for a bicycle in order to lose myself, to escape, to get away from human society.[17]

He is quick to read opposition and criticism as envy:

> But elevated tastes . . . belong to Baudelaire and to me, and are not shared by others. Most people want large paintings. Artists have always praised my etchings and never my paintings, for the ridiculous reason that, not being etchers themselves, they have little to fear from my success in the field, while as a painter they consider me a dangerous winner of prizes, who has become a favorite with private collectors.[18]

His self-adulation becomes unintentionally comic when he narcissistically laments at the sight of an attractive thief: "He seemed an Adonis-like image of physical beauty and I, looking at him, thought with melancholy of my own youth, now past, when I had been as handsome as he" (p. 9). Nothing could be further from the timid, bewildered laborer Ricci in De Sica's film. Yet despite its naked vanity and mean-spirited disgust at the Roman subproletariat, the novella's picture of the economy of survival and exploitation is both more vivid and convincing than any of the films contemporary to it, which could not directly challenge the rigid censorship in sexual matters and consistently idealized their central characters as pure-minded victims of social injustice.

Thus, when Zavattini called his attention to Bartolini's novella, De Sica had in his hands the raw material for a study in egoism. But clearly that was of no interest to him. We must therefore reexamine in the light of the film what he might have meant in calling it "Egoism #2." Ostensibly, *Ladri di biciclette* directly represents the agony of an unemployed man. Unemployment was at its peak in 1948: 2,142,000 of a population of 46,000,000 were out of work. The filmmakers gradually unfold the portrait of a man of goodwill, with strong family affections, whose character has been malformed by prolonged unemployment, although they tell us nothing of his past or of his years without work. The "egoism" that poses obstacles to his forming solidarity with others in his plight, or keeping faith with his sense of honor and justice, seems to be the interiorization of his social defeat. From the very opening when he does not hear his name called after two years of waiting for a job until another unemployed aspirant rouses him from his stupor, he needs the inventions and energies of others in order to act. His wife silently ignores his whining and helplessness as she decides to pawn their sheets to redeem their already pawned bicycle; only his young son, Bruno, who has been earning some money as a gas-station attendant, knows the serial number of the bicycle after it is stolen; his friend Baiocco and his fellow sanitation workers lead Ricci and Bruno around the flea market in his search; and it is Bruno who knows about football teams, how to add accurately in the restaurant, and how to find a policeman to save his father from the mob in the thief's neighborhood. The price of Bruno's superior practicality is a slap from his father when he mildly criticizes how he let an old man whom they glimpsed talking to the thief slip away. In the end Ricci cannot even steal, and again Bruno tacitly saves him in his darkest moment from the angry crowd that caught him.

As De Sica represents him, Ricci is not a fool, nor is he a figure who suggests the New Comedy as do the obese Communist Baiocco and his friends; his failures are so underplayed that he loses neither his dignity nor our sympathy. This is the carefully calculated result of directing a non-actor.

De Sica makes Ricci's passivity and his ineptitude a vehicle for purchasing the viewer's sympathy. His only arena of expression is the family. Despite the indications that even there he lacks the resourcefulness of his wife or his son, the abstract ideal of the nuclear family underwrites the film's sentimentality. Why do the Riccis have no extended family in Rome? Are he and his wife immigrants? Pierre Sorlin, in *European Cinemas, European Societies, 1939–1990*,[19] argues that he may be a northern immigrant and she a Roman, because of her familiarity with offices and her movement about the city. He notes that they live in the suburban development of Val Melaina, a Fascist project for moving the poor five miles from the city center and its shanties. It is there that we first see him sitting on the ground outside the employment office. Sorlin concludes that Ricci does not know his way about the city and therefore he always avoids the monumental center. His speculation accounts for the protagonist's alienation, but the conclusion that his wife is a native opens the question of why she does not call upon her family in the crisis described by the film. Again, I believe that De Sica's fascination with what he calls "egoism" determined this apparently artificial isolation from the solidarity of an extended family. His concern for the plight of the unemployed is secondary to his anatomy of the individual moral crisis his protagonist experiences. Here "egoism" is a term for the shearing off of pride and self-respect that drives Ricci to attempt a theft.

Kristin Thompson has neatly defined the film's relationship to narrative conventions:

[A]lthough *Bicycle Thieves*'s careful script construction resembles that of the classical film, its abrupt changes in tactics help to undermine the conventional hermeneutic line. The question through the first portion of the film . . . is whether Ricci will find his bicycle in time to keep his job. Yet for a lengthy section of the film . . . we are led to downplay that question and wonder what effect the loss of the bike will have on the family. Finally, though we do learn the answer to the original question, the ending seems open and ambiguous, since the theft of the bike has clearly become a secondary issue, and our main concern at the end is the impact of the day's events on the father-son relationship.[20]

The superstructure framing the itinerary of Ricci's and Bruno's Sunday search through Rome delineates a pyramid of rekindled hopes and ironic frustrations. However, De Sica understates the drama so effectively that we are given simultaneously a vision of Roman street life and of an impoverished man nearly blind to it, who can concentrate only on the one tool that will guarantee his employment as a poster-plasterer for the city. Not only does the director refuse to capitalize on the options for suspense that the script provides him; he holds the mutually alienated epicenters of the city portrait—itself a film genre with historical and political resonance since the twenties, comprising such films as *Berlin, die Symphonie einer Grosstadt* (1927), *The Man with a Movie Camera* (1929), and *A propos de Nice* (1929)—and of the sadly unresourceful worker in an equipoise that encourages an analysis of their interaction rather than a simple identification with the protagonist, except in those rather frequent moments when he allows the charm of the child to destroy that delicate balance. The success of De Sica's direction of the Ricci character devolves not only from his refusal to use an international star—Selznick proposed Cary Grant for the role. Rather, by using a factory worker with no acting experience, the director forced himself to invent a protagonist virtually devoid of expressive nuances, into whose gestures and expressions affective tones could be read. Above all, De Sica presented a figure who would not overpower the balance between daily rhythms of an urban landscape divested of all familiar monuments and the isolated individual, so obsessively focused on his material quest that he very gradually, and with considerable resistance, comes to a realization of his own failures—his "egoism"—as he reads them reflected in his interactions with his son.

On the stylistic level, De Sica relies on montage much more than Rossellini or Visconti. In the two comic moments of Bruno's separation from his father a carefully timed cut controls the humor: his thwarted urination and his brash peeping into a confessional, for which the priest gives him a rap on the head. The instantaneity of the cause and effect in two coordinated shots underwrites the humor in both cases. In the more dramatic episodes of the two bicycle snatchings the montage is very elaborate. The first employs some thirty shots in two minutes to delineate the teamwork of the thieves who take Ricci's bicycle and even divert his immediate pursuit by directing him to an innocent cyclist. The second, the conclusion in a large piazza beside the soccer stadium, requires some seventy shot changes in seven minutes. Here De Sica manufactures a decidedly psychological space out of the shot-countershot exchanges of Ricci turning his gaze from the hundreds of bicycles parked outside the stadium to a single, unlocked one on an empty street. The montage-enforced identification with Ricci's moment of decision shifts suddenly with a moving camera shot of wide-eyed Bruno, sitting on the curb because he has missed the tram his father told him to take.

This shot-countershot exchange is the climax of the film and the moment toward which it had been gravitating all the time. In it and in the conclusion which quickly follows it, we can see the moral implications of De Sica's reliance on montage. It contributes to the binary focusing of the identification—primarily with Ricci, secondarily with Bruno. In filtering all the perceptions of the film through them, together or alternately, the filmmakers guide us first in seeing Ricci invested with the authority his son naturally grants him in order to make Ricci's ultimate self-revelation all the more pathetic because he must acknowledge it before Bruno. In this specular relationship Bruno's solidarity with his father (except when he is unjustly punished) and his enthusiastic keeping of faith in their project become the gauge by which we measure the nuances of Ricci's "egoism." In contrast, the long-take and sequence shot style usually favored by Rossellini and Visconti tends to diminish psychological identification and to situate individual action in a larger social terrain. The division of *Paisà* into short episodes with its attendant multiplication of protagonists and the textual strategies of *La terra trema* magnify the distancing of the mise-en-scène.

The narrative premise of the bicycle theft has been amply criticized. Sadoul called it "un accident banal." Baldelli[21] claims that any worker in such a situation would have made a deal with a neighbor who owned a bicycle, offering two hundred of his twelve-hundred-lire monthly salary for the use of the vehicle. Sergio Amidei, who quickly dropped out of collaborating on the script, described the project as politically unsound: "Fundamentally I had my doubts about the whole film, in the sense that I did not find it 'Italian'; I didn't think it true in such a situation that such a man, a communist, a worker who lived in a 'borgata,' and whose bicycle was stolen, wouldn't go to the Party and they wouldn't find him a bicycle."[22]

However, within the film the PCI appears as an inefficient, almost hermetic organization. Seeking out his friend, Baiocco, Ricci gets scolded for disturbing a political speech about unemployment and must wait for the rehearsal of an inane musical revue to end before he can tell him what happened to him. Rather than bring the party machinery to Ricci's aid, Baiocco mobilizes a city garbage truck and its crew to search for the bicycle in the black market. Baiocco's benevolence, which is personal rather than political, does not disguise the misappropriation of civil labor and equipment; in fact, De Sica directs the garbage crew as the stock figures of New Comedy.

Both the police and the Church come under attack as well. The former are unembarrassedly indifferent when Ricci reports the theft of his bicycle; instead, they are absorbed by an action of the Celère against an unspecified demonstration. Later, the pursuit of the old man during the Catholic service for the poor founded by Don Moresco occasions a sustained satire on the efforts of bourgeois laymen and clergy to clean, feed, and evangelize the poor.

In two important articles (1949, 1953) on the significance of *Ladri di biciclette* within Italian cultural life, Franco Fortini, for a long time a Socialist editor and writer, later a figure of the independent Left, argued that *because of its contradictions* it became the preeminent Italian film of its time. The 1949 article begins with a description of an act of violence taken from a news report:

> Antonio Alecci, son of Giorgio, twenty-four years old, tried at nine o'clock
> on the morning of Friday, January 21, in Corso Vercelli, to steal a merchant's
> bicycle. Caught, beaten bloody by the quickly gathered crowd, he was
> handed over to the police. The evening of the same day, the crowd at the
> Odeon paid two and a half million lire to see the first showing of De Sica's
> film and were moved. Life, obviously, does not imitate art. The poor often
> brutalize the poor and they are always brutalized by the rich. The facts belie
> the morale of pity, and not only in this case.[23]

Referring to the contemporary acclaim and criticism of the film as *either* a Christian parable or a Marxist indictment, he finds these "contradictory solutions" underlying the unique strength of the film: "It would seem to us that in these years Italian culture never had an expression of art and truth that actually embodied such contradictions, which are the basis of the Italian people." According to Fortini one audience can exit the cinema thinking that "Ricci, the sinner, is nearer to salvation than Ricci, the honest man," while another audience concludes that it would be best "to remake the laws because no one should have to steal again."[24]

In elaborating the Christian interpretation of the film, Fortini makes the seemingly untenable argument that Ricci's release at the end of the film is a compensation for his "forgiveness" of the thief when he sees him in an epileptic seizure and recognizes his greater poverty. The film throws up formidable obstacles to such a reading: the policeman Bruno finds saves Ricci from the thief's neighbors, and instead of forgiving him, he joins the policeman in a search of his apartment. Despite this error, Fortini is justified in seeing that the film invites a Christian reading as much as a political one. The undialectical simultaneity of those options becomes for him "the noose that strangles Italy; we see no way out of it. But the face of the unemployed Ricci when he gets hit, that hardened and pale face, guarantees that the noose will be tightened."[25]

Fortini's mystical Christianity is far from Rossellini's liberal Catholicism. He was born a Jew and converted from conviction to Waldensian Protestantism in 1939. Thus Ricci's poverty, suffering, and simplicity might correspond to Fortini's religious ideals, and the film's anticlericalism would not pose any obstacle to his Christian reading. In fact, Fortini's position closely corresponds to the occasional religious references in the writings of Zavattini. He is outspoken in his condemnation of the clerical influence on politics, but he acknowledges the importance of social justice in the teaching of Christ.

Addressing the issue of realism in 1953 for the journal *Cinema nuovo*, Fortini restated his admiration for the film:

> In cinema, a fruit of the neopopulist poetics that takes realism as a value is
> *Ladri di biciclette*. The quality of the film is in the meeting between film
> technique and the *reality* of a vast category of Italians (men, almost all of us)
> who at once believe or don't believe in heaven, consciously suffer the injustice of others and of their own guilt, live at once as oppressed (the denial of
> justice) and as oppressors (the theft and the final chastisement).[26]

He prefers to "neorealismo" the term "neopopulismo" to emphasize that the representation of the working class and the unemployed in the post-Liberation cinema repeated nineteenth-century views of poverty held by the Italian bourgeoisie. The films I have discussed so far in this book incorporate many of the aspects of neopopulism that Fortini includes in his definition: "regionalism, dialect, components of revolutionary and Christian socialism, naturalism, positivistic verism, humanitarianism." However, in a "realist" cinema, as he defines it, 'Ntoni Valastro, Ricci, Umberto D, Totò the Good, the partisans of *Paisà,* and several of Antonioni's upper-class characters (among others he catalogues) would "meet and collide, in all their complexity." Therefore, from his perspective in 1953 he held that the strength of De Sica's film has nothing to do with its vision of a working-class situation; it comes from the intersection of the filmic process (which he considers necessarily implies class conflict because of its industrial mode of production) and a moral ambiguity experienced by most Italians.[27]

Fortini's testimony helps us to understand the enduring achievement of De Sica's and Zavattini's major films, despite their stylistic and narrative conservatism. The comprehensive realist cinema that he imagined never materialized. (Guido Aristarco thought he saw it taking shape in Visconti's work of the forties and fifties, but he was misled by his partisan conviction that such a synthesis would be the accomplishment of a filmmaker tied to the PCI.) Fortini recognized that De Sica's *ideological ambivalence* made him the most representative of the major filmmakers of his generation in Italy.

Miracolo a Milano

With the internal emigration of southerners to the large cities in central and northern Italy, shantytowns grew. By the time *Miracolo a Milano* was released (February 1951) there were more than ninety thousand people living in the shanties of Rome alone, but by situating the film in Milan, the richer Lombardian capital, De Sica and Zavattini exploited the growing contrast between the very rich and the very poor. Zavattini's 1943 novella, *Totò il buono,* on which the film is based, occurred in the imaginary city of Bamba. Actually, a film subject from 1938, "Diamo a tutti un cavallo a dondolo" ("Let's give everybody a hobbyhorse") had been reworked as a novella when the war aborted the making of the film. After the artistic but not commercial successes of their first two postwar collaborations, De Sica returned to the altered project in homage to Zavattini. In the meanwhile the fantastic premise of the plot, that oil gushing in a shantytown brought capitalist expulsion of the residents, nearly became an Italian reality when vast oil and natural gas deposits were discovered in the Po Valley in 1949, through the efforts of Enrico Mattei, a former partisan activist and DC member, who was vice president of the state-owned oil company AGIP. De Sica's choice of Milan as the location for his film of Zavattini's novella may owe something to its being the center of Mattei's activity.[28]

The revival of the prewar fable suggests the filmmakers recognized the continuity and continuing relevance of the social conflict schematized in the novella. The aged Lolotta finds an infant, whom she names Totò, under a cabbage plant and raises him until her death, whereupon he is placed in an orphanage. Released, he becomes the innovative and unceasingly generous leader of a shantytown where oil is discovered. But Mobic (Mobbi in the film), the richest man in the city and owner of the land on which the shantytown stands, tries to evict the inhabitants with the assistance of the riot police. Totò, leading the resistance, would have soon been overpowered had not two angels (in the film, the spirit of Lolotta) given him the power of magically executing his will.

At this point the novella and the film begin to diverge more and more. Both trace the extension of Totò's defensive magic into an attempt to ameliorate the poverty of his fellow shanty citizens made futile because of their "egoism," a wide spectrum of variations on greed and pride. In the novella the government of Bamba co-opts Totò's popularity, making him a puppet governor until an accident apparently kills him. When he steals back to Bamba in disguise and bereft of his magical power, a growing crowd recognizes him. His power returns outside a shop where he arms his followers with brooms and leads them off toward "the very spot where Signora Lolotta had disappeared [in a vision], straight toward the kingdom where *buon giorno* really means *buon giorno*." The film replaces the final chapter of the novella with a chase sequence in which the angels recapture the magical dove, the gift from Lolotta which is the source of Totò's miraculous power. Thereupon the police try to arrest the squatters. But Lolotta restores the bird to Totò in front of the Milan cathedral in time for him to reprise the original conclusion, leading his followers into the sky on the brooms of street sweepers.

The novella located the magic power in the word "tac." The replacement of an Arabian Nights' magic word by the emblem of the Holy Ghost lends an ironic Christian dimension to the film fable. We see Lolotta, in superimposition, delivering the stolen bird with two transparent angels in hot pursuit of her. Thus to the implication latent in the revival of the project—that is, that capital controls police power as much in the republic as in the Fascist state—has been added the idea that the spirit of genuine Christianity has to be stolen from its institutional guardians to be of service to the poor.

Officially the dominant Christian Democratic party took the paternalistic stance of supporting the family and the poor in a traditional and anti-Fascist culture. But the evangelical voice of the party, Giuseppe Dossetti, wrote in 1945:

> Christian Democracy does not want to, and cannot be a conservative movement. It wishes to be a movement permeated by the conviction that in choosing between the ideology and experience of liberal capitalism on the one hand, and the experience, if not the ideology, of the mass anti-capitalist movements on the other, it is the first, not the second, which is the more radically anti-Christian.[29]

But by 1950 it became clear that the De Gasperi government, the United States' most loyal NATO ally, had chosen the "more radically anti-Christian" option in everything but its rhetoric. Dossetti himself left political life in 1951 to withdraw to a monastery. The more fantastic and extra ecclesiastical act of withdrawal by the defeated poor of *Miracolo a Milano*— flying off from the Piazza Duomo on broomsticks—does not allude to his repudiation of the political arena; the film was finished just before he retired. Although the film is no more an allegory of Dossetti than of Mattei, it refracts the tensions between capitalist exploitation, nationalistic modernization, and Christian idealism that had been only slightly rearranged by the fall of Fascism and the consolidation of the conservative republic.

Insofar as *Miracolo a Milano* suggests themes of the national religion, it points obliquely to the Church's social failures. Within the context of the film, the dove spoofs its Christian symbolism. Far from being a member of the Holy Trinity, it is just a magical prop. Totò's goodness is innate, unmediated by Christian doctrine, and if it owes anything to nurturing, it is the result of Lolotta's playful education, which is exemplified in another act with iconographical ironies: when the child spills milk, Lolotta pretends the mess on the floor is a river beside which she places toy houses. The Promised Land, where milk flows like rivers, turns out to be a trope for the playful imagination rather than a divine gift to a chosen people.

The lesson of Lolotta is more vivid than that "there's no use in crying over spilled milk." It is the acceptance of a broken and ruined world as the starting point for imaginative invention. For the filmmakers themselves this means the exploitation of a range of purely cinematic options at odds with the repertory of illusions that constituted the rhetoric of filmic realism in the forties, and to which their earlier films subscribed. Within the political economy of the film, the experience of Totò's childhood accident and Lolotta's subsequent invention instruct him in turning the violence of Mobbi and the state into harmless parodic gestures; and his "education" furthers his acceptance of the "egoism" of his cohorts as challenges to his meliorating inventiveness.

Thus, the independence of the visual and the sound tracks inherent in all films easily allows De Sica to give us a vivid realization of an inventive highlight from the novella: the order to attack issued by successively higher ranked police officers and soldiers loses its meaning when Totò makes a soprano's operatic voice come from their mouths. Pasolini elaborated this moment, just as he appropriated and further transformed the iconography of the dove, in *Uccellacci e uccellini* (1967).

In 1949 Zavattini wrote of the situation Italian filmmakers faced five years earlier:

> In the midst of the terrible rubble we realized we had spent too few images
> to open the eyes of our neighbor and help him face, if not prevent, the mon-
> strous events. To put it bluntly, the cinema had failed in choosing the way of
> Méliès and not the way of Lumière where the path was sown with the thorns
> of reality. . . . We seem to be on the eve of rediscovering our original mean-
> ing. For that matter, the cinema *was* our original meaning; from the first lens
> that opened to the light, everything was equal to it, this was its most uncon-
> taminated and promising moment, the reality buried under myths was slowly
> emerging; a tree, an old man, someone eating, sleeping, weeping, but then
> they preferred plots, to avoid too-surprising equations: the close-up of a poor
> man's eye might be taken for a rich man's, or vice versa.[30]

Although Zavattini here criticizes the tradition of Méliès, identifying it with narrative cinema in general (within which Zavattini *always* worked), *Miracolo a Milano* pays enthusiastic homage to the imaginative technical tricks invented by Méliès. The tear gas thrown at the shanty dwellers flows back into the canisters by reverse motion. The power of the magical bird usually manifests itself through stop-motion editing: Totò initially tests it by making a plate of fried eggs suddenly appear. The transparent angels are superimpositions. Such an extensive and flagrant utilization of the vocabulary of Méliès's fantasy emphasizes the purely cinematic illusionism in which all references to social ills and follies are purely symbolical: when Totò distributes his magical gifts, one follower demands a million lire only to be inflated by the next who wants a million million; a single black man (an iconic figure in neorealist cinema of the Occupation) and a single white woman, who have eyed each other throughout the film, whisper for favors individually only to be frustrated when Totò satisfies each's desire to change skin color; a suicidal young man is saved by the love of a Venusian statue brought to life; and in accord with the novella, Rappi, who betrayed the community's oil secret to Mobbi for a new top hat, loses his prideful mark of distinction when Totò gives everyone hats. The film insists that a purely benign man, or perhaps a true Christian, can exist only in a world of fable.

De Sica and Zavattini consistently focus their attention on the people left out of the benefits of the reconstruction of the republic. No political party magnifies their voices. The problem, De Sica seems to contend, resides in the inescapable "egoism" of all adults. Political parties and organized religion imply solidarity, but they are as incapable of keeping faith as the people who make them up.

CHAPTER 5

Between the
Vital Crises

The Christian Democrats maintained power throughout the 1950s at the cost of the alienation of the intellectual and artistic forces that had invigorated the cultural life of the new republic immediately following the war. But the Communists were also losing their moral authority as the oppositional power. Actually ever since Elio Vittorini broke with the PCI in 1947, there had been increasing protest against its cultural Stalinism. In 1949 the party expelled Pier Paolo Pasolini for homosexuality. Eventually the anti-Stalinist revelations by Khrushchev at the twentieth congress of the Russian Communist party in 1956 delivered a decisive blow to the PCI; that same year the suppression of the Hungarian revolt further damaged Togliatti's counterforce. Italo Calvino resigned from the party the next year. Similarly, Franco Fortini took progressively more critical positions in the PSI, the Socialist party, until quitting it in 1958.

The DC was not the beneficiary of the disillusionment with the organized Left. Its Interior Ministry was so prone to using excessive force in suppressing strikes and demonstrations that it often disgusted even sympathizers to the party. Then, just before he retired in 1953, De Gasperi tried to push through what his opponents called "The Swindle Law" (*la legge truffa*) by which a simple majority would guarantee two thirds of the seats in the Assembly, a frightening echo of Mussolini's Acerbo law. A mere 0.15 percent of the vote defeated the "swindle." Ironically, the increasing strength of the dissenting neo-Fascists, the fastest growing political force in the fifties, made the difference.

Allegiances with the traditional parties of the Right allowed the DC to control the Assembly without neo-Fascist support until 1957. But control meant stagnation: "the second legislature (from 1953–58) came to be known as the 'legislature of immobilism,'" according to Paul Ginsborg. Immobilism, steady economic growth, and the entrenchment of Italy's vast Byzantine system of *enti pubblici*—government agencies controlling transportation, communications, natural resources, electricity, sports, and cultural activities—typified the period.

Equally characteristic was the prolonged Montesi scandal: the death of a young woman on a beach near Rome in 1953, initially called an accident, became the subject of a national obsession for four years. Revelations of aristocratic drug addicts and smugglers, accusations of government cover-ups and the politically motivated manipulation of evidence by the highest-level officials of the DC, and the involvement of prominent film actors and producers drove up the circulation of the more vulgar leftist newspapers and all the gossip journals. Political life had become a theater of decadence.

The cinema world was itself a center of scandal, glamor, and affluence. In 1950 the pregnancy of Ingrid Bergman and her marriage to Rossellini attracted more attention than any of his films. His former star Maria Michi (Manfredi's lover in *Roma, città aperta* and the prostitute in *Paisà*) married the millionaire Duke Torlonia; Silvana Mangano (who won international fame as the sexy star of the Communist director De Santis's *Riso amaro*) married Dino De Laurentiis. Cinecittà became an outpost of Hollywood for the production of spectacular costume dramas like *Ben Hur*.

Yet this was also a period of intense cultural criticism in such intellectual journals as *Officina, Nuovi argomenti,* and the PCI-sponsored *Il Contemporaneo.* Film journalism too flourished in *Film critica, Bianco e nero, Cinema nuovo,* and other shorter-lived periodicals. In short, the contradictions operating in Italian culture became manifest.

With the Christian Democrats securely in power, labor remained inexpensive and industry grew at unprecedented rates. By that time the combined successes of Mattei's ENI, Fiat (the automobile producer), and the Italian steel industry (Finsider) led to massive building and road construction projects and pointed toward the rapid growth in private automobile ownership. Italy's gross domestic product grew at an average 5.5 percent per year from 1951 to 1958, then leaped to an average 6.3 percent for the next five years, as industrial production more than doubled.[1]

I cannot recount the history of Italian cinema in the 1950s *in nuce*, nor is it necessary to rehearse here the achievements and complications of that period, which are chronicled in available histories in English as well as Italian.[2] Let me make, however, a few observations about the activities of the protagonists of my narrative during that decade.

Two important filmmakers emerged from the penumbra in which we noticed them in the forties and began to make feature films in the fifties. They were Michelangelo Antonioni and Federico Fellini. Erotic life was the central preoccupation of the films of both. Antonioni centered his attention on the dramatically enlarging wealthy class. Turning away from the "neopopulist" milieu, he also committed himself more seriously than any of his contemporaries to a modernist inflection of narrative. Thus his first long film, *Cronaca di un amore* (*Story of a Love Affair*, 1950), an elegantly constructed and elliptically ambiguous variation of a film noir, posits a working-class protagonist entering the world of the Milanese rich emblematically as a salesman of expensive sports cars, abetted by his former girlfriend and now adulterous lover. Her marriage to an industrialist has elevated her to the world of fashionable parties and elegant dress salons.

The boutiques move to the center of Antonioni's fourth feature, *Le amiche* (*The Girlfriends*, 1955), an adaptation of Cesare Pavese's novel *Tra donne sole* (*Among Women Only*), set in Turin. His affinities with Pavese were numerous, but it is especially significant that he filmed Pavese's novel about suicide five years after the author killed himself. There is a suicide, or an attempt at it, in every film Antonioni made in the fifties.[3] Although this fixation is fundamentally existential, and explicitly related to erotic despair, it often has political overtones. This is dramatized at the end of *Il grido* (*The Cry*, 1957) when Aldo, this time a rejected lover from the working class, kills himself on the day of a demonstration against a NATO base. Within the repeated dissection of affluent vacuity, suicide becomes a protest against the national obsession with consumption and the futility of organized efforts at reform.

Fellini, for his part, chose marginal protagonists: vaudevillians, actors, aspiring artists, swindlers, prostitutes, carnival performers, but even the most disenfranchised of these nourished fantasies and projects which reflected the consumer society around them. The confidence man of *Il bidone* (*The Swindle,* 1955) mercilessly exploits the hopes of a shantytown dweller and a woman in a charity kitchen (as well as a cripple); the prostitute of *Le notti di Cabiria* (1957) sells her shack and hands over her savings to a bogus suitor. However, Fellini's films are not polemics for social justice so much as parables of grace found among sinners and the wretched. In an open letter to Massimo Puccini, he rejected Marxist criticism of his lack of political commitment in the form of topical commentary: "Sometimes a film, while avoiding any precise representation of historical or political reality, can incarnate in mythic figures, speaking in a quite elementary language, the oppostion between contemporary feelings, and can become very much more realistic than another film in which social and political matters are referred to more precisely."[4]

One sign of the disengagement of the national cinema that came with the waning of the postwar political films was the appearance in the early fifties of works addressing the moral impoverishment of the film and entertainment industry. Fellini's *Lo sceicco bianco* (*The White Sheik,* 1952, from Antonioni's script) punctures the illusions of *fumetti,* rather than cinema, when a naive provincial newlywed, on a honeymoon in Rome, struggles with the seductions of a star of the photo-romances to which she is addicted. In *La signora senza camelie* (*The Lady without Camelias,* 1953) Antonioni himself analyzed the breakdown of the marriage of a film producer and an actress, whom he briefly turns into a star. He depicts the film industry as a paradigm of the vacuous world of the Italian upper bourgeoisie.

Visconti contributed to this critical self-reflection on the film industry when he directed a Zavattini script in making *Bellissima* (1951), a film about the failure of an ambitious mother (played by Magnani) to get her young daughter into motion pictures. But his most ambitious project of the fifties was *Senso* (1954), a historical drama shot in color and set in the period of the battle of Custoza: it challenged the triumphalistic mythology of Garibaldi's liberation and unification of the nation, while at the same time diagnosing an operatic glorification of defeat at the core of the Italians' revolutionary impulses. Into the melodramatic story Visconti inscribed an allegory of the failures of the postwar Resistance. The still unsettled status of Trieste, which had been claimed by both Yugoslavia and Italy after the war—to the considerable embarrassment of the Communists and the political profit of the neo-Fascists—may have made *Senso*'s critique of upper-class patriotism and its goal of driving all foreign forces from Italian territory particularly thorny. The film was attacked, censored, and vigorously debated in the polemical journals. For the remaining years of the decade Visconti avoided explicitly political issues, concentrating on directing plays and operas and filming an adaptation of Dostoyevsky, *Le notti bianche* (*White Nights*, 1957).

De Sica and Zavattini attempted to prolong the spirit of the Resistance-bred cinema into the fifties. With *Umberto D* (1952) De Sica finally achieved the fusion of "egoism" and social commentary he claims had been his aim in his first postwar films. His protagonist is a fussy and very proper pensioner who worked for thirty years in the Ministry of Public Works, whose manners and attitudes preserve the mentality of apolitical monarchists from before the war. His bureaucratic career slightly predated and extended continuously with the Fascist regime. Neither a Fascist himself, nor a partisan, he represents a generation of Italians who were comfortable with the nationalist rhetoric and the traditional public morality of Mussolini's regime. In the course of the film Umberto finds himself unable to live on his minimal pension. The landlady in whose apartment he lived since long before the war has evicted him.

The set of the apartment is emblematic of the social and political ambience of the film as a whole. The restoration-in-progress suggests the societal transformation of Italy under way at the beginning of the economic miracle. The theater of neorealism, centered in a kitchen which has yet to be restored, has all but disappeared, ironically superceded by the affluence of the owner of the commercial cinema that keeps Umberto awake at night. The landlady is even uglier in her aspirations to bourgeois respectability as the cinema owner's wife than in her career as a pander or, formerly, perhaps even a prostitute.

Through the opening titles we see a massive protest march of old men demonstrating for higher pensions, shot from high above. Scelba's Celere easily disperse the crowd under the legal pretext of demonstrating without a permit. Although the police rush into the line with jeeps but without guns, Italians in January 1952, when the film opened, would still vividly remember the slaughter of six workers at a demonstration in Modena two years earlier which had aroused sufficient disgust to force De Gasperi to reshuffle his cabinet, dismissing the rightist PLI (Liberal party) and incorporating followers of Dossetti from the left wing of the DC. Furthermore, 1950 and 1951 saw a staggering 11 percent inflation rate after steady declines since 1948. (In fact, inflation would not reach such proportions again until the mid-1970s.) The trenchant topicality of this opening was confirmed when Giulio Andreotti, then undersecretary of entertainment, vigorously protested the exportation of De Sica and Zavattini's film as "washing Italy's dirty linen in public." Guido Aristarco has amply demonstrated that the DC journals of the fifties tended to label all films dealing with poverty or social injustice Communist propaganda.[5]

For De Sica the protest demonstration is merely a futile gesture:

> The economic condition of Umberto is not what concerns us. What concerns us is his moral and human relationship with society. What concerns us is the loneliness of an old man. Men do not communicate with one another, how then can they communicate with Umberto, who, moreover, is an old man? . . . Human beings have this primitive, perennial, ancient fault of not understanding one another, of not communicating with one another.[6]

Curiously, the purest example of Zavattinian neorealism is also among the latest, his own episode for *Amore in città* (*Love in the City*, 1953), the only number of a filmed "magazine" of shorts by different directors bound by a common theme. In "La storia di Caterina" he re-creates a newspaper item about an unwed mother from Sicily reduced to homelessness in Rome. Although Zavattini focused his attention on the social and economic difficulties the southern woman encountered in the capital, the selling point of the whole anthology was its common theme of love. Eros had played a very minor role in the films I have been discussing in the first three chapters of this book. But it reemerged naturally as the dominating theme of even the more ambitious Italian films of the fifties. *Amore in città* did not have the participation of Rossellini, Visconti, or De Sica, who were all making erotic melodramas of different sorts that year (all of them with Hollywood stars in their casts!), but Fellini and Antonioni contributed episodes. By 1956 the "neopopulism" of De Sica's collaborations with Zavattini reached its point of exhaustion in *Il tetto* (*The Roof*), their drama of southern immigrants trying to construct a shanty on a roof in Rome.

Immediately after making *Paisà* Rossellini made *Germania anno zero* (1948) in Berlin. Between 1948 and 1955 he made another nine features and contributed to three omnibus films in a spectrum of genres—comedy, fantasy, operatic oratorio, dramatic monologue, and melodrama. Fellini worked with him on the two scripts that examined simple Catholic piety:

Amore (*Love,* with Magnani, 1948) and *Francesco, giullare di Dio* (1950). In three of them, he used Ingrid Bergman to show aspects of Italy through a foreigner's perspective: *Stromboli, terra di Dio* (*Stromboli,* 1950), *Europa 51* (*Europe 51,* 1952), and *Viaggio in Italia* (1953). The machine in the title of his *La macchina ammazzacattivi* (*The Machine to Kill Bad People,* 1948–1952) is a magical still camera that can eradicate "bad people." In this subversively antipolitical fable a well-meaning photographer eliminates the politicians and economic exploiters in his village only to see their vices replicated by the poor. *Dov'è la libertà?* (*Where is Freedom?* 1954) was a vehicle for the comic personality and revue heritage of Totò, who plays a convict who cannot bear the horrors of society when he is released for good behavior. The unifying tenor of these spiritual biographies is the importance of sacrifice and service in the inevitable confrontation with a materialistic and greedy community; Rossellini suggests that the reward for such service is a heightened awareness of divine mystery.

Rossellini spent much of the second half of the fifties making a film in India, but his *Il generale Della Rovere* (1959) signaled a change that predicted the revitalization of Italian filmmaking and the recovery of its international preeminence. The very fact that so preeminent and prolific a filmmaker was back in Italy working on an Italian subject was stimulating; furthermore, his choice of a Resistance drama, starring De Sica—another icon of the postwar cinema—as a confidence man mistaken for an underground leader who attains heroic stature by accepting his role and playing the inspiring patriot to his death, gave symbolical significance to his return.

A harbinger of a turning point, *Il generale Della Rovere* was still a spiritual biography with closer formal and moral ties to Rossellini's films from the early fifties than to the ambiguous, connotative narrative mode that was soon to become the predominant new style. Curiously, that new mode bypassed Rossellini himself. He struggled to regain his artistic authority throughout the half decade in which his contemporaries were flourishing. Only when the boom waned did he abandon the various attempts, mostly at historical fiction, which marked his failures of the early sixties—*Era notte a Roma* (*It Was Night in Rome,* 1960), set in the period of *Roma, città aperta; Viva l'Italia* (*Long Live Italy,* 1961), about Garibaldi; *Vanina Vanini* (1961), an adaptation of Stendhal; and *Anima nera* (*Black Soul,* 1962), a contemporary melodrama. He then began the remarkable series of television films on great men and historical moments that constituted his final achievement.

CHAPTER 6

Annus Mirabilis

The year 1960 was the most remarkable for film premieres in the history of the Italian cinema. On 5 February Fellini's *La dolce vita* opened. Immediately a controversy arose concerning its alleged "immorality." Soon it was the most successful Italian film made in the sixty-five years of the native industry. At Cannes, in April, Michelangelo Antonioni's *L'avventura* scandalized traditionalists and mobilized the support of an emergent international core of cinematic modernists. In September the presentation of *Rocco e i suoi fratelli* signaled the return of Visconti to preeminence as a filmmaker and set off another furious debate over censorship. Finally, if we move beyond 1960 to take in a full twelve months, the opening of Antonioni's *La notte* on 24 January 1961 confirmed the artistic triumph of Italian cinema.

La dolce vita

Although Federico Fellini has declared that in making *La dolce vita* he depicted the dilemma of a private man, with no political considerations, his film reflects the dynamics of Italian politics during the years of its conception and production, 1957–1959. The conservatives of the DC were finding it harder and harder to maintain control of the Assembly without seeking the support of the parties of the Left, a solution the liberal wing of the DC would effect in the early sixties. In February 1957 the votes of the neo-Fascist MSI were needed to maintain the Segni government. In May of the same year the dedicated anti-Fascist Adone Zoli initially repudiated neo-Fascist support in forming a government but was forced to capitulate, with public humiliation, when he fell just one vote short; that vote the MSI provided. By the time the film was ready to be exhibited in April 1959, the government led by Fernando Tambroni held a cozy alliance with the far Right, amid rumors of an imminent rightist coup d'état.

In the film we are told that Marcello, the reporter and gossip-hound protagonist, works for a semi-Fascist newspaper. In this capacity he earns the disapproval of his liberal friend, Steiner, the host of a grotesque intellectual salon. Steiner himself turns out to be the film's most sinister figure, when he kills his young children and himself. Fellini slyly criticizes the journalism of the Left, as well, by showing the *Paese sera,* a Communist paper, ready to sensationalize Steiner's tragedy. For Fellini the degradation of Rome at the height of the economic miracle of the late fifties is not a partisan matter: Fascists and Communists are cashing in on violence and scandal.

He considered calling the film "Babylon—2000 years after Christ." Such a title would have directed the viewer to the infernal vision of the city which became the seat of the Roman Catholic Church. Instead, *La dolce vita* ironically picks up a popular periphrasis for the idle, and often scandal-prone, style of the loose coalition of aristocracy, celebrities, and lavish beneficiaries of the economic miracle who partied in Rome. Peter Bondanella has shown that Fellini incorporated into the film several of the most memorable events of 1957 and 1958 involving celebrity and scandal photographers: Anita Ekberg's wading in the Trevi fountain, a striptease in a restaurant, and fights between celebrities and photographers.[1] The astounding success of the film both in Italy and in the world was due, in part, to fascination with these phenomena and a deafness to the moral tone of the film. The Church shared this deafness, and characteristically its vain attempts to suppress the film only increased its success. However, this obtuseness was not universal. The Catholic mayor of Florence, Giorgio La Pira, a pious maverick, championed the film defending its Christianity to the outraged Tuscan hierarchy, while in the other direction Padre Baragli in *La Civiltà cattolica* offered a sophisticated repudiation of the film, after acknowledging its religious references and a "few genuinely human values": "We must mistrust condemnations which for the most part are concerned with erotic and sexual immorality and we mistrust even more the condemnations of those who, in the denouncements, do not lose money, but profit by them."[2]

The novelist Elio Vittorini, whom Fellini tried unsuccessfully to cast in the role of Steiner in the film, accused the clerical detractors of disguised fascism:

> I find this a profoundly Catholic film. . . . The Catholics don't under-
> stand anything; they don't recognize their own son; they don't hear their
> own language. Actually I have to say that these Catholics who rebel and take
> a stance against this film are simply Fascists. They speak as Fascists and not
> as Catholics.[3]

By centering the film around the activities of Marcello Rubini, a gossip journalist whose sexual aggressiveness brings him into as many diverse situations as his work does, Fellini elaborates an epic vision of the decadence of the capital, using for the first time a modernist, paratactic structure. Such forms were coming to the foreground of the most ambitious European narrative films in the late fifties and early sixties. The film's thirteen episodes are so autonomous that they seem outside of sequential time: the events could take place over months or in just a few days—actually a careful calculation of nights and mornings indicates at least seven days must pass, but the film can give the impression of occupying an even shorter timespan. Fellini and his scriptwriters abrogated the conventions of plot development and suspense: some figures (besides the protagonist) appear in several episodes, but no important issues of their character or their actions are left unresolved until they reappear, giving the impression of a work that could be expanded indefinitely. Thus, the film's most dramatic event, Steiner's suicide, not only occurs offscreen, but has been unanticipated; in fact, because we expect no decisive action by him, it is all the more striking, when we learn of it.

Marcello's duties include spying on a prince in a nightclub, escorting the movie star Sylvia (Anita Ekberg) around Rome, covering an alleged epiphany of the Virgin Mary to two young children, and studying the crowds on the Via Veneto. The attempted suicide of his girlfriend, Emma, and his encounters with Maddalena, the daughter of an industrialist, who makes love to him in a prostitute's flooded basement apartment, are interwoven with these professional duties. When he rushes off to a castle with a car full of Via Veneto friends to a party of aristocrats or ends up as one of an orgy-bound party breaking into a friend's villa at coastal Fregene, the distinction between his work and his private life dissolves.

Fellini subtly suggests the resurgence of Fascism through a casual comment of Marcello's father, a successful champagne distributor who meets him on the Via Veneto. In the Kit Kat nightclub which they visit together, he asked the waiter if he were there in 1922, suggesting that he was last in the club during the year associated with the Fascist March on Rome. Later, one of the guests at the aristocratic castle of Bassano di Sutri will actually acknowledge that he was part of the March on Rome. But all this would be trivial and irrelevant if it did not guide us into the moral infrastructure of the film. In the scene in the Kit Kat there is an incidental, unemphasized phrase quoted by Marcello's father, a phrase any Italian might innocently use, which is of great significance to the tone of the whole film. To the chorus girl, Fanny, who politely tells him he looks like a young man, he responds, "Non rinnoviamo 'disperato dolor che il cor mi preme.'" (Let's not renew "the desperate grief that rings my heart.")

By quoting from canto 33 of Dante's *Inferno*, and alluding to the darkest moment in the *Commedia*, he is making a joke. To him his lost youth is as bitter as Count Ugolino's miserable starvation, eating the flesh of his dead sons. At the moment the quotation merely characterizes the humor and the culture of the retired wine merchant. But as the film progresses the allusion grows more resonant. On the grand scale of the *Commedia* the story of Ugolino is a countertype of the uncompleted sacrifice of Isaac by Abraham, which, of course, is itself a type of the sacrificial passion of Jesus. Ugolino is frozen in the bottom of hell because he was a traitor, but also because he was a literalist. Instead of reading the typological pattern in his son's offer of his own flesh to quell the hunger of his father, and turning to the Son for the salvation of his soul, he blindly (*già cieco*) ate his dead sons' flesh before he too died.

American criticism of *La dolce vita* has long recognized the centrality of Dante here. John Simon astutely observed that Fellini culled citations from the *Commedia* and from *The Tempest* uttered by "monsters" in their original contexts.[4] John P. Welle explored the importance of the citation of Ugolino for the theme of fathers and children in the film. However, he tries strenuously to demonstrate that *La vita nuova* is the guiding model for the film.[5] In an article devoted to the relationship between *Otto e mezzo* and the *Purgatorio* Barbara K. Lewalski outlined an allegorical reading of *La dolce vita* as a version of the *Inferno:* Steiner as an anti-Virgil becomes "a false guide" and Paola, the young waitress who appears again at the end of the film, Beatrice. She concludes:

> The imagery too is transposed from Dante. The film begins with a huge statue of Christ, its arms ironically extended in benediction, being carried, it seems, away from the city by airplane; it ends with a shocking inversion of a traditional Christ symbol in the monstrous, hideous dead fish holding in its mouth a swarm of smaller dead fish—a transposition of the Satan figure at the pit of Dante's hell, his three heads mocking the Trinity and his three mouths gnawing on the heads of the notorious damned.[6]

Finally, Anne Paolucci anticipated me in identifying Paola, not with Beatrice as Welle and Lewalski do, but more accurately with Matelda whom Dante placed at the summit of the mountain of Purgatory. Unfortunately, Paolucci did not elaborate on this reading.[7]

At the very moment at which Marcello's father utters his citation of Ugolino, Fellini and his director of photography, Otello Martelli (who had shot *Paisà* and most of Fellini's earlier films), frame one of the many statues of naked women decorating the nightclub with a Venus motif in the wide Totalscope image behind the old man, almost as if the statue represented his thought. Yet from the opening images of the statue of Jesus being flown by helicopter through the Roman sky, the filmmaker announced a disjuncture between statues and what they represent. The statues and the paintings of *La dolce vita* are false idols, signs that point to what has been lost, such as the statues of Roman emperors and the family portraits of ancestors in the castle of the decadent aristocrats.

Here Marcello's father dangerously idolizes his fantasy of an erotically vigorous youth. It is dramatized twice: first by the pantomime skit of the nightclub entertainer, an old clown with a phallic trumpet, who like a failed Orpheus or Pygmalion attempts in vain to impress or seduce another of the nude statues. Nevertheless, he has the magical power of making balloons follow him as if he were the Pied Piper, and this allusion to power over children, with its overtone of destruction, is cogent. The second dramatization occurs within the plot itself when Fanny seduces the old man, apparently to curry favor with Marcello, whose gossip articles could help her career. But the seduction turns sour; the Dantean joke about his "grief" becomes grim when the patriarch either fails to perform with her at her apartment or suffers a mild heart attack. The situation is ambiguous:

the old man, now sullen, humiliated, takes a cab to a train station, refusing his son's help.

Marcello, like his father, is a persistent womanizer, and perhaps like him will eventually suffer the fate of physical incompetence. The analogy of Ugolino, as the typological model for the fathers in the film, becomes even more striking when the apparently benign Steiner kills his two children. Sinister parents appear all through the film: Maddalena alternates her nights between erotic adventures and games of cards with her rich father; in the castle of Bassano di Sutri there is a momentary confrontation between the feeble owner and his equally feeble adult son, before we see that they are both dominated and infantilized by the elderly family matriarch who summons them to Mass; the parents and grandparents of the children who claim to have seen the Madonna nakedly exploit the sensational interest it arouses.

The episodic structure of *La dolce vita* tends to camouflage the inner logic of its sequences. The scene of Marcello and Steiner looking in on his sleeping children would immediately abut upon the meeting of Marcello and his father on the Via Veneto, as it did in the original screenplay, if the filmmaker had not chosen to insert the presence of the charming young Paola into the film. (She will turn up in the very last episode as part of a crucial Dantean allusion.) Hereby montage both sets up and defuses a parallelism which the fabric of allusions subterraneously supports.

The visit to Steiner's salon is as pivotal to the film as the meeting between Marcello and his father. Only in retrospect, however, can we come to understand the sinister undersong of Steiner's self-deprecation and of his often fatuous ponderousness. His final speech (written after the scenario was finished), to Marcello alone, occurs at the end of a sinuous long take, in which the camera (with an unconventionally close lens for a version of Cinemascope, as many critics have noted) follows him to the curtained beds of each of his two children as he seems to bless them in their sleep:

> Sometimes the night, this darkness, this silence weighs on me. The peace frightens me, perhaps I fear it most of all. I feel as if it were only an appearance, hiding Hell [*l'inferno*]. I think of what will happen to my children tomorrow. The world should be marvelous, they say. But from whose viewpoint, if one telephone call could announce the end of it all? We need to live

outside of passion, beyond feelings, in the harmony of a finished work of art. . . .

As Steiner and Marcello enter the children's bedroom, the camera glides past a Rouault painting of Christ's face on the wall to which neither pay heed. In contrast, as he finishes his speech, Steiner turns toward his reflection in the window behind him as if to confront his own image, that is to say, as if to face up to the meaning of his words and of his metaphor in his own life; yet when the scene occurs, viewers can hardly suspect that he will murder his children and himself within days. But when we see the film a second time, there is a new resonance in the linkage between his metaphor of the work of art and his previous comments, one in admiration of his Morandi still life—"such power, precision, and rigor. You could say art has left nothing to chance"—and another warning Marcello that he cannot find "salvation" in an insulated "esthetic" existence like his own—"a society in which everything is organized, everything predictable, everything perfect."

The apparently benign blessing of the children—Steiner kisses his fingers, then touches the child's forehead—is part of a chain of false benedictions in the film. When Marcello joins the movie star Sylvia in the Trevi fountain, she sprinkles water on his head in a parody of baptism, which the director emphasizes by having the fountain shut down at just that moment. Then Marcello performs his own counterbaptism in the penultimate scene of the film, not with water but an iconographic emblem of the Holy Ghost: ripping up a pillow, he tosses feathers over the revelers.

The party is the climax of a frustrated carnival celebrating the marriage annulment of one of the female guests. Just before she completes her striptease, the owner of the villa they invaded enters, cutting short her performance. Marcello's consequent attempt to orchestrate an orgy by assigning new partners to all the celebrants fizzles out as he becomes a stale parody of Dionysius, riding on the back of a drunken woman whom he tries to "turn into a chicken" with the down feathers. His "baptism" of the guests as they file out of the villa is the last of several travesties of the sacraments, scattered throughout the film: Sylvia had nearly baptized him; Steiner confirmed his children, annealing their heads with his fingers; Marcello heard Maddalena's confession in the castle; an annulment party takes the place of marriage; Sylvia disguises herself as a priest visiting St. Peter's;

there are two versions of extreme unction: a priest genuinely performs the last rites for the trampled child during the riot of the false miracle, and the police enact their investigative ritual over the dead Steiners. Only Holy Communion, the fundamental sacrament, is pointedly missing. Whereas the sacramental subtext of *Roma, città aperta* had served to reinforce the explicit valorization of the conjunction of religion and Resistance, in *La dolce vita* the parodies of the sacraments, like the works of plastic and graphic art in the film, are a set of "mere appearances, hiding Hell." Or more accurately, because the façade is so easily penetrated, the disguises *reveal "l'inferno."*

If indeed *La dolce vita* describes a modern Inferno in which the half-hearted neo-Fascist Marcello repeats the sins of his father—driving his girlfriend, Emma, to attempted suicide, and copulating with his rich friend, Maddalena, on a prostitute's bed, thereby perverting the redemptive sign of her name—where then are the typological marks of "salvation" in this film, if there are any? I take it that the opening and closing sequences are as explicitly Dantean as the quotation from Ugolino. Furthermore, they are parallel constructions. In both there is a shot-countershot alternation between Marcello and an attractive woman he does not know; in both a roaring noise makes verbal exchange impossible.

As the film opens, a helicopter totes an enormous statue of Christ across the city to the Vatican. Marcello and his photographer companion, Paparazzo, follow in another helicopter, presumably to cover the curiosity for their paper. In a mock ascension, the shadow of the effigy rises up the wall of an apartment building in an image reminiscent of the finale of *Miracolo a Milano*. If we are reluctant to see a statue of Christ as a type of Dante's Medusa, (so I shall argue) the strong cut that marks the transition to the next episode makes the association more explicit: when we can expect the stone face of the statue with outstretched arms in countershot to the aerial view of the Piazza San Pietro, instead we have the jarring shift to a dancer in a Siamese mask in an exotic entertainment in a restaurant where Marcello snoops on a celebrated aristocrat.

John Freccero points out the centrality of the Medusa in canto 9 of the *Inferno* to the theology of reading in the *Commedia*. The poet warns the reader:

> O voi ch'avete li 'ntelletti sani, / mirate la dottrina che s'asconde /
> sotto 'l velame de li versi strani.

[O you who have sound understanding, mark the doctrine that is hidden under the veil of the strange verses.] [8]

According to Freccero, to read literally is petrification. I want to suggest that the statue itself is a petrified literalization of Christ. One of three women, sunbathing on a roof, comically confirms this: "It's Jesus," she says. Marcello tries to pick her up, gesturing that she should give him her telephone number. In this opening, shot/countershot emphasizes both the perversion of intersubjectivity in the encounter of person and statue and the subsequent reification of sexuality, which introduces Marcello to us (for that is the first time we see him) as a man who tries to conquer a woman whom he has only seen at an unapproachable distance.

Fellini delays the naming of the Medusa until the very end of the film, and then smuggles it in French. As soon as the Fregene party breaks up, stragglers wander to the beach where a large, strange raylike fish has been dragged to the shore. It is the counterpart of the statue of Christ, as Lewalski observed. However, in stressing the importance of the "swarm of smaller dead fish" within its mouth, she missed a crucial allusion (absent from the original scenario). Domino, a transvestite, introduces the idea of "penance" as he walks to the fish beside Marcello. He talks of changing his life. When he sees the fish he says, "Il est plein de Meduses." ("It is full of jellyfish.") The jellyfish, or *meduse*, draws its Romanic name from a metaphor of petrification its poison induces. Amid the babel of voices around the spectators of the fish, we hear that it has been dead three days. This Christological allusion is wedged among questions about its financial value, its interest for television, its sex, and from one transvestite the suggestive puzzle, "Which is the front and which is the rear?"—as if he were speculating on its sexual mechanics.

From this ambiguous emblem, Marcello turns to a young woman shouting to him across the din of the sea. She is separated by a short inlet of water. He cannot hear her, nor can he reach her. Failing to communicate by signs, he shrugs, and turns from her to embrace a young and amorous woman in the final shot of the film. He had once met the girl across the water, Paola, in a restaurant between the scenes of Steiner's party and meeting with his father; she was listening happily to the very tune one of her countertypes, the divorcée, would later use for her striptease. In the Dantean web of allusions she is a figure for Matelda, the emblem of innocent sexuality the Dantean pilgrim encounters at the summit of Purgatory. The topology of the conclusion of *La dolce vita* recalls that of *Purgatorio* 28: a pine forest and a stream across which the pilgrim sees a young woman, like Proserpine. In the *Purgatorio* the gentle noise of the stream does not inhibit speech: Matelda tells him the place is Eden and sings a line of Psalm 31 [32] in the next canto, "Beati quorum tecta sunt peccata" (*Purg.* 29, 3). Although Eden is never mentioned in the film, its counter-type, Prospero's island, enters the mélange of Steiner's grotesque salon when a young Englishman responds to Steiner's tape-recorded collage of natural sounds with the words of Shakespeare's Caliban: "noises, sounds and sweet airs that give delight and hurt not." Furthermore, it is at Steiner's that the concept of redemption becomes thematic. Yet, as I have claimed, the episodic structure of the film covers up its inner logic: we hardly notice that Steiner's party follows immediately upon the disaster of the children who claim to have seen a vision of the Virgin Mary, which ends in a riot—largely induced by the television exploitation of the "miracle"—in which a boy is trampled to death. The perversion of religion and revelation is obvious in the earlier episode, but the parallel perversion of art and intelligence at Steiner's is deliberately made harder to read.

Throughout *La dolce vita*, and especially at the end, a Catholic theory of sin (*peccata*) and forgiveness (*tecta*) informs the plot. Sin is not only a violation of goodness, but it contains a medusan element of its own hardness. Each repetition of a sin inures the sinner to commit the same sin again. Confession, then, blots out the past chain and makes recurrence more difficult. Marcello repeatedly chooses to lose himself in erotic wandering. He must blind himself again and again to the violence around him. He must ignore the signs and allusions of redemption. Opening with a Dantean warning in the image of Christ turned to stone, and ending with Marcello's refusal to understand the call of a Mateldan innocence, Fellini's "sweet life" is a vision of the glamor of sin.

There is a polyglot concatenation of voices throughout the film, compounded by the accents of foreigners speaking Italian. This linguistic pastiche reflects the new centrality of Rome as a playground for rich Europeans, a workplace for American moviemakers, and a haven for alienated foreign intellectuals. An exchange between an American poetess, speaking in Italian with a heavy accent, and Steiner recurs three times: first, as part of the pretentious talk of the salon; a second time immediately following that, when an English guest plays it back as "dialogue between feminine wisdom and masculine uncertainty," having secretly recorded it over an old tape of natural noises made by Steiner; and finally, played back again by the police investigating Steiner's suicide. The recorded versions end with a thunderclap.

> Poetess: . . . Primitive as a Gothic steeple, so high up you can't hear the voices below.
> Steiner: If you could see my real stature, you will see I am no higher than this. [He makes a gesture with his index finger and thumb.]

Behind her perceptive simile of Steiner as an aloof Germanic type out of touch with human voices (or those of his children), and specifically incapable of understanding *her* poetry, there is a disturbing reinterpretation of the Gothic church which in Dante's time—he was roughly contemporary to the High Gothic—strove for unity and totality, symbolizing the human and divine natures of Christ and embodying a microcosm of the City of Heaven. If the steeple were a bell tower, it was meant to be heard—a variation on the thunderclap—not to hear voices below. The poetess reduces the Gothic edifice to merely human scale, and Steiner continues the process, confessing his smallness among men. Lost in the doubly egocentric exchange is any vestige of the divinity that provided the impulse to Gothic construction, or even of the fusion of nature and human ingenuity represented by the recorded thunderclap, vivid enough to wake the children. By repeating the dialogue three times, Fellini challenges the viewers to find meaning in it, to wake up to it, while he hints that we will probably be as lost as the police who listen to it for forensic evidence.

Pier Paolo Pasolini criticized the film precisely for its "Catholic irrationalism," while at the same time extolling its importance and its formal and moral similarity to the great literary success of the day, Carlo Emilio Gadda's baroque novel, *Quer pasticciaccio brutto de via Merulana* (*That Awful Mess on Via Merulana*), a work largely written during the Fascist period, but published in 1957. For many it ranks with Svevo's *La coscienza di Zeno* (*The Confessions of Zeno*, 1923) as the major Italian novel of the twentieth century. In 1958 Pasolini, following a Spitzerian paradigm, had analyzed four levels of dialect in the novel, but his formulation of a related ideological aporia has relevance for his comparison to Fellini's film:

Thus Gadda presents himself in *Pasticciaccio* as beside-himself and crushed between two errors: the surviving naturalistic positivism of a pre-Fascist liberal of the Right, and the compulsory distorting lyricism of an anti-Fascist worn down and broken by the unequal struggle with the state.

His anguish—which is social anguish—is thus without remedy, and his style will always be a tragically mixed, obsessive style since, in accepting the institutions he believes to be good, he is driven into a fury without respite against the institutional agencies which are effectively bad.[9]

He repeated this method of analysis on *La dolce vita*, brilliantly dissecting its style as a complex function of (1) actor, cast against type (e.g., Dannunzian Annibale Ninchi playing Marcello's father) beside those virtually playing themselves (e.g., most of the characters in the three parties); (2) expressionistic use of costumes (particularly women's hats and dresses), Roman locations, and "amplification" (e.g., the miracle amid klieg lights and rain) beside documentary-like situations; (3) "paratactic" camera movements beside "the most simple kind of shot[s]"; and (4) the slow, expansive development of scenes that end with "lightning-like rapidity," such as the scene in which Marcello's father departs. Bondanella justifiably calls the essay "one of the most original analyses of *La dolce vita* ever written."

Comparing the film to Gadda's novel, Pasolini noted:

There is not one significant communication in the film which is presented purely functionally; it is always excessive, overcharged, lyrical, magical or too violently veristic. That is to say it is semantically amplified. . . .

Like Fellini, Gadda violated word-roots, always in the service of a meaning that reinvents those terms with a language that is altogether subjective, grotesque, violent, visceral, and distorting, and yet combined with passages of veristic realism angrily slapped into the text. Like Fellini, Gadda possesses a lexicon that is the greatest pastiche imaginable.[10]

He understood his distinction between Gadda's pastiche "on internal surfaces" and Fellini's "placed in the foreground" as functions of the authors' political formations; for the novelist was molded in the rationalistic, "positivistic" mode of Italy before Fascism, while the filmmaker, despite his antifascism, was formed by provincial Fascism, so that "[h]is political opposition rests completely on the uniqueness of individual fantasy, on anguish and on joy, as on an intimate and almost mystical patrimony."

Fellini reduces the sweet life of the economic miracle to a fabric of individual temptations: the temptation of fascism for the industrialists and aristocrats; the temptations of sexual indulgence in a consumer society declaring its moral independence from the Church; the temptation of easily acquired money for frivolous work. The moral agon is not so much interiorized within his protagonist as it is revealed in his contradictory behavior in different episodes. Therefore the filmmaker invokes, albeit covertly, the Dantean model as a means of suggesting a moral order to the chaos of characters, behavior, and symbols in the film. What astonished Pasolini, however, is the affection and enthusiasm with which Fellini depicted his infernal world:

> What counts in Fellini is that which endures eternally and absolutely in his broadly Catholic ideology[,] his loving and sympathetic optimism. . . . Look at the Rome he describes. . . . It is an exhibition of the Italian petty bourgeoisie in its own ambience which exaggerates its traits. . . . With this bourgeoisie there mingle disconnected and indescribable monsters from above and below. . . . It seems to me an incredible thing to succeed in seeing purity and vitality even in the petty bourgeois mass that squirms in this *parvenu,* scandalous, movieland, superstitious, and fascist Rome. And yet there is not one of these characters that does not emerge as pure and vital, always presented in his moment of almost sacral energy.[11]

Later we shall see how Pasolini himself fashioned a Dantean drama of inner conflict in the diametrically opposed economic environment of the Roman shantytowns in his first film, *Accattone* (1960). A few years later still Antonioni would weave Dantean allusions into his picture of the neurotic instability of the industrial class, *Il deserto rosso* (1964). In 1960 his model for the interiority of moral conflict was Kierkegaard. Only Visconti, of the major figures of 1960, sustained the social vision of his earliest cinema, and that gave his film a somewhat antiquated look.

Rocco e i suoi fratelli

The economic dominance of American "superspectacles" such as *Ben Hur* in the late fifties inspired the slogan "il superspettacolo d'autore" to identify the prestigious and for the most part popular films of Fellini, Visconti, and Antonioni. While Fellini and Antonioni capitalized indirectly on the public's fascination with the sexual confusions of the very rich, Visconti drew his widest audience in seventeen years from an analysis of sex and violence among the poor.

Like *Ossessione, La terra trema,* and *Senso, Rocco* was a large-scale project, somewhat truncated by the expenses of production and by censorship. Visconti attempted once again to create the cinematic equivalent of a realist novel of a family's fortunes. Dostoevsky's *Idiot* suggested some of the plot, and *The Brothers Karamazov* and Mann's Joseph novels loom in the penumbra of the title. Georg Lukács, whose literary essays drew considerable attention from the Italian Left in the fifties, had recently championed Mann as the progressive counterpoise to the "static" modernist view of society found in both Joyce and Kafka.

Franco Fortini described the pervasiveness of Lukács's ideas on "critical realism" in Italy in the 1950s:

> There was an often unacknowledged, but most evident influence: some . . .
> spoke of the imminent movement "toward realism" in literature and the arts.
> And really there was the impression, in that period, that neorealism, a worn-
> out literary movement, had been definitively wiped out, that the tenacious,
> programmatic residue of naturalism and the avant-garde had been surpassed
> or was about to be surpassed; . . . and that Lukács' idea of "great realism"
> permitted not only a rethinking of Italian literary and critical issues of the
> preceding thirty years, but would encourage a return to nineteenth-century
> bourgeois literature with new eyes, substituting for the decadent mode an-
> other kind of reading.[12]

For the Communist critics Carlo Salinari (of *Il Contemporaneo*) and Guido Aristarco (of *Cinema nuovo*) the concept, virtually the slogan, "from neorealism to realism" applied especially to Vasco Pratolini's historical novel, *Metello* (1955), and to Visconti's heavily censored film of the Italian Risorgimento, *Senso* (1954). Unlike many of whom Fortini wrote, Aristarco was an avowed Lukácsian, who consistently championed Visconti as the great "bourgeois critical realist" of the Italian cinema. The critical and political debates over *Metello* and *Senso* may have confirmed Visconti's commitment to fashioning a cinematic equivalent to the realist novel.

In fact, he had already put Pratolini and the screenwriter Suso Cecchi D'Amico to work on the scenario of *Rocco* when he read Giovanni Testori's *Il ponte della Ghisolfa* (*The Bridge on the Ghisolfa*, 1958), a volume of loosely connected stories about subproletarian life in Milan. He incorporated elements from stories—the love of a prostitute, the difficult relationship between a boxer and a promoter, the animosity of two brothers over one's successful career (in Testori's stories he is a singer, called "Sinatra")—and hired Testori to authenticate the dialogue of Milanese low life, much as Pasolini had done for Fellini when he was making *Le notti di Cabiria* (1957) about prostitutes and pimps.

In *Rocco* Visconti uses melodrama to delineate the gap between the northern industrial milieu and the operatic modes of emotional expression he attributes to the southerners. The Parondis are a family of emigrants from the southern coast of Lucania, in the instep of the Italian boot, where the most dire of Italian social and economic conditions had not changed significantly since Carlo Levi described the region in *Cristo si è fermato a Eboli* (1945). (In describing the Parondis I am drawing on details found in the published script which are sometimes not apparent in the film.)

First the eldest of five sons, Vincenzo, moved to Milan. After the death of his father, his mother, Rosaria, sold everything she had to pay for the train tickets for herself and her other four sons—Simone, Rocco, Ciro, and Luca. The film begins with their unannounced arrival in Milan on the very evening Vincenzo was celebrating his engagement to Ginetta Gianelli, the daughter of a Lucanian family successfully reestablished in Milan and very likely of a higher social and economic status than the Parondis in the first place.

Rosaria and her four sons, as we see them at the opening of the film, represent the lowest stratum of "terroni," as the southern emigrants are derisively called. In the late fifties almost two million southerners relocated in the North, largely in the industrial triangle of Milan, Turin, and Genoa. According to the script, the action of *Rocco e i suoi fratelli* takes place in stages between October 1955 (the arrival of the Parondis in Milan) and February 1960 (Rocco's boxing championship). During this period the annual influx of "terroni" to Milan increased from fifty-four hundred to more than thirteen thousand (the statistics are confused after 1958). For the most part, these newcomers settled in public housing built at the periphery of the city; they held the poorest paid jobs, and suffered from the regional prejudices of the Lombardians.

It was commonly observed at the time of the film's release that it continued the story of *La terra trema* into Italy of the late fifties. The choral present that Visconti adapted from Verga certainly has its equivalent in *Rocco e i suoi fratelli*. The very choice of the boxing milieu conveniently surrounds first Simone, then Rocco, who are the epicenters of Visconti's melodrama, with a screaming crowd, or a busy gymnasium. The set designer, Mario Garbuglia, has said that the party for Rocco's victory in Rosaria's apartment in which the neighbors from the courtyard join in a toast "was inspired not so much by the actuality of Milanese apartment courts with their inner balconies but above all by the idea of having a chorus, as in the Greek theater, for the tragedy that unfolds in the foreground."[13]

If the film is a tragedy, it lacks both an articulation of hubris and a moment of recognition. Instead, it turns on the incompatibility of southern and northern sensibilities and the expectations they entail. This is particularly vivid in the stormy, triangular relationship of Simone, Rocco, and the prostitute, Nadia. Simone's passionate violence and Rocco's equally excessive endurance, a saintly passivity, derive from the temperaments of Rogozhin and Prince Myshkin in Dostoevsky's *Idiot*, by way of Testori's chapters, "Cosa fai, Sinatra?" and "Il resto, dopo," in which Attilio rapes his brother's girlfriend in front of him and then beats him up.

Simone cannot adjust to the sexual code of subproletarian Milan. Once Nadia has slept with him, he thinks he has a claim on her. So, when he learns that Rocco is seeing her two years later, he attacks them at night at the Ponte della Ghisolfa with the help of a "chorus" of his criminal friends. As they hold Rocco down, Simone rapes Nadia, throwing her panties in Rocco's face. Visconti portrays Rocco paralyzed with horror, crying, as Nadia leaves begging for his comfort under the heavy emphasis of Nino Rota's music. In the vicious fight which follows, Rocco hardly defends himself. The filmmaker used no music at this point. He shot this night scene for the most part in distant long shots but recorded the blows so that they seem to be auditory closeups.

Although the plot required that Simone murder Nadia without a witness, Visconti brilliantly obtained his choral effect by parallel montage, carefully intercutting the final encounter with simultaneous scenes of Rocco's championship bout. Simone's emotional confusions are refracted through Rocco's performance: when Nadia hysterically rejects Simone's advances, Rocco staggers under his opponent's blows; when Simone stabs her to death, Rocco scores a knockout. Rota's music, at its most melodramatic during the murder, which Nadia seems at first to accept in a gesture of crucifixion, collides effectively with the sound texture of the blows and shouts of the ring at each montage shift. There is even a verbal overlapping when Rocco's trainer urges him to "cover up" against punches to the head while Simone tells Nadia to "cover up" as he wraps around her the coat he pulled off as she tried to escape from him.

A detailed look at the shot structure here will be indicative of Visconti's stylistic shift from the intricate composition in depth of *La terra trema* of twelve years earlier. From a series of closeups of Rocco and his opponent boxing, the scene shifts to a tight shot of Nadia and Simone, held for a long time. At first Nadia, backed against a tree, tries to resist his kisses as he covers her with the coat. Then, giving up, she tells him how much she hates him, over the music coming onto the sound track. As her speech continues, Simone stops kissing her; he is clearly staggered when she tells him how she loved only Rocco and that now she does not care what he does to her. When she moves off frame, the camera stays on Simone; the music intensifies, dramatizing a downward tilt to his pocket as he slowly takes out a switchblade knife and opens it. This long shot ends with a tilt back up to his face. The music drives to a crescendo over the next five brief shots—a medium shot of Nadia some distance from Simone, a long shot of the two of them as he approaches her, another medium of her, a countershot of Simone, and finally a tracking shot behind Simone as he reaches her. She opens her arms as if crucified, then puts them around his head. Just as we are expecting the stab, the scene changes to the ring, where the sound of the crowd and punches replace the music. A few tight closeups of the fighters precede a long shot of Rocco delivering a decisive blow, and a very long shot from the back of the stadium of his opponent hitting the mat.

Throughout the film, Visconti prefers to open episodes with details, saving very long shots for the climax or the termination. This is true of the beginning of the film, which shows the Parondis closely packed in a train and saves a long establishing shot for their exit from the Milan station; similarly Rocco's meeting with Nadia after the rape, on the top of the Duomo, begins with close shots of their pained exchange—he is urging her return to Simone to "save" him—and ends with a very high and distant shot from above as Nadia runs away from Rocco. It would appear that Giuseppe Rotunno shot the film with a zoom lens even though there is very little zooming, and a good deal of tracking for short distances to take in the interactions of several characters in a room. Generally, the zoom lens follows the actors closely in their movements, in a compressed depth often like that of a telephoto lens. Usually the director favors intense close-ups and static portrait shots at middle distance: when Nadia appears in the first and more squalid of the Parondi apartments, her image is intercut with portrait shots of each of the brothers; Rocco's troubled confessions to Ciro that he cannot help translating the hatred he feels into aggression in the ring occurs in a long closeup, as does his nostalgic speech at the victory party, longing for a return to the southern "land of olive trees and moon sickness . . . and of rainbows," while the affected members of the family listen in closeups and portrait shots. The long shot of the full table at the end of the speech is a small-scale version of the montage shift Visconti and his editor Mario Serandrei use repeatedly in this film. The rhythmic alternation of isolating closeups, fluid interpersonal scenes, and sudden shifts to the distanced perspective befits the novelistic scale of *Rocco e i suoi fratelli* which intermixes individual psychological vignettes, family melodrama, and an overview of emigrant life in Italy's economic capital. This constitutes a strong alternative to the microcosmic focus on the Valastro family, and the preference for allegorical types over psychological portraits, that emphasized the insularity and suggested the typicality of the community in *La terra trema*.

The division of the film into five chapters named for each of the brothers in order from eldest to youngest helps to deflect some of the attention from Simone and Rocco. In the opening chapter Vincenzo rather resents the disturbance of his upwardly mobile life caused by the unanticipated arrival of his family. His mother's histrionic behavior at the engagement party temporarily estranges him from Ginetta. He has to learn the baroque mechanisms of the welfare system in Milan to find a home for his family. It is he who first flirtatiously brings Nadia to the apartment when she is fleeing from the anger of her father, disgraced by her prostitution. He too has tried boxing, a sport dominated professionally by southerners, and vainly warns Simone against following that route.

In essence, Vincenzo is the assimilated southerner on the lower scale of the Milanese economy. The very first thing we hear him say is that he has no intention of returning to Lucania. Late in the film, he seems on the way to satisfying his modest ambitions when he purchases a van on credit from Ciro's prospective father-in-law. His moral strength is focused on escaping from his mother's dominating jealousy, which is so fierce she tries to stop his marriage and refuses to attend the baptism of his first child. The sign of his ability to adjust to the standards of the North is the ease with which he abandons his mother's traditionally southern sexual politics—"a man who truly wants a woman . . . takes her without asking permission from her or anyone else"—when Ginetta asserts she will not live by that Lucanian code.

Simone is already a more vivid character when his chapter begins, at the time of his first boxing victory. More precisely, it starts in Nadia's room; he has gone off with her without telling his manager, the homosexual Morini (a figure from Testori's book), who had arranged a celebratory dinner. Thus Visconti draws him to the center of the narrative as a disloyal and narcissistic figure. With ironical symbolism, his first fight for the Aurora club of Milan is against a club from Lucania. There Ginetta's brothers mercilessly deride Simone as they, fully assimilated to Milan, cheer as fans of the Lucanian fighters. Nicknamed Apollo because of his good looks, preferred by Rosaria as her greatest hope for financial success, Simone expects rewards without discipline. He smokes, drinks, and misses his training sessions whenever he can be with Nadia, who quickly rejects him. Simone's callousness toward the sinister Morini prefigures his misuse of his genuinely altruistic brother, Rocco. Simone asks Rocco to borrow money for him as an advance on his minimal pay as a laundry delivery boy; he charges dry cleaning against Rocco's salary, and even steals an expensive shirt from the laundry. When he returns the shirt, he seduces the woman who owns the laundry and ends up stealing her jewelry, letting suspicion fall on Rocco. His chapter concludes when Nadia returns the jewels to Rocco because she wants nothing more to do with Simone.

The contrast between Simone and Rocco generates the "moral manichaeism"[14] of the film's melodramatic tone. The elder brother, seduced by fantasies of easy money, sex, and glory, continually challenges the younger to find ways to extricate him. At his worst, Simone is the pawn of his criminal friend, Ivo (another Testori character), who goads him to violence for the amusement of his gang, the darkest of Visconti's "choruses."

The night Nadia had returned the jewels, Rocco told Simone that he had been called up to do his military service. His own chapter begins, then, after a two-year hiatus. A letter from his mother and a chance meeting with Nadia (who has just been released after being imprisoned for prostitution) make this central moment of the film a deceptive idyll. Short scenes illustrate details from Rosaria's letter while we hear her voice reading it. She regrets Vincenzo's marriage and the economic strain of Rocco's military service, but boasts of a new apartment, Simone's boxing success, and Ciro's move from garage work to the Alfa Romeo factory as a result of his studying in night school. She stresses here, and later in a bleaker moment of doubt (then to Ciro), that she is known in the neighborhood and called "Signora" in the shops. Contemporary American readers and viewers of the film might not understand her pleasure at so simple a form of respectful address unless they realized the deplorable treatment of peasant women in the South as late as the 1960s. Joseph Lopreato gives one example of a peasant woman ignored and refused service in a post office, mocked by both the clerk and a policeman, until she gave up pleading for service and retreated cursing, "May you die with rabies, arrogant cowards!"[15] Another of his examples tells of a woman pushed to the ground and harassed by teenagers, to the general public's amusement, for trying to protect her daughter from a boy's caresses. Milanese social services and the courtesy of northern Italian life fulfilled Rosaria's fantasies; in the North, going to a city was not a dangerous risk per se for a peasant woman.

Rocco disarms Nadia from the first by extending to her the unqualified sympathy he gives to his family; he refuses to be repelled by her prison term, and even subtly suggests that he sees her imprisonment in political rather than moral terms by telling her the story of his friend from Lucania who was jailed for protesting the injustice of land reform. Nadia, in turn, betrays her vulnerability for the first time under his sensitive probing. She is perhaps the most fully articulated instance in Italian cinema of the enduring icon of the good prostitute. With the intensification of the debate which finally led to the closing of the brothels in 1958, this figure flourished in major Italian films: *Le notti di Cabiria* (1957), *Il grido* (1959), *La dolce vita* (1960), *Accattone* (1961).

The chapter under Rocco's name spans the two years—according to the script from April 1957 to February 1959—in which he assumed the financial support of the family by reluctantly becoming a boxer. At first he merely accompanied Simone to keep him in training, and sparred with him. As Simone grew more lax, and then lost an important fight, Rocco took over and immediately surpassed him in his métier. Thus, Simone's exhibitionistic rape of Nadia and his beating of Rocco, at the heart of the chapter, manifests his rage and rivalry toward his brother, just as Rocco's paralytic silence toward Nadia immediately afterward registers his guilt for unwittingly inducing it. Consequently the chapter ends with his confession to Ciro of his horror of the repressed hatred that makes him a successful fighter.

But Ciro, whose chapter begins at that point, fails to understand him or to take him seriously. For him, Simone is a "bad seed" who must be expelled from the family, in a formula that varies a New Testament parable. Rocco's eventual triumph and Simone's homicide occur in the context of Ciro's growing prominence in the family. He is the fully successful emigrant—educated at night school, a foreman at Alfa Romeo, and engaged to a Milanese woman. An early version of the script made him a leader in a strike at the factory, but Visconti realized the shortcomings of so schematic a political outline. It is to Ciro that Rosaria theatrically expresses her sense of failure, when Simone moves Nadia into her apartment and Rocco leaves to live with Vincenzo (she does not know of the fight between the brothers, and thinks Simone is the victim of the evil eye, which she in turn tries to put on Nadia). Gian Piero Brunetta calls the film a tragedy in five acts, identifying Rosaria's speech to Ciro as the moment of recognition.[16] But it is ultimately an empty rhetorical gesture by Rosaria; she blames Nadia for all of Simone's failings and only questions her own emigration as a hyperbole of anxiety to elicit the automatic reflex of reassurance that Ciro gives her.

His chapter describes the stages that prepare Ciro for his decisive rush to the police to denounce Simone as a murderer which marks the conclusion. He argues against Rocco's offer to continue boxing in order to pay the dubious debts Morini claims as a victim of Simone's beating and robbery, but he nevertheless delivers money to Simone to facilitate his departure from Milan. This meeting in the seedy hotel room to which Simone has retreated is played out before the youngest brother, Luca, who clearly idolizes Rocco and sides with his feeling of family loyalty over Ciro's morality.

Ciro's identification with the life of the industrial city has its significant linguistic dimension. At the victory party he falters in his turn at offering a toast: he cannot continue the rhyme in dialect as Vincenzo and Rocco have done, and must finish in official Italian. This linguistic gesture complements the moment on the tram in the second episode of the film when Rosaria can barely communicate with the conductor and resorts to showing him a photo of Vincenzo as she seeks help in finding out where to get off to reach his address.

In an article for the PCI journal *Vie nuove* (22 October 1960), which Gianni Rondolino suggests may have been a collaboration with the Communist ideologue Antonello Trombadori,[17] Visconti wrote of the importance of Ciro to the film:

My endeavour had been to draw from the very roots of Verga's method the prime causes of the drama and to present at the culmination of the downfall (in *La terra trema:* the financial embarrassment of the Valastro family; in *Rocco:* the moral collapse at the moment of greatest economic leveling) a character that clearly, almost didactically (I am not afraid to use the word) illuminates it. Here, in *Rocco*, it is no accident that this character is Ciro, the brother who became a worker, who has not only demonstrated an unromantic, not transitory ability to insert himself in life, but who has become conscious of the different duties connected with different rights. Altogether, and I have to say without my realizing it, the conclusion of *Rocco* turned out to be a symbolical finale, that is to say, emblematic of my convictions about the Southern Question: the worker talks to his youngest brother of a future vision of his country that reflects the ideal union Antonio Gramsci conceived.

Actually, the filmmaker has here rephrased the script of the short finale, Luca's chapter: when Luca reports how the police seized Simone, Ciro tells him of his love for his brother who taught him to "learn his rights and duties" but then forgot his own lesson. I do not know if this speech was ever shot; it is in no version of the film I have been able to see. He does tell Luca, who clings to a fantasy of returning south with Rocco, that Rocco is as dangerous in his way as Simone, because saints cannot live in human society without provoking disaster. Luca himself instantiates the icon of the child as a figure for the future of Italy. His short chapter designates him as the moral repository of the family conflicts and successes. If the Gramscian ideal of an alliance of southern farmers and northern industrial workers is to occur, Visconti suggests, it will be fed by the experience of those who have known both worlds.

In an interview in 1958 Visconti had said:

Melodrama has had a bad reputation ever since its defenders abandoned it to schematic and conventional performances. In Italy this genre appeals to the natural predisposition of the people, but it also suits the tastes of the

European public because its structure is so unified and direct. I love melodrama because it locates itself right on the border between life and theater.
I tried to portray this predilection of mine in the opening sequence of *Senso*.
Theater and opera, the baroque world: these are the themes that bind me
to melodrama.[18]

Even if we interpret the melodrama of *Senso* as a criticism of the shortcomings of the bourgeois revolutions of Garibaldi, as if Visconti were implying that Italians were in danger of seeing their history as melodrama, it
is difficult to accept Visconti's implication that the "unromantic" and un-
fickle nature of Ciro makes him the Gramscian hero of *Rocco e i suoi
fratelli*. Rather the film illustrates the emotional richness of the southern
heritage, locates the conscience of Italy in the moral conflicts of southerners, and implies that melodrama, occupying "the border" between political
actuality and art, is the most vital mode of representing and understanding
those moral conflicts in their richness.

Visconti has artfully built a network of rhyming and contrasting
scenes into his large panorama of the city life and instinctual passions of
the poor: the two tram scenes contrast the brothers' wonder at the night
lights of the great city with the brief amatory happiness of Rocco and
Nadia; Luca goes to Vincenzo's work site to tell him of the eviction that
will mean a better apartment for the family, then to Ciro's to bring him an
announcement of night-school courses, and finally again to Ciro's to announce Simone's capture; the film nearly begins with the interrupted party
celebrating Vincenzo's engagement and nearly ends with the even more
fatal interruption of Rocco's victory party; the two most violent scenes,
the rape and the murder of Nadia, occur in the bleak landscape at the
periphery of the city, at night and in fog. The careful architectonics of
the scenario shapes the explosiveness of its melodrama into an epic of
southern aspirations in terms of fragile romantic enthusiasms and frustrated triumphs.

L'avventura

Michelangelo Antonioni's *L'avventura* was the third film of 1960 that signaled the dramatic revival of the Italian cinema. In the final speech of that
film, Patrizia, a friend of the heroine, Claudia, tells her "there is certainly

no point in being melodramatic." Even though she refers to Claudia's intense conflict, brought about by falling in love and starting an affair with Sandro, the fiancé of her closest friend, Anna, who disappeared during a yachting party to the Eolian Islands just two or three days before, the resistance to melodrama can be heard as a programmatic declaration of a principle of Antonioni's mature style. In fact, the international prestige of *L'avventura* may have been as much a function of the ultimate suppression of the melodramatic tensions that had been at work in Antonioni's earlier films as it certainly was of its refinement and extension of their visual elegance.

L'avventura shares an aesthetic with the phenomenological, psycho-analytical, and avant-garde currents emergent in Italian culture in the late fifties, but which previously had no significant representation in film. When Guido Aristarco of the journal *Cinema nuovo* circulated four questions about the status of the new Italian cinema (specifically the three new films of Fellini, Visconti, and Antonioni) among novelists and critics, Luciano Anceschi, the professor of aesthetics at the University of Bologna and founder of the journal *Il Verri* (who was the godfather of the Italian avant-garde of the sixties), responded that Antonioni "touched him, personally, more deeply than all the others"; and that *L'avventura* was "a coherent vision, not a mechanical one; in fact, it is at once delicate, fast, deep, and light. Or to put it another way, its truth and invention seem unlabored." [19]

Umberto Eco, the most prominent apologist of the Anceschi circle, devoted several pages of *Opera aperta* [20] (*The Open Work,* 1962) to a discussion of "the openness of *L'avventura*" but nowhere else in that influential book does he dwell on cinema. For both Anceschi and Eco formal research in art can be a political activity. For instance, in a later essay on "Form as Social Commitment" (included in the 1972 edition of *Opera aperta*) Eco wrote of *L'eclisse:*

> This movie about a useless and unlikely love affair between useless and un-
> likely characters tells us more about contemporary man and his world than
> a panoramic melodrama involving workers in overalls and countless social
> confrontations, structured according to the logical, rational demands of a
> nineteenth-century plot—whose very denouements would imply the resolu-
> tion of all contradictions into a universal order. In fact, the only order man
> can impose on his situation is the order of a structural organization whose
> very disorder allows the apprehension of the situation. [21]

Similarly, in the journal of the phenomenologist Enzo Paci, *Aut-Aut,* where issues of psychoanalysis, American pragmatism, and Heideggerian thought were frequently debated, cinema was rarely discussed; but whenever it was, Antonioni was the dominant focus of attention.

At the end of the fifties and through the early sixties the Frankfurt school, the French *nouveau roman,* the aesthetics of chance operations, abstract art, and psychoanalysis attracted considerable attention in Italy. The development of Antonioni's cinema was of particular interest to those most open to these currents, just as, conversely, his work was attacked from factions opposed to them. For example, Alberto Moravia, whose realist novels the critics of *Il Verri* disparaged, criticized *L'avventura* in his column in *L'Espresso* for its lack of social and political vision. Ironically, Moravia's novel *La noia* (*The Empty Canvas,* 1960) would turn out to be the literary work most frequently aligned to Antonioni's worldview, and Moravia himself would soon come to champion his films.

To a large degree Antonioni shared a sense of the modernist tradition with the Anceschi circle. Lorenzo Cucco lists the following profound literary and figurative allegiances: Flaubert, Gide (whom he translated), Camus, Joyce, Pavese, Adorno, Fitzgerald, and De Chirico.[22] This list clearly associates him with the antimelodramatic tradition, which Brooks describes in terms of "stoic materialism and a language of deflationary suspicion."[23] His summary of this mode of fiction can bring us to the details of *L'avventura:* "Plot and action are de-dramatized, voluntarily insignificant. Desire, the relations of intention to action, the coherence of subjectivity, ambition as the self's project are all stripped of significant status, shown to be inauthentic or illusory."

I shall start my analysis of *L'avventura* by drawing attention to a decidedly unemphasized moment near the end of the film in which "nothing happens": Sandro is wandering about the San Domenico Palace Hotel, actually a converted monastery, apparently in search of his fellow architect Ettore, for whom he has the profitable but unfulfilling job of providing building estimates. He has just left Claudia in their room to sleep. When the film began in Rome a few days before, Claudia and Anna, his girlfriend, stopped to pick up Sandro for a cruise on a private yacht. He had just returned from a month away which had made Anna very anxious. After a painful conversation on the first Eolian island they visited, Anna disappeared without warning. After a day of searching for her in vain, her friends had only inconclusive hypotheses: she may have killed herself, drowned accidentally, or somehow got off the island with a passing fishing boat or even with smugglers. In the midst of the search Sandro makes a play for Claudia, who rejects him, insisting that they go to the mainland to pursue the tenuous clues offered by the police and the press. When he persists in pursuing her, she leaves him to join the rest of the yacht party at a villa. Filled with anxiety about his arrival there, she rejoins him in his search, this time responding to his advances. By the next day she has fallen in love with him. Therefore, with intense guilt she came to fear Anna's return.

So it is on the second night of their affair that I want to begin my examination of the film. In his wandering, Sandro briefly passes a Mannerist painting and a woman looking at it. Neither the painting nor the woman will appear again in the film. Here is Seymour Chatman's description of the scene from his lucid analysis of the filmmaker's stylistics, *Antonioni; or, The Surface of the World:*

> Sometimes the found object comments on the story in a more lighthearted way, as when we see, from Sandro's point of view, an old master painting in the lobby of the luxury hotel in Taormina. The decadence implicit in the depiction of a patriarch king taking refreshment at a lady's breast is ironically mediated by the jaded, complicitous gaze of the young woman, another guest at the hotel. Her eyes convey both boredom and invitation, and though Sandro refuses her, he is soon to accept the favors of Gloria Perkins.[24]

Sandro looks briefly at the painting and exchanges glances with the woman held in its spell. He turns away, disgusted or bemused, but the camera fixes him for several seconds, his head blocking our view of the image of the elderly man sucking the breast of a young, dressed woman. Just as the scopic flirtation of the woman looking at the painting suggests an offer to reenact the baroque scene in a more private place in the hotel, the very oddity of the glances within the painting seems somehow relevant to the eyeline matches in the scene's montage. Both the painted woman and the old man are looking off to the right, instead of acknowledging each other, but the object of their gaze is not within the canvas, which suggests that it might be a fragment of a larger painting or part of a larger unit.

Chatman's description of the scene and his interpretation of the scopic interplay are, as usual, accurate; but from an art-historical, iconographic point of view he could not be farther off base about the painting, as he subsequently acknowledged in his notes to the published filmscript. It depicts "Roman Charity," or the story of Pero, a dutiful daughter who sustains her starving, imprisoned father, Cimon, with her own milk. The story, recorded in Valerius Maximus, has been painted since the Pompeian frescoes. By the seventeenth century it became a combined image for feeding the hungry and visiting prisoners in representations of the Seven Acts of Charity. Thus we find Pero and Cimon on the left of Caravaggio's great painting of this theme in Naples.

What relevance does this iconography have to Antonioni's film? At first sight, none. Certainly Chatman is correct in foregrounding the play of invitation and refusal between the viewers of the painting. When Sandro does not respond to the tacit solicitation, we may assume for the moment that it is because he is so much in love with Claudia, just as in the shots to follow he does not seem to react to the stares of the exhibitionist Gloria Perkins. But soon the film will demonstrate the error of such readings. For when Claudia wakes at dawn and does not find him in the room, she first goes to Patrizia, to see if he has stayed with her and Ettore, and then finds him embracing Perkins on a couch in the hotel lobby. There is just one more scene in the film: when Claudia runs out of the hotel, Sandro gives Perkins the money she asks for ("just a little memento") and follows Claudia in despair. In the final shot *she* consoles *him,* caressing his head as he sits on a bench.

Merely as an expensive baroque object the painting contributes to the opulence of the hotel. As an image of an old man sucking the breast of a young woman it is a curiosity, all the more fascinating because of the indication of a sight off the canvas. In the sexually charged environment of the lobby, it mediates a failed seduction. The obscurity of the subject, Roman Charity, and the fragmentary and suppressed allusion to the Seven Acts of Charity in the Gospel of Matthew underlines the gaps between Roman and modern morality, Christian charity and psychosexual dynamics, iconography and pornography.[25] In this film of ellipses that parades one loss of meaning or certainty after another, the painting and its multiple interpretations allegorizes the status of the cinema.

The nominal subject of the painting, the devotion of Pero to her father, brings us back to the opening shots of the film in which Anna's father confronts her about her yachting trip. He is a wealthy diplomat whose thirty years of "diplomacy and lying" (in his own phrase) subtly attest to the continuity of Fascist and DC foreign ministries. When she tells him where she is going, he gives three responses in ascending critical order: First, he asks her if it is not the custom to wear a cap with the name of the yacht, indicating how out of touch he is with fashion. Then, he observes that he is used to being left alone, implying that Anna has not been a dutiful daughter. Finally, he criticizes her relationship with Sandro: "He'll never marry you." When she counters that she is the one who refused him, he insists, "It's the same thing." The coupling of his hostility to Sandro with his feeling of desertion directly reverses the tale of Pero and Cimon, in its incestual undertones as well as its overt moral exemplum. Actually, we hear Sandro propose first to Anna, then to Claudia in the film. According to Spinazzola, "In a very Italian way, he wants to marry all the women, because marriage would satisfy his bourgeois aspiration for stability and would offer a justification for his renunciation of any professional ambition."[26]

When Anna disappears she leaves behind a copy of the Bible and F. Scott Fitzgerald's *Tender Is the Night,* a novel about the relationship between a psychiatrist and his patient-wife, who suffers from schizophrenia brought on by an incestuous relationship with her father. Anna's father significantly pays no attention to the novel, but takes the presence of the Bible as a good sign that she has not killed herself.

The first of many triangular relationships operative in the film is that of Anna, her father, and Sandro. But no sooner is their discussion concluded than we discover that Claudia has been a witness to this scene. It is of course a characteristic of Antonioni's style to use such hysteron-proteron structures on both a formal and a narrative level. For example, the premises of Sandro's reaction to the woman at the painting become clear only after it and the subsequent scenes in the hotel are over. Throughout the film, Claudia witnesses such scenes of conflict and the eros of others. The primal scene schema at work here has a long history in Antonioni's cinema. In *Il grido* he literalized the trauma, depicting the moment when Rosina comes upon her father, Aldo, making love to his mistress, Virginia, as a turning point in Aldo's troubled passage to suicide.[27] Claudia must wait in the piazza while Anna impulsively and angrily has sex with Sandro as soon as they meet; her sudden erotic impulse can be seen as a revenge for Claudia's persuading her not to keep him waiting when they arrive at his apartment. Claudia witnesses Raimondo's failed attempt to seduce Patrizia on the yacht: here the impassive Patrizia tells her to stay while Raimondo looks up her dress and slips his hand onto her breast without any reaction on her part. Later she spies on a young Sicilian as he attempts to engage a female passenger on a train in a discussion of love; she even draws Sandro into enjoying this display of erotic ethnology. Furthermore, the couple, Corrado and Giulia, constantly fight in front of her and everyone else. Giulia drags her along as a witness to the seduction attempt of an absurdly smug teenage painter of nudes, then throws her out of the room when she is ready to submit to him. The wife of a druggist (who claims to have seen the missing Anna) puts on a hyperbolical display of jealousy before Claudia and Sandro. And climactically Claudia catches Sandro on a couch with Gloria Perkins.[28]

The psychoanalytic orientation of Antonioni's mature cinema underscores his representation of antiheroic characters who cannot focus their wills. They are beneficiaries of the economic miracle who associate with the nobility (at the villa of the teenage painter) and the heirs of the rich (e.g., Anna). Claudia tells Patrizia, in their discussion of their mothers, that she had a "sensible," that is to say "poor," childhood, yet she travels along with the rich without any apparent economic problems; there is no mention of her work. Sandro describes his adolescent fantasies of creative genius, without money, but admits he has achieved nothing but affluence (apartments in Milan and Rome).

The nearest either of them come to the articulation of an ambition is Sandro's response to the seventeenth-century architecture of Vincenzo Sinatra and Rosario Gagliardi at Noto. He gushes: "What imagination! Look at all the movement. They were interested in the stage effect. Extraordinary freedom!" Encouraged by Claudia, he recklessly declares that he will give up making estimates for Ettore and return to creative architecture. But the next morning, unable to get into the Duomo to see its interior, he jealously knocks over an ink bottle on the scale drawing of a detail made by a young architect, who has to be restrained from fighting with him. Translating this rivalry into sex, he nearly rapes Claudia when he returns to the hotel room. Even his infidelity with Gloria Perkins, after promising Ettore to have estimates for him the next day, has an element of revenge against Claudia because she shared his moment of delusive enthusiasm.

In the intricate texture of reflected speech and gesture interlocking parts of the film, the confrontation with the young architect at Noto inverts an earlier instance of restrained violence in the custom house at

Milazzo, where the police were interrogating smugglers for information about Anna. In a hysterical outburst Sandro began to attack one of the smugglers, but immediately after he was stopped he diverted his attention to the architectural curiosities of the customs house (actually Tommaso Maria Napoli's bizarre Villa Pallagonia at Bagheria). Both architecture and landscape become "stage effect" in this film. The baroque architecture of Noto is a textbook example of the interplay of building and landscape, but the rest of the film is permeated—from the opening glimpse of the diplomat's villa, with St. Peter's deep in the center of the image and high-rise apartments encroaching on the space—with a range of isolated and urban landscapes that dwarf the contemporary figures even when they are stage sets for their drama. The distances as they near and separate from each other, and from the camera, reflect their relationship as much as do their gestures and words.

With an exquisite sense of blocking and reframing in long takes, Antonioni reduces the baroque freedom and movement as well as the romantic isolation of the Eolian Islands to an elegant modernist grid. This is one of the reasons the paintings of De Chirico are so frequently cited in discussions of this film.[29] Stanley Cavell succinctly described the De Chirican tone of the film:

> An innovator will have his own manner of projecting the future. Antonioni gets it, beginning with *L'Avventura*, with his spacing of film time, in particular by his fermata over single shots, which enclose an air of *pressentiment*. This is the autograph emotion of surrealist painting; and one is reminded of iconographic or thematic features of Antonioni's films that show him the inheritor of surrealism from painting. There is his obsession with the façades of uninhabited, new buildings (the town development in *L'Avventura* . . . is a transcription of Chirico); they are not haunted, we know nothing is present inside them, they have no past. . . . Absence is obviously a root topic in Antonioni as it was in surrealism. In both it is registered by the sheen or finish of the frames, which, along with the clean, deep lines of perspective, perfects the avoidance of human clutter or arbitrariness; nothing is behind this space.[30]

A number of different visual strategies at work in the film have sources in De Chirico's paintings from the period 1910–1918. Many of his haunted townscapes articulate depth by drawing in perspective and the abstraction of arches and galleries. Often the architecture bisects or tri-sects the canvas with well-defined vertical lines (*Piazza con Arianna* [1913], *L'Enigme de l'arcade* [1913], *La Lassitude de l'infini* [1912–13]), or an arched façade will run parallel to the picture plane (*L'enigma dell'ora* [1911]). In all of Antonioni's films of the early sixties he uses the strong verticals of arches, walls, doorways, and pillars to section the rect-angular screen into two, three, or more zones of human action (or mere human presence) and empty space. Often the human figures are as isolated and dwarfed by the setting as are De Chirico's people and statues.

De Chirico frequently inserted a train in the distance of his townscapes (*La meditazione del pomeriggio* [1912–13], *Les Plaisirs du poète* [1912–13], *La Récompense du devin* [1913]). One of the striking visual shocks in *L'avventura* comes from the placement of the train in the scene in which Claudia first submits to Sandro's lovemaking. They have just left the un-inhabited town Cavell correctly identified as a transcription of De Chirico. They embrace each other in a field through a series of extreme closeups before the camera cuts away to a distanced shot of a train passing from right to left. The shock occurs in the next shot, again of the lovers in middle distance, into which the train shoots surprisingly close and moving from left to right.

The lovemaking recalls the way in which the earlier sex between San-dro and Anna had been photographed. Their heads had been so near to the camera that they evoked De Chirico's placement of a plaster head in the lower foreground of paintings such as *L'Arc des échelles noires* (1914). Even the cluttered studio of the teenage painter of nudes bears a resem-blance to the compositions of easels and paintings in several of the can-vases called *interno metafisico* of 1917 and 1918.

If Antonioni has moved his beneficiaries of the economic miracle into a "metaphysical" landscape carefully constructed from a mélange of Sici-lian islands, towns, villas, hills, and both baroque and modern architec-ture, he understated the De Chirican "air of *pressentiment*" with one ex-ception: at the end of the brief visit to the empty town, the camera tracks forward from a shadowed street toward the sunny piazza and church in the distance as Sandro and Claudia drive away. The mood and chiaroscuro is overtly De Chirican, as in *La Tour rose* (1913) or *La Tour rouge* (1913). The tracking movement in this situation is familiar from mystery and hor-ror films, suggestive of the point of view of the missing Anna.

A similar tracking shot in *La notte* (1961) has a very different tone.

The camera moves forward and upward after the protagonists, Giovanni and Lidia Pontano, drive away from the hospital where Tommasso, their friend, lies dying of cancer. Perhaps the generic signals of *L'avventura*, a "giallo a rovescio" (mystery inside out) in the filmmaker's words, reinforce the De Chirican mood of the shot and the whole film. Perhaps the cinematography of Aldo Scavarda, who had shot *Cronaca di un amore* and *La signora senza camelie* as well, with its somewhat more intense use of whites and darks makes a psychological difference. (Gianni Di Venanzo shot all the other black-and-white films of Antonioni. They have the same compositional patterns, but aside from a few notable sequences—Lidia's stroll in Milan, the conclusion of *L'eclisse*—the "metaphysical" mood is less pronounced.)

The analogy to De Chirico has been one of the many commonplaces of Antonioni criticism since the release of *L'avventura*. Another was the similarity of his films of the sixties to Alberto Moravia's novel *La noia* (*The Empty Canvas*, but literally translated *Boredom*). *La noia* is the first-person narrative of a wealthy painter, in the midst of a crisis he attributes to "boredom." He reacts to it with an erotic obsession with Cecilia, the model of a fellow painter, an older man who had died of a heart attack while making love to her. In many ways, *La noia* is a version of Luigi Bartolini's postwar novel, *Ladri di biciclette,* updated in the atmosphere of the economic miracle.

Italo Calvino may have been the first to make the comparison in his defense of *L'avventura*:

> As a description of society *L'avventura* is just perfect. Its Southern Italian setting, for instance—the inferno of underdevelopment contrasted with an affluent inferno—is the most truthful and the most impressive that ever appeared on the screen, without the least indulgence to populism or local color.[31]

His one objection is that the script is "uneven," which brings him to a parenthetical remark about Moravia's novel: "*La noia* is the exact opposite: as perfectly constructed as a clock, it is too dogmatic in defining its own meaning, which by the way is often wrong."

In contrast, Pier Paolo Pasolini praised *La noia* at the expense of *La notte*: "Both works express the anguish of the modern bourgeoisie: but through two quite diverse poetic methodologies . . . which precisely reveal a genuine difference of ideological formation." According to the axis of difference that Pasolini perceived, Antonioni's vision is ahistorical, his characters are unaware of their bourgeois anguish, and his bourgeois audience hypocritically identify with his world while refusing to see their own anguish as a form of Dino's (*La noia*'s protagonist) erotic obsessions. However, as Pasolini sees it,

> [Moravia] knows that psychology is not only psychology: but also sociology. He knows that the "complex" of which he speaks, even if it is a strictly personal fact, is also a social fact, derived from a mistaken rapport between social classes, from a mistaken rapport, that is to say, between rich and poor, intellectual and worker, between the refined and the uncultured, between the moralist and the ordinary person.[32]

Elio Bartolini (to be distinguished from Luigi), a novelist and sometime collaborator with Antonioni who worked on the script of *L'avventura,* made an interesting effort in a symposium in Rome in 1961 to refocus the debate on Antonioni from the critical formulae he identified as "Antonioni narrator and moral historian of the bourgeoisie" and "Antonioni or the flight from the banal" by pointing to the influence and affinity of the director to Kierkegaard, and particularly *Either/Or*.[33]

Bartolini, who contributed to the script of *Il grido,* suggested that its hero Aldo was the sole Antonioni protagonist to face up to a genuine ethical dilemma before collapsing in the "dilettantish" evasion of suicide. Suicide, in fact, is an obsessive theme in the early films of Antonioni, here ambiguously suggested in the disappearance of Anna. For the most part, the Antonioni hero cannot escape from what Kierkegaard called the "esthetic" mode of the erotic life to the "ethical."

Curiously Kierkegaard seems to have been an unacknowledged source for Moravia in writing *La noia* as well. In the hilarious "Prologue" of the novel, Dino describes his aborted project of a history of boredom:

> My universal history according to boredom was based on a very simple idea: the mainspring of it was neither progress, nor biological evolution, nor economic development, nor any of the other ideas usually brought forward by historians of various schools; it was simply boredom. Burning with enthusiasm at this magnificent discovery I went right to the root of the matter. In the beginning was boredom, commonly called chaos. God, bored with chaos,

created the earth, the sky, the waters, the animals, the plants, Adam and Eve; and the latter, bored in their turn with paradise, ate the forbidden fruit. God became bored with them and drove them out of Eden; Cain, bored with Abel, killed him; Noah, bored to tears, invented wine; God, once again bored with mankind, destroyed the world by means of the Flood; but this in turn bored Him to such an extent that He brought back the fine weather again. And so on.[34]

In *Either/Or* we find:

Since boredom advances and boredom is the root of all evil, no wonder then, that the world goes backwards, that evil spreads. This can be traced back to the very beginning of the world. The gods were bored; therefore they created human beings. Adam was bored because he was alone; therefore Eve was created. Since that moment, boredom entered the world and grew in quantity in exact proportion to the growth of the population. Adam was bored alone; then Adam and Eve were bored together; then Adam and Eve and Cain and Abel were bored *en famille*. After that the population of the world increased and the nations were bored *en masse*. To amuse themselves, they hit upon the notion of building a tower so high that it would reach the sky. This notion is just as boring as the tower was high and is a terrible demonstration of how boredom had gained the upper hand.[35]

Like Kierkegaard's *Symparanekromenoi*, the figures of *L'avventura* are the living dead who seek to escape from boredom by the pursuit of pleasure. Their yachting voyage to Cytheria follows the Danish philosopher's ironic advice to treat human relationships as a farmer would rotate his crops and to derive pleasure from accidental, rather than planned, occurrences. But Anna's disappearance is the grim price this proto-surrealist doctrine exacts in Antonioni's narrative.

As I have already noted, Antonioni is particularly sensitive to the compositional power of vertical elements—the corners of buildings, door jambs, and so on—to isolate characters in the larger, horizontally extended form of the widescreen image. He repeatedly uses these verticals to bisect, or trisect the screen, often doing both by moving the camera in a long take. The final image of the film vividly illustrates this principle. We see Claudia and Sandro from behind in a long shot. He is sitting on a park bench; she stands to his left, caressing his head. To the right a third of the mountainous vista before them is blocked by the masonry wall of a building, from the edge of which the delicate tracery of a metal balcony on an upper story slightly protrudes into the white sky at dawn. The double black horizontal lines of a guardrail run across the frame at the level of Sandro's shoulders, his head is in line with a dark curve of mountains, while Claudia's silhouette reaches over that line into the white sky. To her left, the snow-covered cone of Etna gradually rises to the line of her head.

Here as elsewhere in *L'avventura* the elegant composition contributes to the distancing effect which encourages us to ponder and analyze the affective gesture rather than empathize with it. Claudia's stroking of Sandro's head does not indicate the rebirth of love so much as the acknowledgment of his infantilism. She can console him for the reckless betrayal of their incipient romance because she knows that there is no one to console her for her sense of having betrayed her friendship with Anna. In *Il Verri* Franco Valobra wrote at the time of the film's release:

> The 'pity' [pietà] of Antonioni, nevertheless, is not sentimental or irrational; it isn't the saccharine and anachronistic pity of the character of Rocco, for example (or even that to be found in certain De Sica films: the hand of little Bruno that squeezes his father's in *Ladri di biciclette*): in sum it is not a "pity that produces disasters." However, it is the realistic, bitter, but courageous awareness of a situation and of the impossibility of evading it.[36]

Valobra's intertextual allusion is apt. Antonioni, in fact, had contrasted his film to De Sica's in "La malattia dei sentimenti," a colloquium published in *Bianco e nero*.[37] In *L'avventura* Antonioni discovered a narrative form and perfected his visual style to the point where a culminating affective gesture—of the sort both Fellini and Visconti studiously avoided in ending their 1960 films—labors to divest itself of the sentimentality of its prototype in De Sica. Furthermore, if we can hear in the carefully chosen word "pietà" a reference to the pictorial iconography of Mary mourning the dead Christ, he has also located the maternal dimension of Claudia's gesture, albeit ironically, in this fully secular film. But that is the very irony Antonioni clearly inscribed in the film by placing the baroque painting of Roman Charity, displaced from its Christian context iconographically, so conspicuously in the prelude to Sandro's betrayal.

Antonioni's Psychoanalysis of the "Boom"

Antonioni alone of the major filmmakers formed by the war and the Resistance found in the social contradictions of the economic miracle the material for several films. Visconti undertook to film Giuseppe Tomasi di Lampedusa's best-seller, *Il gattopardo* (*The Leopard,* 1963, from the novel of 1958), and thereby focused again on the Risorgimento and on Sicily; Fellini examined his private fantasies and fears in *Otto e mezzo* (*8½,* 1963); they both contributed episodes to the omnibus film *Boccaccio '70* (1962). Antonioni, on the other hand, produced four films in four years with upper-middle-class protagonists—in each of the first three one is an intellectual of some sort—in the milieu of the very rich. Seymour Chatman calls these four films "the great tetralogy" and treats them as a complex unit in his book. More reservedly, Sam Rohdie refers to the first three as "a loose trilogy." Since neither the same characters, families, nor communities appear in even two of the films, I see no point to either term.

What these four films do hold in common is the presence of actress Monica Vitti, as the female protagonist, in fact, of *L'avventura, L'eclisse,* and *Il deserto rosso.* This casting recalls Fellini's use of Giulietta Masina in five of his films of the fifties, and even more pointedly, in consideration of the roles Vitti played and their milieus, Rossellini's use of Ingrid Bergman in five of the feature films he made from *Stromboli, terra di Dio* (1950) to *La paura* (*Fear,* 1954).

Rohdie sensitively described the formal relationship between Rossellini and Antonioni without mentioning casting; after comparing the suicides in *Germania anno zero* and *Il grido,* he wrote:

> In so far as Antonioni relates to Italian neo-realism and perhaps most
> of all to Rossellini, it is partly here in this reticent narration and documentation of objects, events, figures on the side of the camera without immediately
> functioning as signs and objects of a pre-known, pre-organized narrative.
> But there is another element in common, as well with, if not neo-realism,
> certainly Rossellini: the documentation of the "writing," the presence of
> the camera seeking to find, and waiting to find, its subject. In the case of
> Rossellini the subject is more certain and the apprehension of it relatively
> unproblematic; in Antonioni, the uncertainty and slippage of the subject becomes the drama of the narrative.[1]

To this I would add that Antonioni refined and nuanced the Bergman heroines. In Rossellini's films she plays a foreigner through whose eyes he is able to see afresh the Italian landscape, manners, and natural piety. Antonioni's Vitti is always the Italian beauty through whose intelligence, alienation, and once, neurosis "objects, events, and figures" manifest their strange resistance to meaning or their numinous superabundance of it. (In *La notte* that power extends to Lidia, played by Jeanne Moreau, when she is alone.)

Antonioni's use of Sicily and the Eolian Islands in *L'avventura* owes something to the landscapes of *Stromboli, terra di Dio* and *Viaggio in Italia,* although he systematically divests them of Rossellini's Catholic mysticism. There are also similarities in the narrative situations of *Europa 51* and *Il deserto rosso.* It is difficult to determine if the filmmaker was aware of such homologies. However, there can be little doubt about the similarities between *La notte* and *La dolce vita;* in fact, the former in its finished form can be seen as Antonioni's response to Fellini's film.

La notte

Before making *L'avventura* Antonioni had written a script, *Baldoria (The Party),* about eight couples who, after flirting through a dinner party, decide to drive to a large seaside villa to pursue their pleasures. But the beauty of a sudden snowstorm diverts them once they arrive, and in enjoying it, the partners remain together. Although he had the financing to make this film after *L'avventura* he decided, according to his collaborator, Tonino Guerra, to abandon it because of similarities to Fellini's film, especially to the penultimate scene. Antonioni had also written a script about a woman who comes to believe that her marriage is disintegrating because of her lack of beauty. This had been put aside when Giulietta Masina, Fellini's wife, was not available to play the part.

Ultimately he incorporated elements of both scripts into a double portrait of a husband and wife in the milieu of Milanese industrialists. He hired Enno Flaiano, a satirist and chronicler of Roman urbanity who had played a large role in shaping the scenario of *La dolce vita*, to work with him and Guerra. The resulting script takes place within a twenty-four-hour span.

The successful novelist, Giovanni Pontano (played by Fellini's star, Mastroianni) and his wife, Lidia (Jeanne Moreau), stop off on the way to a party for his latest book to visit a friend, Tommaso, an intellectual dying of cancer, in his hospital room on the morning of his last day. The problems of their marriage become immediately apparent when Giovanni, who lingered with Tommaso longer than Lidia, allows himself to be embraced by a psychotic nymphomaniac who easily lures him into her room. Before they can make love attendants rush in and violently pull the woman away from him. In the car, Lidia does not want to hear his confession. But when he insists, she returns the verbal equivalent of Claudia's final caress: she says, "I understand. You were upset," referring to the news they had just received that Tommaso's cancer was inoperable.

Later she slips away during the book party to stroll in the outskirts of the city. In the evening they visit a nightclub and reluctantly attend a party in a millionaire's villa celebrating the first victory of his daughter's racehorse. The party lasts until dawn and occupies the longest stretch of the film. Pontano listens to the offers of Gherardini, the owner of the villa, to become a writer for his corporation and he flirts unsuccessfully with his daughter, Valentina (Monica Vitti). Meanwhile Lidia learns of Tommaso's death and succumbs to the seduction of a guest at the party, only to back down after he has driven her to his apartment. Like *L'avventura* the film ends at dawn. The Pontanos have left the villa by way of its golf course. After listening to Lidia's reading of an old letter that he does not recognize as his own, Giovanni makes love to her, despite her resistance, in a sandtrap.

Although this synopsis betrays no trace of the earlier scenarios out of which *La notte* developed, there are subtle verbal and gestural hints scattered through the film itself that point to an occluded counternarrative that might be crudely retold as follows: The imminence of Tommaso's death has forced Lidia to consider her past and her marriage. For instance, in the golf-course scenes at the end of the film she tells Giovanni, perhaps for the first time, that Tommaso had been in love with her but never spoke of himself. She admits he often might have made love to her before she married Giovanni; she was so bored with everything that she would not have resisted, even though she did not love him. More indirectly, we learn that Lidia was a rich girl, born to the ambience of the Gherardinis, and that she was considered ugly when she was young. (A long forgotten acquaintance, whom she met at the party, openly expresses surprise at how attractive she has become.) She chose the handsome and narcissistic Giovanni Pontano, then a poor and talented young writer, over the intellectual Tommaso.

While Lidia is absorbed by the past, Giovanni is focused on his grim future. It is the publication day for his latest novel, but he feels he has lost his vocation. Intensely narcissistic, he is obviously used to being attractive to women and admired by men. He is particularly eager to hear Tommaso's praise of his new book, and he admits to Lidia that he mistook the nymphomaniac's psychosis for passion inspired by him. At the book party, his publisher asks him to sign a copy for Salvatore Quasimodo. The presence of the 1959 Nobel laureate underscores the difference between Pontano's successes and the sustained achievement of a major author's lifelong poetic project. He knows that Gherardini will make him an offer to put his talent and reputation at the service of his corporation. His narcissism drives him to hear the offer at least. Gherardini, himself a "self-made" millionaire, shrewdly points out that employment as director of cultural activities in his corporation would allow Pontano to be "independent" of his wife's wealth. This suggestion both deflates Pontano's egoism by revealing how he is considered among the wealthy and offers an economic anesthetic to the dissolution of his marriage. By now he has realized that Valentina is Gherardini's daughter. So there is a hint of revenge on the father when he intensifies his seduction, confessing to her that he is in an artistic crisis and that she is the one who can revitalize him. When she rejects his advances, saying she does not sleep with married men, he begins to display contempt for Gherardini's guests.

In the final minutes of the film Lidia articulates what Valombra read into Claudia's caress: "I don't want to exist any longer because I cannot love you. This is the thought that came to me while we were in the night-club and I annoyed you." When Giovanni insists that this is a "sign" that she still wants him, she says, "No, it's only pity." Antonioni himself observed: "In *L'avventura* [the characters] do not communicate beyond this *trait d'union* of pity. In *La notte* the characters speak to each other, communicate, are conscious of what is happening to them. But the result doesn't change." [2]

Antonioni takes *La notte* a step beyond the expression of pity that had terminated his earlier film. Lidia reads him a text, describing an earlier dawn in which the writer ("I") eventually names the sleeping addressee as "Lidia." Although Antonioni told Charles Samuels that "[i]t's a modestly written letter, showing how correct he was to think his talent unsatisfactory . . . not even a nice [letter]," the letter clearly exemplifies a writer's effort to extend a momentary feeling into a timeless epiphany. For Lidia it is a vestige of the passion for which she is nostalgic; for Giovanni, when she tells him that he wrote it, it is another reminder of his alienation from his past feelings and from his own writing. In the panic of his wounded narcissism he insists on making love to her, in cumulative revenge for having been confronted that day with mortality, genuine literary achievement, loneliness, economic humiliation, failed seduction, and finally the power of time to mock his timeless epiphany.

Organizing his narration around the epicenters of two protagonists who are seldom in precisely the same place, Antonioni refined his editing strategies. This is particularly evident early in the film when they are each alone. The first shots of Lidia after she leaves Tommaso's room exemplify the dynamics of such montage: a long shot of the exterior corner of the hospital in which she is dwarfed, almost unnoticeable, beside their automobile, precedes a high-angle view of her sobbing, her back flat against the hospital wall, which bisects the frame. Her position in the right half of the shot matches the corresponding shot, immediately following it, of Giovanni entering the corridor outside Tommaso's room—we do not see his leavetaking—and pausing to lean against the door in the left half of the frame. He too is overwhelmed by the realization that he has seen his friend for the last time. When he turns to walk to the elevator the camera follows him until he encounters the nymphomaniac. The first index of the decay of their marriage is that he and his wife cannot share or even discuss their parallel reactions to the loss of their friend. [3]

La notte can be broadly divided into two main parts with a prologue in the hospital and an epilogue on the golf course. Lidia's departure from Tommaso's room initiates what I am calling the first part; throughout it the anatomy of the marriage gradually reveals itself behind a surface of accommodation without signs of overt hostility. That part terminates in Lidia's undisclosed "thought" in the nightclub. The second part of the film takes place at the Gherardinis' party. Insofar as the first part traces through images and gestures an emergent thought, or two different thoughts if we take Giovanni's confession of his artistic sterility as more than a seductive ploy, the nuances of montage and composition play a greater role in the first part of the film than in the second.

As they maneuver through a traffic jam between the hospital and the publishing house, dialogue plays the central role, so that Antonioni is content to alternate four camera positions—framing the two speakers from either side of the car, through the windshield, and from the back seat. This transitional episode presents Giovanni's confession of his experience with the nymphomaniac and, above all, Lidia's ironic observation: "An experience like that could make a good story, entitled *The Living and the Dead.*" Even though she is accusing her husband of reducing his moral and psychic life to alienated material for his career, the title is nevertheless her own invention; with it she describes her vision of their life at that moment, ambiguously leaving open the identification of the two poles. Similarly, the title of Giovanni's new book, *La stagione* (*The Season*), hints at the frailty of temporal continuity and thereby at his anxiety over his continued productivity. Later, Valentina will be introduced as the reader of Broch's *Sleepwalkers,* which title can be taken as a label for the Gherardinis' circle.

The language of *La notte* is an elaborate web of titles, hints, approximations, and cautious confessions, framed by Tommaso's blunt acknowledgment of his failures and the poeticized delusion of an atemporal epiphany in Giovanni's letter. When Tommaso tells them that he has "the impression of staying at the edge of an enterprise" and of lacking the intelligence to go deeper, Giovanni reveals more than he intends in his smiling consolation: "If you talk that way, the only thing for me to do is give up writing and find a good job"; for he is precisely on the verge of such a decision.

In marked contrast to the superabundance of idle chatter at the book party and the Gherardinis' soirée, the extraordinary passage of eighty-five shots, representing the parallel observations of Lidia after she leaves the book party and of Giovanni when he returns alone to their apartment, is nearly wordless. The passage naturally subdivides into five parts: thirteen shots of Lidia wandering through the nearly deserted city center, eleven shots of Giovanni returning to the apartment and taking a nap, thirty-seven of Lidia when she takes a taxi from the center to explore a neighborhood at the periphery, another fourteen shots from the moment Giovanni awakens until Lidia telephones him, and ten more, including four when he meets her.

The images of Lidia in central Milan, both before and after the scenes of Giovanni in the apartment, evoke the surrealist *flâneur*. The familiar cityscape becomes strange: amid the glass boxes of high-rise offices and within the studied geometry of the sleek corner building and the arc of a fountain basin, Lidia suddenly pays attention to a parking attendant eating a sandwich as he leans against a wall, a couple of workers convulsed with laughter as they turn a corner, a sole man at a desk barely visible through the glass wall of an office, and in the most De Chirican of images in the film, an old woman avidly eating a cup of ice cream as she stands in a row of concrete posts demarcating a pedestrian walkway. The tall concrete and glass structures seem to intensify the sounds of helicopters and jets that alternate with bells and sirens in the acoustic environment. Lidia instinctually comes upon a pocket of poverty in Italy's richest city when she walks into a yard opened up by the incomplete demolition of a building. A child is crying and wash hangs on a line, suggesting the presence of squatters. Three successive images in the yard shift the tone of the sequence from that of accidental encounters to symbolical representations, as if in a dream. Lidia's failed attempt to console the child, followed by her noticing a broken clock, discarded amid debris, and finally an exquisite closeup of her ringed hand flecking a layer of rust from a wall taken together suggest that her apparent childlessness, her age, and the disintegration of her marriage are on her mind.

We cannot realize in the shot that follows that the center of attention has shifted to Giovanni until he emerges from his car. His environment is more linguistically oriented than that of Lidia's wanderings, but equally vain: he greets a neighbor, falsely claiming he cannot get out of the city for the weekend because he has too much work; he picks up mail that he does not read; in the apartment he turns off a recorded English lesson to which no one is listening. The bilingual catalogue of objects and infinitives neatly parodies the paratactic abstraction of the sequence of which it is a part:

"the journals," "the door," "the window," "to speak," "to open," "to shut." His exchange with the maid could not be more rudimentary: after determining that Lidia did not come home or call, he lets her go. In his office neither the page in his typewriter nor the piles of journals and clippings hold his attention. The most fascinating of the montage alternations of protagonists occur when he lies down for a nap. He moves the blind to look upward into the space beyond his window. The countershot is false. A blank concrete wall seems at first the object of his gaze until the tiny figure of Lidia appears in a small open space in the lower left corner, forcing us to realize that we are actually looking down from a great height at a skyscraper and a segment of the pavement over which it extends.

This deceptive matching cut dramatizes the incongruence between Giovanni's view of Lidia, whose absence from the home makes him uncomfortably aware of the necessary loneliness of his métier, and her view of herself dwarfed in the most oppressive of the film's many images of the alienating city. Her flight to the periphery is inscribed within the unpunctuated series of shots without preparation or motivation; a taxi stops and she gets out, leaving the viewer to infer gradually where she has gone and why. Yet a subtle verbal framing device binds an important part of the segment. She tells the cabdriver to wait ("Aspetti qui") while she looks around. Immediately a gang of young men attract her attention as they enter a lot where two will fight. Theirs is the Milan of *Rocco e i suoi fratelli* without the melodrama. Her curiosity turns to horror when one boy falls and his antagonist, sitting on his chest, brutally punches his face until she yells "stop" ("Basta"). At this point the pivot of elementary verbal commands shifts. The fighter, taking her interest as a sign of attraction, approaches her and urges her to wait ("Aspetta") but she runs off to the cabdriver just as he completes the verbal round, saying "enough" ("Basta") to the man pumping gas into his taxi.

This echo contrasts the purely functional language of the taxi driver, who is merely doing his job, with the tension between expectation and satisfaction at work in Lidia's voyeurism. Chatman justifiably criticizes the crude interpretation that Lidia "is looking for sex, that she is 'cruising,' " in the scenes at the periphery of the city.[4] However, the sexual charge of her encounter with the bare-chested boxer is palpable. Undeniably that is how he understands her intervention and why he attempts to stop her by calling "aspetta." Furthermore, as soon as she telephones Giovanni from a café, asking him to meet her, the woman behind the counter offers her a nearby *pensione* where she can hold her rendezvous. Although Lidia politely declines, the suggestion gives her an amused smile.

Between these two moments Lidia joins a group of onlookers watching boys set off amateur rockets. In fact, no sooner does she escape to the taxi driver than the thrust of the rocket attracts her attention, drawing her into the group of spectators in a dreamlike elision of events. The scene is indeed "beautiful" as she tells Giovanni over the telephone, especially the culminating images in which the cloud of exhaust engulfs the boys firing the final rocket. The rockets are linked to the fight, especially in the sexually ambivalent perspective of Lidia. Antonioni does not reduce these images to systematic sexual allegories, above all, because he forces the viewer to experience them with an ambivalence akin to his protagonist's, and in a parallel mood of frustrated anticipation.

The filmmaker added two speeches to the script in shooting the meeting of Lidia and Giovanni in this zone. In both the script and the film, Lidia opens their meeting with a lie, saying she came there "by chance." The improvisations follow.

> Giovanni: "How strange! Nothing has changed here."
> Lidia: "It will change. It will change very soon."

Soon after, looking at rusted rails, Giovanni observes: "When we used to come here this track worked." The added dialogue can be taken as a reference to sociological transformation of the neighborhood under the pressure of the economic miracle; for Lidia has seen both the working-class fighters and the middle-class rocketeers, no longer on the scene in the twilight moment of Giovanni's appearance. More poignantly, these exchanges point chiastically toward the final scene on the golf course, in which Lidia's recognition of change and loss confronts Giovanni's erroneous dilation of an unchanging moment.

Although it would be an error to read Lidia's visit to this former site of assignation as a sexual quest, it would be just as wrong to deny the erotic nostalgia encoded in the primal scenery of the fight and rockets. The ambiguous erotic nostalgia and ambivalent voyeurism of these scenes subtly prepare us for the alienation and frustration implicit in the two scenes that follow: Lidia bathing before her disinterested husband, and his analytical absorption in the striptease in the nightclub. Here, as often, when we read an Antonioni film from the early sixties backward, the explicitness of later scenes illuminates the abstractions and ambiguities of the earlier ones. In *L'eclisse* this will become a dominant principle of composition.

Near the end of *La notte* the triangular relationship between the Pontanos and Valentina calls forth an extraordinary series of triadic compositions in shot-countershot, hinted at in the prologue in the hospital. In fact, an unusual shot-countershot pattern marked the very introduction of Valentina, early in the party sequence: Lidia noticed her reading Broch's novel at the foot of a long staircase. The camera framed them both from behind Lidia. The reverse angle showing Valentina's silent acknowledgment of Lidia's attention included the whole staircase again from behind Valentina. This exchange of shots anticipates a later alternation when Lidia and her unsuccessful seducer, Roberto, return from their drive. Just as they enter the villa they confront Valentina and Giovanni in a potentially embarrassing encounter, which Valentina defuses by inviting Lidia to her room to dry her clothes and hair.

Despite their tentative intimacy, expressed in their corresponding declarations of existential anguish, Lidia and Valentina do not face each other in the shot-countershot exchanges. At first, Valentina naturally stands behind Lidia to dry her hair, but even when she has finished the two women repeatedly reposition themselves to face the camera at different planes of distance from it. Giovanni's intrusion into these manneristic compositions occasions an elaborate choreography, in which he or Lidia alternately approach Valentina while the other assumes a spectator position in the background.

At the climax of this elaborate leavetaking Valentina says, as if articulating the viewer's response, "This evening, you two have worn me out." As soon as they leave, she switches off the light in her room with her foot. With the gesture of her foot the composition in depth suddenly becomes a silhouette of Valentina's full figure posed against the light of the dawn outside her window. Synchronized to her withdrawal from the three-dimensional theater of erotic competition and marking her transformation into a flattened icon of pure cinematic image and sound, the jazz that had been heard throughout the previous scene increases in volume and clarity, recalling the music of the striptease. This gorgeous moment concludes the body of the film and announces the epilogue.

The relationship of *La notte* to *La dolce vita* is complex and elaborate. Flaiano collaborated on both films; Mastroianni plays a writer in each.

Both films depict the decadent aspects of the economic miracle with afflu-ent parties, nightclubs, and hospital scenes. The revelers jumping clothed into the Gherardinis' swimming pool rhymes with Sylvia (Anita Ekberg) wading through a Roman fountain. But two iconographic details indicate that the parallels might not be accidental. Early in the film a helicopter appears outside of Tommaso's hospital room, for no obvious purpose to the narrative, but calling to mind the opening of Fellini's film. Even more striking is the belletristic tape recording Valentina plays for Giovanni's criticism, then erases before he can hear it a second time. It is a prose poem about sounds: a television, a dog barking, an airplane, the silence of a tree. Steiner had played his guests a taped collage of natural sounds the night before he killed himself and his children in *La dolce vita*.

Notably missing in this catalogue of similarities are references to reli-gion. Antonioni is a strictly secular filmmaker. When Charles Samuels asked him if man could "conceive of a new morality," he responded:

> Why go on using that word I loathe! We live in a society that compels us to go on using these concepts, and we no longer know what they mean. In the future—not soon, perhaps by the twenty-fifth century—these concepts will have lost their relevance. I can never understand how we have been able to follow these worn-out tracks, which have been laid down by panic in the face of nature. When man becomes reconciled to nature, when space be-comes his true background, these words and concepts will have lost their meaning, and we will no longer have to use them.[5]

Although *La notte* went into production just a month after Tambroni was forced to relinquish the premiership to Fanfani, the political tremors of the summer of 1960 are almost invisible in the film. Tangential refer-ences to the work of the Jewish intelligentsia of Weimar Germany—in ad-dition to Valentina's reading of Broch, we learn that Tommaso had just published an article on Adorno—hint at vague historical analogies. In fact, in showing the unconsciousness or indifference of his protagonists to the political tensions operating in Milan in 1960 Antonioni revises Fellini's Roman carnival of grotesques, just as he distances himself from Visconti's melodrama of class struggle. Yet, above all, he resists Fellini's flirtation with fantasies of redemption. Thus, when the final shot of *La notte* re-frames the previous image of Giovanni forcing Lidia to make love to him in a sandtrap so that the couple are in the distance to the extreme right of the frame, the camera, as if seeking to refind the symmetry of the final image of *L'avventura,* cranes to the left and rises slightly, finally settling for a long view of the artificially manicured landscape with a mass of trees to the right and low hills on the left; but unlike the previous film it is now depleted of human presence. The alfresco amours are only a grim parody of the revitalization Lidia sought.

L'eclisse

The publicity for Antonioni's films of the early sixties implied a unique intellectual status for his work. The advance advertisements for *L'avventura* which began to appear in the *Corriere della sera* in mid-October 1960 unconventionally quoted from a poem by Apollinaire:

> O my heart, I have known
> The sad and beautiful joy
> Of being betrayed in love
> And love again . . .

Then, 25 January 1961, the day after *La notte*'s premiere, an advertisement two columns wide and three quarters of a page high quoted the endorsement of nine intellectuals, including Salvatore Quasimodo, Carlo Levi, and Enzo Paci.

Paci himself, a professor of philosophy at the University of Milan, Italy's most prominent phenomenologist and editor of *Aut-Aut,* conducted a public seminar on Antonioni's next film, *L'eclisse,* the day after it opened (13 April 1962). Antonioni and Monica Vitti attended the seminar, and it was covered, with texts and a photograph in *L'Europeo.*[6] A public seminar, with press coverage, cannot possibly take place spontaneously the day after a film opens. In one sense this was a publicity stunt, yet the very nature, and the seriousness, of the gesture is an index of the integral place of Antonioni's cinema in Italian intellectual life in the early sixties.

Paci, citing Lukács's *History and Class Consciousness,* emphasized the notion of reification in the film. Beginning with a discussion of the remarkable final scene, in which both protagonists fail to keep a rendezvous and the camera dwells on the site of their proposed meeting, he states:

But the gestures of that human being who was Vittoria are no longer present: only things remain. Again we see the whole neighborhood appear to us in a rigorous sequence in which the posthumous testimony of the missed appointment negates itself even as testimony. Things become ever more thinglike, things made by man but not completely fabricated. Bricks, for example.

. . . .

It seems to me that the film indirectly compels us to become aware of objectification so that we might change, become human, and avoid *disintegrating* into things or objects. It teaches us to *return to the subject*.[7]

A second "dibattito sull'*Eclisse*" was published in the leftist journal *Il Contemporaneo* in June 1962. The editor Carlo Salinari invited Galvano Della Volpe, Luigi Chiarini, and Alberto Carocci to discuss the now controversial film with him. Even though Salinari acknowledged that *L'eclisse* may be the "most advanced" of Antonioni's films, "ideologically . . . because this time he clearly indicates capitalistic society as the society in which the dispersion of personality, the exhaustion of feelings, and the incapacity to communicate occur," he criticized the filmmaker for having "continual recourse to allegory (not to symbols) to express himself; that is to say, he had to superimpose from outside a purely intellectualistic ideological meaning, in place of the ideological clarity that he fails to attain through his poetic language as such."[8]

These two discussions share a good deal of common ground: they grant Antonioni's artistic preeminence, even though Della Volpe insisted that his is a decadent art; they focus centrally upon the final scene of the film, a series of images of a street corner in Rome's EUR neighborhood, calling forth parallel discussions of reification; and for both the inescapability of a Marxist perspective is assumed, although Paci's group utilized a Husserlian vocabulary and frequently cited Sartre's then recent *Critique of Dialectical Reason*.

Chiarini, who had read the transcript of the panel at the University of Milan, complained at Salinari's "dibattito" that the concept of alienation has become "like mayonnaise" which the critics of *L'eclisse* spread over everything. Along with Salinari he called the film a frigid allegory that fails because Antonioni, whose sensibility seemed to him more of a writer than a filmmaker, attempts to do what is contrary to the nature of cinematic "language": or in Carocci's concordant terms, to make "a film totally based on concepts."

For Paci and his students, debating in the presence of the film's maker and its star, the aesthetic success of *L'eclisse* went unchallenged. Paci claimed that the film's dissection of alienation and reification "teaches us to return to subjectivity"; Giairo Daghini found it more sophisticated than Antonioni's previous works because of the emphasis it places on repetition and the power of things in capitalist society; Paolo Gambazzi extended Daghini's argument, contending that the erotic-emotional drama at the core of the film was a key to its political view rather than an intimist psychological study; and Andrea Bonomi stressed a Husserlian view of temporality as key to the film's study of money. This examination of temporality led to a concurrence of voices defining the philosophical depth of *L'eclisse* in comparison to *L'année dernière à Marienbad* (*Last Year at Marienbad*).

The differences between the two sessions illuminate the shifting arena of the discussion of film. The *Il Contemporaneo* forum continued the tradition of the ideological examination of important films which had been part of Italian cinematic culture, especially on the Left, since the late forties. Typically, its participants resisted the acknowledgment of a decisive change in the temper of the best Italian films in the early sixties. At the same time, Paci's seminar represented an opening toward the consideration of cinema in academic, philosophical circles and, conversely, a new willingness to explore the possibilities of understanding films with the help of a philosophical framework and its technical vocabulary. I shall return to the subject of these debates at the end of this chapter.

The phenomenological approach to art exemplified by Paci's seminar was not an isolated occurrence; the trimestral journal *Il Verri* had privileged such a tack, as its editors promoted a new avant-gardism in Italian literature, publishing the authors who would eventually form Gruppo 63, and opposing both narrative neorealism and the hermetic poets. At the theoretical core of the journal there was a commitment to exploring the parameters of literary language, informed by developments in linguistics, anthropology, and psychoanalysis.

Conversely, the wariness expressed by the panelists assembled by the orthodox PCI review, *Il Contemporaneo*, reflects a growing crisis in aesthetic discussions on the Left. New journals had emerged to accommodate and spur on important shifts in the cultural terrain. From Bologna, Pasolini, Fortini, and other "heretics" of the Left published *Officina* between 1955 and 1959. The year it folded Vittorini and Italo Calvino started up

Il Menabò in Turin. These two journals challenged the aesthetic ossification of the PCI orthodoxy as forcefully but with more diversity than *Il Politecnico* had in the late forties.

While Antonioni was shooting *L'eclisse, Il Verri* devoted a special issue to "La Condizione Atomica" (including a text by Paci), a motif latent in the film. One could say that by 1962 Antonioni's work had more affinities with this emerging force in Italian culture than that of any other filmmaker, certainly of those of his generation, even though the economic and artistic compromises necessitated by feature film production kept his work outside of the avant-garde orbit championed by *Il Verri*. The atomic theme is touched upon directly in the final montage: a man steps off a bus at the corner of the anticipated rendezvous reading a newspaper. For a split second, it seems he might be Piero, *L'eclisse*'s male protagonist. The filmmaker shows us both the headline of an issue of *L'Espresso,* the organ of the Radical party, and an internal page. We can easily read "Peace is in a weak position," and "The Atomic Competition." The newspaper sets up a reading of the final image, of a glowing streetlight, as an allusion to an atomic explosion.

The film was shot during Fanfani's third government, one of the last purely DC regimes before the opening to the Left in December 1963. By this time the flirtation with neofascism and the fears of a military coup had passed. A month after the PSI failed to mount a no-confidence vote in the DC government, Fanfani and his foreign minister, Segni, went to Moscow on a diplomatic mission which took place without drama. However, shortly after they returned, the newspapers featured Khrushchev's announcement of an H-Bomb "of unheard-of power" (10 August), immediately followed by his threats to attack Italy because of the placement of NATO warheads in the South (11 August). With black humor he spoke of his best wishes for the Italian people and of his countrymen's love of their oranges, but he warned that, if attacked, the Soviet Union would have to destroy missiles wherever they are to be found, even among the oranges. The First Conference of Non-Aligned Nations, meeting in Belgrade early in September, kept the topic of atomic brinkmanship in the newspapers. The issue of *L'Espresso* that Antonioni filmed covered the Belgrade Conference. American readers may get a sense of the political tension of the moment by recalling that that was the period of the Berlin confrontation of Kennedy and Khrushchev and of the Cuban missile crisis.

L'eclisse depicts the brief affair of Vittoria, a translator, and Piero, a stock market jobber, from the morning that Vittoria breaks up with her lover, Riccardo, a leftist intellectual and editor, until the evening a few days later when they both fail to keep a rendezvous. The eclipse of the title might describe this curious and very brief coming together of two human bodies as well as it describes the potential eclipse of human life through atomic war. As this story is told against the backdrop of a temporary decline in the Rome stock market, the title can also be construed with good reason to describe the economics of the period of the brief affair. In fact, the couple meet by accident when Vittoria seeks, vainly, the consolation of her mother, who plays the market daily. Thus their chance meeting takes place in capitalism's emblematic theater of chance, at a moment when death, too, is at issue; for a minute of silence declared for a dead broker allows them to whisper together.

These metaphors of eclipses, the erotic and the economic, are counterbalanced by geological and apocalyptical intimations that human life itself might be a minute phase of cosmic history; the former was substantially eliminated from the film when the producers, the Hakim Brothers, demanded it be shortened: Antonioni cut out an episode in the Verona museum of natural history in which Vittoria and a woman friend are corrected by a guard about the age of a fossil and forced to realize the relative brevity of the human presence on the planet; only Vittoria's use of a fossil as a decorative wall hanging elliptically suggests the geological chronology in the released film.[9]

The film takes place in Rome with a brief excursion to Verona. By showing Vittoria, Riccardo, and perhaps even Piero as apartment dwellers in the EUR and by shooting much of the film on location in that same display zone of contemporary architecture and city planning, Antonioni situated his story in an arena of cultural politics. The Esposizione Universale of 1942 became an autonomous public corporation, Ente Autonomo Esposizione Universale di Roma (EUR). Initially a grandiose project initiated by Mussolini for a world's fair in 1942, celebrating the twentieth year of Fascism, its construction was suspended during the war. With the consolidation of the DC rule in the 1950s it was reactivated, serving the economic and ideological interests of the conservatives and neo-Fascists who urged civic expansion toward the Mediterranean with luxury and middle-class housing, against the Left's pressure for eastward expansion with housing for the increasing poor population emigrating from southern Italy. By locating an arena and sporting facilities in the EUR for the Seventeenth

Olympics (August 1960), again with neo-Fascist support and leftist opposition, the district became a showpiece for the Italian economic miracle. It attracted residents from the international community, middle-class intellectuals, and affluent Italians without access to the grand apartments in the center of the city traditionally passed down to the heads of well-established Roman families.

The conflict between the Right and the Left was particularly intense in Rome at the end of the fifties and in the early sixties. In May 1959, Mayor Cioccetti (DC) caused a furor by canceling the annual June 4th Liberation Day celebration. A motion from the Left to remove him from office was defeated by a coalition of the DC and parties of the extreme Right. On the city council during those years the MSI was surprisingly strong, holding ten (1956) and twelve (1960) seats. The DC controlled twenty-seven, then twenty-eight; the PCI twenty/nineteen; PSI nine/eleven; PSDI, three; while the Republicans and Monarchists held first eleven, then four between them. In July 1961 the city council was replaced by an extraparty prefect, Francesco Diana, because the Church opposed a coalition between the DC and the parties of the Left, while alliances with the neo-Fascists had been banned. In this respect Rome resisted the pattern of Center-Left urban governments emerging in the northern cities. Even though there are no allusions to party politics or to the administrative crisis of the summer of 1961 in *L'eclisse,* Antonioni's very choice of Rome—virtually for the first time in his career as a maker of feature films[10]—at that volatile moment refracts our understanding of the politics of the film as clearly as his situating *La notte* in affluent Milan had done the previous year.

Setting the film in Rome enriches the scenes at the Stock Exchange. In the first place, the Roman Borsa is a remarkable building, unlike any other in Italy. In the elegant Piazza di Pietra, it is built from the remains of the Hadrianeum (sometimes identified as a temple to Neptune) built by the Emperor Hadrian's son in 152 to honor his deified father. Pope Innocent XII had it transformed into a customhouse at the end of the seventeenth century; two centuries later it was remodeled as the Stock Exchange.

Furthermore, the Roman Borsa has little of the economic prestige and power of the Milan exchange which dominates Italian commerce. This suits Antonioni's emphasis on the role of players with small capital in the minor panic of collapsing prices. As he depicts it, the Rome stock market becomes the focus of chance operations and addictive anxieties which reflect the anxieties of national and international politics. Vittoria's mother, who compulsively speculates, is precisely such a small investor. Her daughter knows she can find her every day at the Borsa. More liberally and capriciously than in America, Italian brokerage firms allowed their clients 100 percent margins on purchases for a week; and then they collect only 30 percent. Buying and selling within a week was quite popular because it opened the possibility of making a profit that would not necessarily be reported to the taxation authorities. After seven days the brokerages are required to declare all their transactions on margin. Therefore, investors who want to hold on to stocks often pay cash.

Antonioni's passion for composing images in rapport with architectural forms spurred him to exploit the implications of a classical, sacred precinct transformed into a massive, boisterous arena of fast profits and panicky losses. This is never more dramatic than in the moment when the principals first make contact. A broker has died: the announcement is followed by a minute of silence, literally represented by a minute of film time which the filmmaker divided into fourteen shots. Seconds before, Piero had introduced himself to Vittoria on the floor of the Borsa, where she had come in search of her mother. The funereal minute freezes Vittoria and her mother on one side of a large column, while Piero and two members of his brokerage stand at the other. When he leans around to whisper to her, the broad column fills the left half of the widescreen image; in countershot it occupies the right half; when the short exchange ends and they step back to their memorial stances, a new shot fixes the column in the center of the screen with the two figures isolated in the left and right quarters of the screen rectangle. A few seconds later, the frenetic cacophony of trading recommences the very instant the buzzer sounds the minute's end.

Here the mass of the building and the energy of the institution dwarf the individuals as they make the first steps toward their erotic liaison. The physical barriers underline the temperamental differences of Vittoria and Piero of which there are hints in their fragmentary conversation. She asks if he knew (*conoscere*) the dead broker; "Sure," he responds, "but here seconds are worth milliards." The rest of the film will turn around Vittoria's problems with acquaintance (*conoscere*), knowledge (*sapere*), and memory (*ricordarsi, nostalgia*) in contrast to Piero's translation of time and objects into money.

Antonioni focuses on the world of short-term investors, like Vittoria's mother, anxious to cash in on the bull market of the economic miracle. When prices suddenly drop, she blames political manipulators, obliquely alluding to the widespread belief that the plunge just before the 1960 municipal elections was engineered by the Socialists' financial news agency.[11] Many of the clients of the brokerage for which Piero works seem to be such minor investors. By way of contrast, he points out a genuine capitalist to Vittoria after he lost fifty million lire (about eighty thousand dollars at the time). She follows him into a pharmacy. Susceptible to the mythology of dramatic speculation, she seems to think he may be planning suicide. But he merely purchases and takes a tranquilizer as he doodles a flower on a paper napkin.

The napkin is one of several objects she picks up. From the very closeup that introduces her in the opening scene, she caresses objects. However, under her touch a vase, a fossil, an elephant-foot end table, a piece of wood, the column of the Borsa, or this napkin loses meaning. The night of her breakup with Riccardo she tells a friend: "There are days when holding a piece of cloth, a needle, a book, a man, all are the same thing." Ironically, although she is a professional translator, she lacks an idiom in which to refer to the things that attract her touch and gaze. Piero's brutal alacrity in appraising things and even people, as when he calls one of his lovers "the beast," simply highlights Vittoria's painful suspension of meaning. She is happiest as a mimic, either dancing in black body paint as an African (oblivious to her racism) or imitating silly lovers, including herself and Piero. Although she is alienated by the nature of things, she turns her alienation from people, even herself, into an occasion for play.

A tension between mimesis and the raw presence of things extends to the aesthetics and economics of Antonioni's filmmaking. The casting of the costars, Delon and Vitti, reflects the French and Italian investments in the film, as Moreau and Mastroianni had in *La notte*. Well-known, attractive actors and actresses dominate cinematic mimesis in the feature film industry. Therefore, at the end of *L'eclisse* when Vittoria stands up Piero, and Piero stands up Vittoria, it is actually we, the audience, who are stood up: for five and a half minutes, fifty-eight shots, Antonioni concentrates on the now familiar corner in the EUR where the principals have been meeting each other. It is a stretch of cinema without stars, but not without people. Perhaps five times the montage introduces a figure who, for the fraction of a second it takes to read the image, might be Piero, Vittoria, or even her mother. As we wait for the rendezvous, eventually realizing that it will not occur, we experience a site divested both of movie stars and of narrative; it is the everyday world mercilessly reflected back at us, alienated. Films often begin with situational montages of this sort, although they are never so long; we accept them as overtures to the narration to come. Yet it was a radical departure to end a film this way. Nevertheless, it is consistent with the thematic development of the strangeness of things and the reification of people, and it is the vehicle through which Antonioni finally situates his narrative within the framework of a possible global disaster.

L'eclisse is very much a film about architecture and the growth of Rome. The historical mutation of the Borsa has been discussed. Often in the film we see the traces of a building boom. An arrangement of cinder blocks and the straw protective matting of a building under construction in the EUR are backdrops to the early meetings of the lovers and ominous witnesses to their failure to show up at the end. When we last see Vittoria, pensively descending the stairs from Piero's brokerage office, we see that the stairwell is under restoration. These and all of the images of the EUR evidence the economic miracle.

Even the personal histories of Vittoria and Piero have their architectural dimensions: they take each other to the apartments in which they grew up. It is in the middle-class apartment of Vittoria's mother that we see photographs of Vittoria's dead father, in military uniform, and of the impoverished southern home where her mother once lived. When Vittoria stretches out on the bed now much too small for her tall stature, Piero attempts to kiss her for the first time. As she resists, her mother comes home, interrupting that phase of the liaison.

They make love for the first time in the affluent apartment of Piero's parents, on the parental bed, under the symbolical gaze of their photographic portraits. Oddly, Piero's crude relationship to things seems to encourage Vittoria to have sex with him. Her curious and tactile address to mute objects, emphasized from the very first time the filmmaker shows her playing with a frame and a vase in Riccardo's apartment, constitutes displaced foreplay. When she asks of an old painting "what is this?" Piero can only answer that they have owned it for a long time. The turning point in this critical phase of their encounter would be Vittoria's distracted discovery of a sexist ballpoint pen as she looks through Piero's room with its adolescent decorations in her solitary tour of the apartment. Held one way the pen depicts a woman in a bathing suit; upside down, she appears naked. Vittoria accepts Piero's advances only after discovering this icon of his emotional immaturity. In the eclipse of her more complex relationship with Riccardo, she submits to Piero's sexual insistence without quite knowing why. The sequence of the pen provides the clue that she makes love to him precisely because he is so immature (and attractive); thus, she will not have to repeat again the emotional turmoil of her breakup with Riccardo.

The opening of the film, with its emphasis on interiors, establishes a tension and an eccentricity of form that only the extraordinary conclusion surpasses. In fact, a set of links and marked contrasts suggest a circular structure. The beginning and end of *Il grido* was obviously circular: we first see the mechanic, Aldo, atop the factory tower from which he can see his fiancée, Irma; in the final scene he jumps from that tower, again watched by Irma. The circularity of *L'eclisse* is more subtle. The film opens with a close shot of a table lamp, some books, a coffee cup, and what turns out to be Riccardo's elbow, as revealed by a slight panning movement. The image of the lamp points to the ultimate shot of the illumination of the street light, while the long, slow-paced opening episode (twelve minutes long, comprising fifty shots) sets up the contrast of the tense interior, occupied only by the couple Vittoria-Riccardo, with the even tenser final cityscape lacking only the couple Vittoria-Piero. Both represent the terminations of affairs.

Perhaps it would be more accurate to speak of the opening as a matrix from which the themes and image motifs of the film develop. The very first shot, panning to reveal an exhausted Riccardo, ends by framing him between two lamps, with a small fan buzzing beside him. It is not long before we discover it is late summer and very hot in Rome. The fan motif recurs in the Stock Exchange: during the minute of silence, only the overhead fans move. In another scene at the Exchange, Piero gives his boss a portable, battery-operated fan.

For ten shots (two minutes) Antonioni retards the cohesion of the interior space of Riccardo's apartment. Rather than clarifying the site with an establishing shot, he accumulates isolated details: of Riccardo's nearly catatonic stasis, of Vittoria, and what she sees and touches; but it is not until after Vittoria peeks out of the curtained window, surprising us that it is dawn rather than night, that Antonioni suggests what has happened, the reason their glances do not meet in the montage, the reason the yet unidentified couple occupy two autonomous cinematic zones even in adjacent spaces: they are exhausted from the psychic turmoil of their nightlong decision to break up.

In a way this opening wearily parodies cinematic creation and viewing: Vittoria first appears composing a rectangular image by moving objects inside an empty picture frame; Riccardo passively sits in a chair, perhaps watching her enervated creation. It is a cinema of sterile reification.

Once the two are linked in a long shot, the reverse-angle cutting relentlessly frames them both, usually from just behind the head of one or the other, for nine of the next eleven shots. They speak without saying much. Vittoria wants to leave; Riccardo tries to hold on to her. This second stage of the episode culminates in a remarkable shot of Vittoria recoiling from her own reflected image and seeking relief from the claustrophobic intensity by opening the curtain, again to surprise us with the uncanny sight of the futuristic tower of the EUR, theatrically unveiled.

This stirs the depressive Riccardo to attempt to make love to her "for the last time," and to demand to know what went wrong. Vittoria responds "I don't know [*Non lo so*]" three times, preparing the viewer to connect her relationships with Riccardo and Piero, who articulates his exasperation with this formular response, as they discuss their feelings following their lovemaking. The lack at the core of Vittoria's self-examination resonates throughout the film. A visual composition reinforces the verbal forecast of the conversation with Piero when Vittoria, telling Riccardo "I don't know" for the third time, turns away from him. The reverse shot composes her face beside a cylindrical lampshade strikingly anticipating the framing of her encounter with Piero beside the columns of the Borsa.

Antonioni's EUR is populated by the well-off children of the owners of traditional urban apartments. It is a strange and antiseptic no-man's-land where people dwell without a sense of home. The first exterior image in the film dramatizes the irreality of the site: although we eventually realize that the film opens at dawn, when Vittoria peeks around the window curtain, we do not see what she sees until later when she opens the curtains, revealing the startling view of a futuristic, phallically shaped tower. Close scrutiny of the shot suggests that the director so wanted an image of this showpiece restaurant, rather like a mushroom cloud, that he faked the shot with a large photograph beyond the window. In any case, it immediately locates the previously interior drama in the EUR for Italian viewers.

The night of the day of the film's opening scene, Vittoria helps her neighbor, Marta, look for her dog, who has run out of the apartment. She momentarily finds herself alone outside the Palazzo dello Sport, listening to the uncanny sound of the wind turning empty flagpoles into an aeolian harp: this is the most numinous of the deracinated "things" in the film. It occurs at the very moment when a new political theme emerges—the "eclipse" of colonialism, seen not from the point of view of an enthusiast of emergent nationalism but from a perspective that locates the EUR as a refuge for an exiled colonist. This same Marta, an Italian plantation owner from Kenya, suffering because her husband does not want to live in Africa, articulates the irony of deracination in the EUR. Even the way she is introduced points out its urban strangeness. She spots Vittoria and her friend, Anita, talking in Vittoria's apartment from her window in the upper story of a nearby building. She telephones to invite them both up to her apartment. This modern, electronic neighborliness marks an implicit contrast to the woman whose apartment faces that of Piero's parents in the traditional center of the city: she peers suspiciously at the couple from the proximity of her window.

Later Vittoria calls Marta out on her balcony to shoot a little helium balloon she and Piero found on their first rendezvous. She obliges them, hitting the balloon with one shot of a rifle used in big-game hunting. This comedy occurs just minutes after Piero callously watches his sports car hoisted out of the EUR's artificial lake with the corpse of a drunk who lifted it for a joyride the night before. With a new paint job, he tells Vittoria, he will be able to sell it.

Marta's apartment is packed with photographs of Africa and trophies of game hunting. A racist and a colonist, she is ironically the only character in the film with a vivid feeling for "home." To her, black Africans are ignorant "monkeys." But Paci has astutely observed that the agents and investors at the Borsa are the ones who behave like monkeys in the film.

During the making of L'eclisse, Kenya was still a British colony despite a decade of Kikuyu rebellion. Jomo Kenyatta had just been released from prison and internal exile. The first gestures toward legislative reform were under way that would eventually bring independence at the end of 1963. Marta worries aloud that the six million black Kenyans will expel the sixty thousand whites, including her family. Almost in exile in Rome, she lives the eclipse of colonial privilege and extols the natural beauty of the African landscape in an artificial urban zone conceived as a monument to Mussolini's colonial fantasies. By 1960 Italy had just lost the last vestiges of its African empire.

Paci summed up the phenomenology of L'eclisse as an investigation of the "disintegrating" power of reification. I have condensed his argument here, omitting many descriptive passages and collateral arguments, and I have rearranged the order of his observations to follow the sequence of the film:

> The interthematic structure is extremely tight. But it's always the theme of relations with the other; it's always the problem which . . . in its simplest form poses itself as the problem of the "couple" in the phenomenological sense of *paarung*. The two subjects, failing to understand each other by effecting a mutual transfer of sense (*Ineinander*), are gradually swallowed up by things, and can no longer act upon the latter. . . .
>
> . . . Vittoria rejects endless discussion, analyses which lose themselves in *serial repetition*. In Piero she seeks a man who acts, not discusses. . . . But in him it is the lack of discussion which becomes non-awareness, the illusory freedom of his own serialization of his actions. . . .
>
> . . . Vittoria approaches things and touches them, almost trying to lose herself in them, in the now insurmountable silence. It seems as if she wants to become an ashtray or an abstract statuette, in order to escape into those unreal conversations which repeat themselves endlessly.
>
> . . . .
>
> At the end . . . the gestures of that human being who was Vittoria are no longer present: only the things remain. Again we see the whole neighborhood appear to us in a rigorous sequence in which the posthumous testimony of the missed appointment negates itself even as testimony.

In the same discussion, Paolo Gambazzi added:

> Things as I live them, or better, as I am constrained to live them in a particular context, which, in the film, is that of neocapitalism, are a kind of "negative epiphany"—an "alienating epiphany." But I want to emphasize it's not just the thing outside myself, but also the thing which returns within: not just objectivity "out there," but above all the objectivity "in here." Vittoria . . . continually repeats "I don't know": the thing, having re-entered the subject, fills it up and creates a kind of impermeability as it lives within. . . . In a word, authentic individuation is missing: I am forced to become myself, to create and individuate my self out of what is other, but not only am I forced, I have chosen to make myself a thing.

Neither Paci's seminar nor the *Il Contemporaneo* panel mention the psychoanalytical bias of Antonioni's filmmaking. Of course, psychoanalysis would have been disparaged by the PCI orthodoxy of the *Il Contemporaneo* group. The Milan phenomenologists had been more receptive to it, despite the polemics of the philosopher Banfi, a founder of their tradition, in the half decade following the war; Paci himself had written sympathetically of psychoanalysis, before and after Banfi's attacks on it as an expression of bourgeois ideology.

There had been a lively discussion of the relationship of psychoanalysis to politics which led to the founding of the journal *Psiche,* which ran from 1948 to 1952. The Rome-based psychoanalyst Cesare Musatti defended the discipline from Banfi's attacks. This same Musatti devoted the first "Quaderno di Psiche" to *Cinema e psicoanalisi,* following up a direction tentatively explored in the October 1947 issue of *Bianco e nero.* Ottiero Ottieri, a novelist I discuss in the next chapter, who often dissects the psychology of industrial work, was coeditor of *Psiche* and a co-writer of the script of *L'eclisse.* Ottieri contributed a criticism of the naiveté of commercial films about psychoanalysis to *Psiche.*

In the early sixties psychoanalytic thinking began to play an important role in Italian cultural life. Elémire Zolla's *Eclissi dell'intellettuale* (*Eclipses of the Intellectuals,* 1959) fused Freudian and Marxian ideas in a widely read analysis of the cultural crises of contemporary industrial society. By 1963 Alberto Moravia could write that all contemporary fiction could be divided into two camps: works informed by Freud and Marx, and works not. Both Moravia and Musatti introduce and dominate Pasolini's 1964 documentary on Italian attitudes toward sexuality, *Comizi d'amore* (*Let's Talk about Love*). Michel David has exhaustively chronicled this history in his *La psicoanalisi nella cultura italiana* (*Psychoanalysis in Italian Culture,* 1966).

I know nothing of Antonioni's experience or knowledge of psychoanalysis. Of the major Italian directors during the twenty years following the Second World War, he has been consistently the most fascinated by psychology and the mysteries of motivation. *Tentato suicidio* (*Suicide Attempt,* an episode of *Amore in città*), *Le amiche, Il grido,* and *Il deserto rosso* deal with attempted and achieved suicides; a suppressed episode of *I vinti* (*The Vanquished*) ended in suicide, and it may be the cause of Anna's disappearance in *L'avventura.* Bankrupt erotic liaisons motivate all of the films he made in Italy. His sole literary adaptation before *Blow Up* had been of Cesare Pavese's *Tra donne sole* (into *Le amiche*), a novel informed by the author's study of Freud. It is possible that the invitation to

Ottiero Ottieri to collaborate on the script of *L'eclisse* was stimulated by the novelist's long involvement with psychoanalysis.

From a psychoanalytic point of view, Vittoria's serial lack of knowledge, nostalgia, or memory can be traced to the loss of her father in her childhood. Actually, the potent vacuum created by the absence of her father may account for the most mysterious and puzzling moment in the film: during the finale the montage puts particular emphasis on a white-haired man, standing at the locus of the abandoned rendezvous, as if *he* were awaiting someone expectantly. In a series of shots starting with the closest—an enigmatic image of his neck and hair—and proceeding with shots progressively more distant, it concludes with a full view of the elderly man, seen only this one time in the film. The brief portrait stresses the unknown man's age, his glasses, and his interrogative posture. Of all of the unidentified figures in the finale, this man is the most demonstratively presented. In fact, there is no other place in all of Antonioni's cinema where we can find a parallel to the eccentric way in which he is disclosed within the scene.

I take this portrait as the equivalent to the confrontational encounter of Sandro with the painting of Roman Charity near the conclusion of *L'avventura;* both are disturbing iconographic cruces. Furthermore, both are emblems of the filmmaker's fascination with the ramifactions of his heroines' relationship to their fathers. In *L'eclisse,* then, Riccardo, the broker whose death indirectly facilitates the meeting of Vittoria and Piero, and this elderly man can function as figurations of the father who died in the Second World War, when Vittoria was a child. Consequently, the ambivalence she manifests toward her lovers contains an element of repetition or "revenge" when she exercises her power to leave or fail to show up. Anna wields such power most dramatically when she disappears from the island in *L'avventura;* Lidia's revenge is the most subtle when she reads Giovanni his old letter at the end of *La notte.* In this respect most of all the Antonioni heroines of the early sixties differ from the characters Ingrid Bergman played in Rossellini's films; for the existential and/or social abysses into which they would fall would always be a source of a mystical revelation, a miraculous reconciliation, or a call to Christian service.

The formal challenge of Antonioni's mature films is a sophisticated version of such "revenge" turned upon the viewer. Gilberto Perez and Sam Rohdie give us precise formulations of the mechanism of frustration and compensation in his work.

Perez:

> Like other modernist works, an Antonioni film designedly disorients us, not to promote confusion but in recognition that our accustomed ways of making sense are no longer reliable, our received assumptions about the world no longer adequate, and in the attempt to find new bearings amid uncertainty, new ways of apprehending and ordering our experience. As seen through Antonioni's camera, our everyday world gives us pause: we're kept from presuming familiarity and made to look with fresh inquiring eyes. . . . [S]o Antonioni's images render the uncertainty of modern life with elegant exactness, and thereby assert, in the face of a puzzling and precarious world, the endeavor of an arranging consciousness.[12]

Rohdie:

> The films [of Antonioni] pose a subject (only to compromise it), constitute objects (only to dissolve them), propose stories (only to lose them) but, equally, they turn those compromises and losses back towards another solidity: . . . a wandering away from narrative to the surface into which it was dissolved, but in such a way that the surface takes on fascination, becomes a "subject" of its own.[13]

If the baroque painting of *L'avventura,* the letter of *La notte,* and the slow-paced catalogue of objects that end *L'eclisse* are among such surfaces, fascinating "subjects," then the proliferation of allusions—political, phenomenological, pyschoanalytical—elicited here are less the result of competing methods of interpretation than of the complex cultural matrix reflected in Antonioni's films of the "boom." He encourages us to slip back and forth between sociological, epistemological, and psychological examinations by the very structure of his films. For example, from the first moment we see her, Vittoria attempts to make an order and sense of the things she casually encounters: with her we direct our attention to a frame, a doodle, a nudie pen; and thereby we come to understand more of her consciousness. But when Antonioni withdraws her mediating presence from the film, to follow the incurious, acquisitive Piero, he reorients the film in the direction of social criticism; and then in a still more demanding way, discarding the mediation of any character at the end of the film, he even calls into question the viewer's construction of both psychological and sociological perspectives. But at that very moment he offers first the newspaper headlines as if a political allegory were at issue, then, amid a concentration of familiar objects and occasions, the old man appears, teasing us with the possibility of a synthesizing psychological perspective only to leave us with another, enigmatic observer; and finally the burden of unresolved meaning is invested in the musical emphasis on the streetlight.[14]

Antonioni's films are the most radical examples of the aestheticizing of anxiety through ambiguity and indetermination in the Italian cinema of the second "vital crisis," the crest of the economic miracle. But they are certainly not the only examples. *La dolce vita* and all of the films by younger filmmakers I shall discuss in the next chapter share in varying degree this principle. In Italy, the stylistic flourish and the underlying anxious uncertainty of modernist forms were the cinematic projection of the superabundant affluence and the political instability of the period.

CHAPTER 8

New Wave Neorealism:
Pasolini, Olmi, Rosi

The epic films of 1960 reflected in the negative light of its moral failures the vigor with which Italian capitalism had refashioned urban life in the fifties. The scale of Fellini's ironic jeremiad, Visconti's reaffirmation of Togliattian principles, and Antonioni's dissection of the co-optation of intellectual life—here I take *L'avventura* and *La notte* as facets of a single cinematic project—indicated simultaneously an optimism about cinema's strength, as part of that industrial expansion, and an intimation of the need for what I have called baroque forms to withstand the engulfing pressure of the transformation. In fact, it would turn out that only Antonioni continued to pursue this direction; Fellini turned toward fantasy and the interrogation of his own creative history; Visconti waited until the spectacular success of Lampedusa's novel, *Il Gattopardo,* pointed a way for him to call upon his own aristocratic origins and operatic experience in a renewed critique of the historical consciousness of the Risorgimento he had attempted in *Senso*. Both the more limited scale of Antonioni's aspiration, when compared to theirs, and his assimilation of the Italian critique of the culture industry provided him with a framework for sustaining the intense energies of that historical moment throughout the early sixties in the four films he made with Monica Vitti.

In the wake of that moment a new generation of Italian filmmakers emerged who rejected the concept of the epic overview, preferring narrowly defined, regional subjects. They enjoyed freedom from the weight of the ideological heritage of the Resistance that conditioned the way their precursors responded to the postwar changes in Italian cultural and social life, and yet they saw their cinematic options defined by the stylistic peculiarities of some of those very precursors. Even in their rejection of the baroque expansiveness of the "superspettacolo dell'autore" they shared the modernist sensibilities that informed such films. Pasolini reinterpreted the postwar cinema of Rossellini; Olmi mined latent dimensions of the De Sica and Zavattini collaborations and took a great deal from Rossellini; Rosi drew upon his apprenticeship to Visconti during the filming of *La terra trema*.[1]

Accattone

Writing an introduction to Fellini's *Le notti di Cabiria*, Pasolini reflected on the social history of neorealism:

> Neorealism is the result of a democratic cultural reaction to the mental stagnation of the fascist period: in terms of literature that consisted of a substitution of a "decadent," hypotactic classicism ordered from above and implying a neat "stylistic distinction" oriented toward a *sublimis* style (in which realism, if it had a place, could be precious realism or the realism of genre) with a taste for paratactic reality, working documentary-like at the level of the represented reality, through a process of mimesis from which emerged the rediscovery of interior monologue, free indirect discourse, and a mixture of styles in which the *humilis* (or dialect) prevailed. At the basis of this literary renewal is a political renewal: and the Marxists—and those who would enter into discussion with them—formed an avant-garde.

> The prime effect of this renewal was the reemergence of an Italy that had been hidden for twenty years: the Italy of daily life, of low life, of dialect, and lower-bourgeois Italy.

> The cinema represented it first: having at its disposal all the necessary requisites for the taste of reality described above; nothing is more paratactic, mimetic, immediate, concrete, or evident than a shot. *Roma, città aperta* already had everything the essayists and aestheticians would slowly discover, theorize, and demand in ten years of study. So it turned out that necessarily in literary as well as filmic neorealism there remained a good deal of what

had been considered wiped out in a single blow as if by a miracle: you find on the neorealistic page or in the frame that there remained the fictive expansion of Pascolian linguistics, which was really a dilation of the self, and a merely lexical enlargement of the world; there remained a populist romanticism, in the De Amicis mode, if you like, which had been imbedded in the cultural layers covered and compressed by nationalistic rhetoric; there remained by deliberate choice hermetic, or decadent and classicizing, language to the extent that the poetic was a precondition, an *a priori* lyricism in handling reality.

It is useless to delude oneself about it: neorealism was not a regeneration; it was only a vital crisis, however excessively optimistic and enthusiastic at the beginning. Thus poetic action outran thought, formal renewal preceded through its vitality (let's not forget the year '45!) the reorganization of the culture. Now the sudden withering of neorealism is the necessary fate of an improvised, although necessary, superstructure: it is the price for a lack of mature thought, of a complete reorganization of the culture.[2]

This critical reevaluation of neorealism in formal and rhetorical terms became the basis of Pasolini's cinematic career. He set out to explore the "paratactic, mimetic, immediate, concrete" nature of filmic imagery and to put into question the "dilation of the self," "populist romanticism," and "classicizing language" of his precursors. Pasolini's first two films, *Accattone* (1961) and *Mamma Roma* (1963), revised Rossellinian neorealism to explore aspects of prostitution. The Merlini law of 1959 finally made prostitution a crime in Italy after decades of Vatican lobbying. The focus on that issue by parliamentary forces elicited from him an examination of the wider social context of the economics of prostitution during the "boom." Thus Pasolini's films reflect the alterations in the icon of the prostitute we would expect to see in Italian films of the sixties. The cinematic prostitute had never actually been a legalized brothel worker in the major films.[3] In fact, the brief moment of near comic relief in *Ladri di biciclette* when Ricci chases the epileptic thief through a brothel, temporarily closed for a work break, is the one representation of that institution to be seen in the films discussed in this book. The Roman prostitute of *Paisà* worked out of a rented room; the streetwalker of *La dolce vita* had her own apartment, to which Marcello took Maddalena; if we are to call Gloria Perkins of *L'avventura* a prostitute, she is both a post-1959 figure and a free-lancer.

Moreover, most of the important cinematic prostitutes appear in films I have not discussed. There is a sympathetic streetwalker in Visconti's *Ossessione* (1943) who seems to be the model for Andreina, the independent and gentle prostitute Aldo meets in Antonioni's *Il grido* (1957); for a great deal of Antonioni's film is an updating and psychoanalytically informed version of Visconti's pioneering work.[4] *Il grido*'s prostitute may have gotten her name from Adriana, the narrator of Alberto Moravia's first-person novel *La romana* (*The Woman of Rome*, 1949). The author gave her the analytical skills of Defoe's Moll Flanders[5] and the kindness of Dostoevsky's Sonia in order to refract a picture of the world of criminals, political police, and anti-Fascist students, represented by her three most regular clients, in Rome in the mid-1930s. More than any of her fictional colleagues in the cinematic tradition, Adriana is the focus of an enlarged and unhappy subjectivity that vacillates between cheerful passivity and a threatening loss of selfhood:

> "My dismay used to make my flesh creep with fear; I used to shudder uncontrollably, feeling my hair stand on end, and suddenly the walls of my flat, the city and even the world seemed to vanish, leaving me suspended in dark, empty, endless space—suspended, what's more, in the same clothes, with the same memories, name and profession. A girl called Adriana suspended against nothingness. Nothingness seemed to me something terrible, solemn and incomprehensible, and the saddest aspect of the whole matter was my meeting this nothingness with the manners and outward appearance I bore in the evening when I used to meet Gisella in the confectionery shop where she waited for me. I found no consolation in the thought that other people acted and moved in just as fertile and inadequate a way as I did when faced with this nothingness, within this nothingness, surrounded by this nothingness. I was only amazed at their not referring more often to it, as usually happens when many people all at once discover the same fact."[6]

Such existential anguish, characteristic of all of Moravia's fiction, is not to be found in the Italian cinema until it surfaces, almost a decade later, in *Il grido*, where the anguish is transferred to the protagonist, Aldo. Yet even in this case, as in his earlier film *Le amiche* (1955), Antonioni undercuts the ontological vertigo by emphasizing erotic unhappiness as the motive for suicide. In *Le amiche* he even had to recast *Tra damme sole*, Pavese's novel of a successful woman's painful alienation from her working-class origins, as a melodrama to foreground this motivation, while his visual composition, isolating figures even when they are in dialogue, smuggled the Pavesian torment of subjectivity back into the film.

Fellini's *Le notti di Cabiria* (1956) moved the icon of the good-natured and "innocent" whore from the periphery to the center of a film for the first time. In an attempt to give a more accurate picture of the world of the newly unlicensed prostitution, Fellini hired Pasolini to work on the film's dialogue. At the time Pasolini was on his way to becoming the most notorious figure of Italian cultural life, its well-publicized, hounded outsider. Born a few months before Mussolini's March on Rome, Pasolini led a dramatic and ultimately tragic life perpetually beyond the norms of Italian acceptability. He claimed that hearing a poem by Rimbaud read in school in 1938, when he was sixteen, converted him from the universal enthusiasm for Fascism. After his father was taken prisoner in Africa in 1942, he sympathized with the Azione wing of the Resistance. His more activist younger brother was a victim of the notorious massacre of Porzus, in which Communist partisans killed those of Azione in 1945. Pasolini had established a reputation as a poet and a champion of Friulian dialect writing by 1950, when he was fired from his post as a schoolteacher and expelled from the Communist party for homosexuality. He moved to Rome where he supported himself very modestly as a literary journalist (his mother, who lived with him, then had to work cleaning houses), until he began to earn more money working on film scripts.

His first major fictional work, *Ragazzi di vita* (*The Ragazzi*, 1955) was initially stopped as pornography. After a year of litigation and growing literary prestige, the tribunal relented. The interconnected stories of the *ragazzi* drew upon the author's intimacy with the subproletariat of Rome's *borgate*. In 1959 he published *Una vita violenta* (*A Violent Life*), a novel of the same milieu.

That milieu, denuded of explicit political references, constitutes the background of his first films. Fellini had offered to finance *Accattone*, but he welshed on the deal when he saw the test footage he had ordered Pasolini to show him. In a sense *Accattone* is a critique and a revision of *Le notti di Cabiria*. Accattone, whose nickname means beggar, has elevated himself to the status of a pimp when the film begins.

Fellini's Cabiria is, characteristically, the sweetest and the least sexual of the long line of generous whores in Italian cinema and literature. The pathos of her exploitation and deception ironically crosses over into the narrative of Christian redemption that the film unfolds. Even after the man she unexpectedly met after praying at the shrine of the Madonna di Divino Amore for liberation from her profession turns out to be a thief who takes all the money she made from the sale of her beloved shack, she cannot resist the redemptive lure of music and festive people. Instead of finding the petit bourgeois paradise for which she prayed, she attains unanticipated Grace in the spirit of the simple-minded lay monk who earlier had offered her spiritual encouragement.

Accattone has neither Cabiria's charm nor her innocence. He will betray his own friends for a meal (somewhat like Augusto, the protagonist of Fellini's *Il bidone*); rob his baby son, whom he does not support, of a gold necklace; force his first woman (Maddalena) onto the street with a broken leg the very day he accuses her of turning in her former pimp (Ciccio), which leads to her beating and consequent arrest; and then seduce, abuse, and exploit a second (Stella) when the first goes to prison. His virtues are limited: he feeds the jailed Ciccio's wife and children after moving into her house with Maddalena, and he is sufficiently moved by the horror Stella feels, after her first night on the street, to try to support her by manual labor or by theft.

The opening titles of the film end with the Dantean quotation of Satan to the Angel of God that took Buonconte da Montefeltro's soul (*Purgatorio* 5, 106–107):

> Tu te ne porti di costui l'etterno
> per una lagrimetta che'l mi toglie. . . .

> You carry off with you the eternal part of him for one little tear which takes him from me. . . .]

Where Vittorio Spinazzola takes the "lagrimetta" to be Accattone's saving kindness toward Stella, I find the idea of salvation by good works runs counter to both Pasolini and Dante.[7] The point of *Purgatorio* 5 is that Grace may come instantaneously at the final moment even of a life that had been immersed in sin. Pasolini, however, generally puts more emphasis on the moment of death than on the concept of sin. As the guarantee of meaning, death marks the conclusion of his 1967 essay, "Observations on the Sequence Shot":

It is therefore necessary to die, *because so long as we live, we have no meaning,* and the language of our lives (with which we express ourselves, and to which we therefore attribute the greatest importance) is untranslatable; a chaos of possibilities, a search for relations and meanings without resolution. . . . *It is only thanks to death that our life serves us to express ourselves.*[8]

The point at which the Dantean model intersects with this Heideggerian, or more precisely existential-ontological, idea of being-towards-death would be hagiography, the lives of the saints. And this may be a part of what Pasolini had in mind when he acknowledged early Renaissance painting and Dreyer's films as the primary sources of his cinematic style. Doubtless, the Dreyer film closest to his project was *La Passion de Jeanne d'Arc* (*The Passion of Joan of Arc*). His memory of the film seems to have sheared away the intricate camera movements which articulate over and over again the figure of a circle with Joan at its center (a Boethian-Augustinian theological geometry); instead, he seized upon the monumental closeups of carefully chosen "types" and the problematic cohesion of the space they inhabit to guide what he called the "sacralità tecnica" of his own initial cinematic style.

Often Pasolini pans from one speaker to another, especially when the *ragazzi* are grouped together. Sometimes the pans describe the movement of a glance. The very frontality of the shot-countershot elements and the autonomy of the panning movements suggest a distillation and an abstraction of the stylistic features of *La Passion de Jeanne d'Arc* without any obvious indication of their linkage to the original. Superficially the film bears a closer resemblance to Robert Bresson's films of the fifties because of the elliptical progress of its narrative—stressing significant accidents and relentlessly driving toward its culminating moment—and its use of a single, culturally prestigious musical source: here excerpts from Bach's *Passion according to St. Matthew* function as Mozart's C-minor Mass did in *Un Condamné à mort s'est échappé* (*A Man Escaped*) and Lully's music in *Pickpocket*. The obsessive use of questions and answers, which Rinaldi explores in his discussion of *Accattone*,[9] may be yet another outgrowth of the influence of the interrogatory form of Dreyer's film.

In 1959 Pasolini had used a similarly skewed hagiographic model to shape his novel, *Una vita violenta,* the fictive life of Tommaso Puzzilli, a *ragazzo di vita* who had been a thug for the neo-Fascist MSI and a day-dreamer of DC respectability before dying a Communist hero. So a year later, making his first film during the most troubling political crisis of post-war Italy—the summer of Tambroni's alliance of the DC with the extreme Right, amid urban riots and widespread fear of a coup d'état—Pasolini narrates Accattone's last days without a single overt reference to the political issues of the moment, as if despairing of any parliamentary solution to the situation of the Roman underproletariat. Instead, the idea of political action occurs only when Accattone attempts to start a conversation with Stella, the first time he meets her; referring to her work as a bottle cleaner as slavery, he says: "Lincoln freed the slaves. But in Italy they put it in place. If I had a machine gun in my hands, anyone would be lucky to be left standing!" Here this is only idle chatter. In the same passage there is a virtual repetition of the final speech of *Pickpocket*: "O Jeanne, what a strange path we took to find each other." Accattone says, "Eh, Stella, Stella . . . Indicheme er cammino!" (Ah, Stella, Stella . . . Show me the way!), adding ironically, "Insegna a 'st' Accattone qual è la strada giusta . . . pe' arrivà a un piatto de pasta e facioli." (Teach this Beggar the right way . . . to get to a plate of pasta and beans.) [10]

Fifteen years later Pasolini recognized two ways in which the film pointed to the "perfect . . . continuity between the Fascist regime and the Christian Democrat regime": the ghettoization of the subproletariat and the criminal violence of the police.[11] Actually Pasolini's most "political" gesture was to relocate the genre of the spiritual biography of the late 1950s (*Il bidone, Wild Strawberries, Pickpocket*) outside of the middle class. *Le notti di Cabiria* may have anticipated this, but Fellini gave his heroine middle-class values and virtues; in short, he transposed her and her world into the framework and the ideology of the spiritual biography. Pasolini's more startling achievement was to deploy the genre without altering the world and values of the criminal underproletariat.

On the most elementary level, this transposition began with the casting of the film. In fact, one of the impetuses driving Pasolini toward film-making was his frustration with the use of actors to play the *ragazzi* in two of the films he wrote for Mauro Bolognini, *La notte brava* (*The Good Night,* 1959) and *La giornata balorda* (*A Dull Day's Work,* 1960), according to his collaborator and informant on Roman dialect and slum life, Sergio Citti.[12] Citti's brother, Franco, played Accattone, and his friends from the *borgate* played the other *ragazzi*. As a first step toward his "sacralità tecnica" this form of typecasting repeated a principle of neorealism, and to some extent a strategy of both Dreyer and Bresson.

The predominance of outdoor cinematography in urban locations, coupled with a distinctively stylized repertoire of compositional and montage strategies that give the illusion of immediacy and simplicity, also distances *Accattone* from the norms of the ambitious Italian films of the late 1950s in ways that suggest a refashioning of neorealism without actually repeating the tropes of films from the 1940s. Pasolini claimed he used only the middle range 50mm and 70mm lenses to "add weight to matter, highlight the depth and the light and shadow,"[13] but there are clearly some minimal zoom movements in the finished film. Perhaps he meant that he never took advantage of the wide-angle and telephoto options of the zoom. When he told his cameraman, Tonino Delli Colli, that he wanted the image "sgranata," which could mean "open-eyed" or "peeled,"[14] Delli Colli used a "hard" film stock from Ferrania and emphasized contrast and grain by printing a dupe negative from the original master. Such rawness plays up the difference between the texture of *Accattone* and the studio polish of *La dolce vita* and the nuanced luminosity of Scarvarda's images for *L'avventura*.

But just as striking were the unfamiliar cityscapes of the Roman *borgate* in the brutal summer sun. Pasolini described the shooting conditions: "Those were stupendous days when summer was still burning in its purest form, and indoors there was hardly a lessening of its fury. Via Fanfulla da Lodi, in the middle of Pigneto, with low shacks, peeling walls, there was a granular magnitude in its extreme meanness; a poor, humble, unknown alley, lost under the sun in a Rome that wasn't Rome."[15] Pasolini punctuated this vision of an unknown Rome with a series of remarkable images: Accattone's dive from the bridge with statues of angels; his drunken, wet face covered with sand, as if in premonition of his burial; his wearing a woman's hat and placing a basket on Fulvio's head; naked babies outside the cemetery; the thieves laughing themselves sick on the curb over Cartagine's stinking feet. The film proceeds through a series of gestural moments, consciously modeled on the fresco panels of the great Florentine masters of the early Renaissance, whom Pasolini studied under the distinguished scholar Roberto Longhi.

The intense summer light takes on *thematic* importance in Accattone's dream: after following a funeral procession which turns out to be his own, he is barred from entering the cemetery. When he scales the wall, he finds only an old grave digger preparing a plot for him in the shade of a tree. He talks him into digging a little farther away so that he will lie in the light. If we take this oneiric desire for light as the "lagrimetta" that saves Accattone's soul, then the "sacralità tecnica" of the film's style coincides with the typology of light in the Dantean allegory.

The musical quotations of Bach, which inject a baroque element within an otherwise antibaroque imposition of a style derived from early Renaissance painting, suggest that the film describes the "passion"—the suffering endurance—of Accattone, his hagiographic agony unto death. Of course, Dreyer had already emphasized this *imitatio Christi* in giving his film of Joan's trial such a title. Pasolini may also have been aware of the Anselmic dimension of Bach's theological polemic in the *Passion according to St. Matthew:* that salvation comes from Christ's willing gift of His death and cannot be earned by the action of men. So Pasolini's protagonist accepts salvation in his dying words ("Mo sto bene"), but he does not earn it.

Broadly speaking there are three movements in the film: Accattone's loss of Maddalena as his source of income, his destitution and attempt to convert Stella into a substitute for Maddalena, and the finale of his passion and death attempting to support himself and her, first by manual labor, then by theft. In all three sections accidents seem to guide the logic of events: at the opening Maddalena is hit by a motorbike, and at the very end a parked motorbike gives Accattone the illusion he can escape; but in a scene structured so much like the ending of *Ladri di biciclette* it must be deliberate, the motorbike he steals becomes the agent of his death. He meets Stella for the first time, accidentally, while conniving to exploit his estranged wife. More significantly, he meets her again at the very moment he is about to reap the reward of a plot against his friends to get their share of food from a church charity.

The spoken language of the *ragazzi di vita* is so embedded with fossilized Christian oaths (themselves layered on a linguistic palimpsest of invocations to Latin gods) that the theological markers in the text are easily disguised as signs of colloquial realism. So Fulvio opens the film with a note of doom: "Ecco la fine del mondo." (Behold, the end of the world.) He carries funereally a bouquet of flowers. The *ragazzi* call his work at a flower stand "martyrdom," and the very word "work" a "blasphemy." Later, after Accattone brutally presses Stella into prostitution, he remarks in exasperation: "Madonna, fateme santo! Chè la penitenza mia già l'ho fatta! E quanta!" (Madonna, make me a saint! What a penance I've already done! and how much!)

Accattone is no allegory of Christ's mission, but it is riddled with Gospel allusions ranging from the farfetched—Accattone's meal and his dive into the Tiber wearing gold ornaments as a parody of the Temptation in the desert—to the blatant—his death in the company of two thieves. In fact, the Christological focus seems to become sharper as the film moves toward its conclusion after the repeated "falla finita" with which the protagonist announces his firm decision to keep Stella off the streets. Fulvio covers the handcart with wilted flowers as if parodying the entry into Jerusalem as Accattone banters that he is on the way to the Madonna of Divine Love (the shrine to which Fellini's Cabiria had made a pilgrimage). The night before, when Accattone had dreamed of his own death, the images literalized the parable of the shepherd: "I tell you the truth, the man who does not enter the sheep pen by the gate, but climbs in some other way is a thief and a robber" (John 10:1). Barred from entering the cemetery as part of his own funeral procession, he scaled the wall to confront the grave digger. So even in his dream Accattone subverts the symbolism of salvation, rendering any orthodox interpretation of his final justification uncomfortable.[16]

Therefore the redemptive narratives of Rossellini's Manfredi-Episcopo and Fellini's Cabiria and Augusto are less problematic than that of Pasolini's hero. Yet, Pasolini's obsession with the *via crucis* dominates all his early black-and-white films: there is the Christ-like death of Ettore in *Mamma Roma,* the film of the Crucifixion in *La ricotta (The Piece of Cheese),* the full-scale biblical narrative of *Il Vangelo secondo Matteo,* and even the parodic trinity of Father, Son, and Bird in *Uccellacci e uccellini.* But this obsession is not a measure of his piety, but almost the reverse, that is, the ground from which he argues with the Church and with the Italian tradition, from the perspective of a self-proclaimed "heretic" or "Lutheran," not in the sense of a Protestant sectarian, but a prophetic rebel.

In the middle of *Accattone* one of the prostitutes seated with the *ragazzi* when Accattone first offers Stella to a man at another table quotes Dante: "Lasciate ogni speranza, o voi ch'entrate" (Abandon all hope you who enter here) as if hell and prostitution were identical. When *Mamma*

Roma picks up the Dantean undersong of *Accattone,* it remains in this Infernal register.

A brief excursus on *Mamma Roma* will illuminate the centrality of the Dantean model for Pasolini's early cinema. The end of that film went through at least two major changes before it was shot. The treatment published in *Alì dagli occhi azzurri* lacks the recitation of Dante in Ettore's prison infirmary cell, but it has an elaborate fantasy, brought on by his fevered delirium, in which Mamma Roma magically crosses a sea and encounters an incarnation of Joy, who enacts with her a parable about a partisan and a soldier, while Ettore is being humiliated by a gang of boys.

In the published script, this complex dream, inspired probably by Bergman's *Wild Strawberries,* shrinks to a superimposed fantasy of elephants attacking and killing Mamma Roma in Guidonia where Ettore was raised, while a Sardinian prisoner recites the end of *Inferno,* canto 18. In the final film there are no dreams or delirious fantasies, but a different Dantean recitation remains: the beginning of canto 4 is quoted.

What do these changes mean? I would surmise that the contextual aptness of canto 18—at the moment of the Pilgrim's vision of panderers, seducers, and flatterers buried in feces—carried too absolute a condemnation of prostitution for a film which bestows so much sympathy on Mamma Roma, who was forced into prostitution as a teenager and whose efforts to escape and boost her son into the lower middle class are systematically frustrated throughout the film. Nevertheless, Pasolini wanted to invoke the *Inferno* within that film, rather than announce his Dantean theme with a quotation in the beginning as he had done in *Accattone.* Therefore, he substituted the more generic opening of canto 4, the first sight of hell in the *Commedia,* for the problematic specificity of 18. Yet for technical or aesthetic reasons Pasolini dropped the dream sequence from the same scene, depriving us of participation in Ettore's subjectivity and rendering his agony in prison the parallel of that earlier moment in the film when his restlessness in his mother's apartment signals his decision to steal and sell her records.

The changes in the ending of *Mamma Roma* point to three lines of convergence with *Accattone:* a moral ambivalence about their shared theme of prostitution, a pseudobiographical form that would have included an oneiric premonition of death, and a carefully chosen allusion to the *Commedia.* The dark irony of Pasolini's second, and less successful, film is that the meliorated world of the INA Casa (public housing apartments constructed in the fifties) and the petit bourgeois ethos of the reformed prostitute make up an even crueller hell than the slums. Mamma Roma's desperate attempts to keep Ettore from becoming a manual laborer, that is, her efforts to frustrate his natural class allegiances, ultimately lead to his death and her despair.

Brunetta identified the motorbike Mamma Roma gave Ettore as both a symbol for the yearning to escape from the confines of the subproletarian ghetto and as a displacement of her own desperation to escape prostitution.[17] She makes her one political statement while riding on it behind her son: in response to his statement of dislike for the middle-class waiters with whom he works—"they think they are somebodies when they have a little of their fathers' money in their pockets"—she worries that he is becoming a Communist.

In Pasolini's first films, upward mobility is a descent into hell. If Accattone is a parodic saint, he owes his salvation to the very horror of his situation; for Pasolini suggests that only the most humble and despised know salvation. Yet the cinematic genre through which he operates, the spiritual biography, had emerged in the European art cinema of the 1950s as the privileged locus of bourgeois sensitivity within alienation. But by inscribing allusions to the *Commedia* in both films Pasolini claims a pedigree for his vision outside of the immediate cinematic context.

Il posto

Displaying a cinematic originality comparable to that of Pasolini, the Lombardian, Ermanno Olmi, concentrated in his first feature films on the ways in which the new conditions of industrial labor in the flowering of the economic miracle took hold of the lives of workers. His emphasis on the centrality of work experience in the sentimental education of his young male protagonists was new in the Italian cinema; it called attention to the peripheral presence of the workplace in earlier films.

Of the fictional characters I have already discussed, Visconti's Ciro Parondi would be closest to one of Olmi's heroes. It is perhaps significant that Visconti gives him only a marginal place in his familial chronicle, as if its melodramatic mode could not adequately represent his experience. And yet he is the only industrial worker depicted in the monumental films of the "superspettacolo dell'autore": Antonioni's Sandro puts off his work estimating architectural costs throughout *L'avventura;* Giovanni Pontano resists the seductions of corporate work in *La notte;* Marcello and Paparazzo can hardly be called workers, so extraordinary are their jobs in *La dolce vita.* In all of the major films of the immediate postwar period work was significant by its scarcity (*Ladri di biciclette*), absence (*Miracolo a Milano, Umberto D*), or failure (*La terra trema*).[18] The opportunity of working was a given by the time of *Accattone:* but the *ragazzi di vita* define themselves by rejecting it, calling "work" an obscene word in the opening scene of the film.

Olmi began making films for the Edisonvolta electric company in 1953. His first feature, *Il tempo si è fermato (Time Stood Still,* 1959) focuses on the first job of a wide-eyed adolescent who is sent to be a watchman in an isolated mountain electrical station, where only one older man works with him. Daily work remains the preoccupation of his next two films, *Il posto (The Sound of Trumpets,* 1961) and *I fidanzati (The Fiancés,* 1963). These films constitute the richest and most complex cinematic contribution to the meditation prominent in Italian intellectual life on the new conditions of labor in the large corporations at the center of the economic miracle of the late 1950s and early 1960s.

The literary and intellectual context of Olmi's cinema included a theoretical discussion of the new conditions of labor in the economic miracle and a range of fictional works centering on factory production and the psychological adjustments of workers. Elio Vittorini and Italo Calvino devoted all of the fourth and some of the fifth issues (1961, 1962) of their annual journal, *Il Menabò,* to the question of "Industria e letteratura," criticizing the inadequacy of the American "slice of life" approach to the representation of the new conditions of industrial life in neocapitalist Italy. They offered the hypothesis that fiction such as that of Robbe-Grillet and the *école du regard* was a more genuine expression of the emerging situation than novels in the realistic tradition which featured workers as protagonists.

In his opening editorial Vittorini stated that "the investigation we are trying to conduct with *Menabò,* in the life of our nation 'through' literature . . . must bring us sooner or later to collect the texts which would let us see to what point the 'new things' amid which we live, directly or indirectly, . . . are accounted for in the 'newness' of the human imagination."[19] In the subsequent issue Calvino wrote of the "shock" that the industrial revolution gave literature and philosophy, changing "things, places, time," so that there are "no longer things but products, mass-produced, machines take the place of animals, the city is a dormitory annexed to the office, time is a clock, man a cog, only classes have a history. . . ."[20]

Il Menabò published essays by both editors as well as Franco Fortini, and novelists Ottiero Ottieri and Luigi Davì among others. In a lucid historical survey of "Temi industriali nella narrativa italiana," Marco Forti focused on the work of Davì, Ottieri, Testori (one of the sources for *Rocco e i suoi fratelli*), Giovanni Arpino, Luciano Bianciardi, and Calvino's stories, "La speculazione edilizia" and "La nuvola di smog." Calvino himself stressed Bianciardi and Arpino and added the work of Paolo Volponi to the discussion. Almost all of the fictional representations of industry discussed were written in the late fifties or the very early sixties.

The longest text collected in *Menabò* 4, Ottiero Ottieri's "Industrial Notebook," began by linking cinema and literature:

> *November 1954.* If fiction and cinema have given us little of the internal life of the factory, there's first of all a practical reason, which then becomes a theoretical one. The world of the factory is a closed world. One doesn't enter or leave it easily. Who can describe it? Those inside can give us some documents but not their explanation: unless they come from artists who are workers or employees, which seems extremely rare. As for artists who live outside, how can they penetrate an industry? The few that work there grow silent, for reasons of time, opportunism, etc. The others don't understand anything about it. Furthermore industry is without expression; that's its characteristic.[21]

Vittorini took exception to this in his opening editorial:

> Could the experience of the factory help a writer today more than the experience of cultivating the soil (or of hunting, fishing, herding, etc.) have helped a writer yesterday or earlier? . . . Industrial truth resides in the chain of effects that the world of the factory sets in motion. And the writer, whether or not he deals with the life of the factory, will be on an industrial level only insofar as his sight and his judgment are interpenetrated by this truth and the examples (examples of appropriation, examples of deeper transformation) that it contains.[22]

By the time his notebooks of the fifties appeared in *Menabò*, Ottieri had published *Donnarumma all'assalto* (1959, *Men at the Gate*, trans. I. M. Rawson [Boston: Houghton Mifflin, 1962]), a novel based on his experiences as a personnel psychologist for Olivetti in a factory outside of Naples. The *Menabò* inquiry was an attempt to make sense of two different, and not necessarily linked, tendencies already apparent in Italian and European literature in the initial years of the sixties: the reassertion of the avant-garde novel, now with a decided predilection for metonymy (the hyperbolic concentration on things and places as a displacement of the constitutive subjectivity of the genre), and the thematic concern with the rhythms and consequences of urban industrialization in a Europe now fully recovered from the disasters of war. The Italian rediscovery of the Frankfurt school, particularly Benjamin and Adorno, at this moment intensified the theoretical speculation of writers, such as Vittorini and Calvino, who had reached maturity in the moment of the Resistance.

Ermanno Olmi, like Ottieri, was one of the rare artists who knew industry from an insider's perspective. He worked as a clerk at the Edisonvolta offices in Milan (where his mother was employed, following his father's death during the war), before moving into the directorship of its Sezione Cinema (prior to the nationalization of the electrical industry at the end of 1962). Between 1952 and 1959 he made a series of about forty short industrial films. The last of them he clandestinely stretched into his first feature, *Il tempo si è fermato*.

The male protagonists of Olmi's first three feature films can be seen as versions of a single type at three sequential moments of entry into the work force. Roberto, who skis and plays in the snow in *Il tempo si è fermato*, is the youngest; his isolation with Natale in the mountainous outpost allows the filmmaker to explore the tensions between archaic traditions of paternal-filial succession and modern modes of employment. Natale's central speech mourning the loss of respect for elders locates more clearly than either of the two subsequent films Olmi's intuition of a troubling divergence of family life and work. Less childlike than Roberto, Domenico, the teenage protagonist of *Il posto*, enters his first job wholly absorbed in an unfocused erotic quest, yet without any preparation for independence from his parents; his very awkwardness solicits and requires maternal guidance from most of the women in the film. Giovanni, the protagonist of *I fidanzati*, is not only older and more mature than the earlier Olmi heroes; he enters the film with both a job, as a welder, and a long-term erotic relationship.

The novelist Paolo Volponi, like Ottieri, worked for the personnel office of Olivetti for many years. When he ventriloquizes the factory worker of his 1962 novel *Memoriale* (*My Troubles Began*), he gives examples of the eccentric situations of his co-workers:

> I know that one of the men who work with me has a crazy mother whom he has to lock up in the bedroom during the day so he can come to work. Another fellow I know gets drunk with his mother. He leaves his wife and goes with his mother to a tavern where they spend the evening drinking and hugging each other like a couple of drunks. Often they disappear for months, they rent a bedroom in some hotel, drink like crazy, and go to all the shows in town.[23]

· Olmi gives us a comparable picture of the eccentricities of otherwise apparently "normal" office workers in *Il posto*. Once the young protagonist, Domenico Cantoni, obtains a mail delivery position in a large company, Olmi suddenly suspends the otherwise consistent identification of the camera and editing with the perspective of the naive Domenico to give us a comic picture of the office into which he will eventually move, and even more unexpectedly the filmmaker cuts from the office to typical moments in the private lives of the clerks: there is a nearsighted man who writes a novel at night in his rented room, trying to hide the light from his landlady; another is embarrassed when a neighbor comes to the door as a woman (his wife or mistress[24]) is cutting his hair; he quickly hides the evidence of his economy; a third refuses to respond to his landlady when she tells him someone wants to buy his uncle's magazine collection, as if he were a capitalist or a mafioso; yet another sings operatic arias in a cafeteria for old people. The only woman represented in this montage suffers from her grown-up son's thefts from her purse. In Jeanne Dillon's terms: "In all, we have a failed writer, a failed bourgeois, a failed speculator, a failed singer, and a failed mother."[25]

Olmi seems to be at one with Volponi and Ottieri in suggesting that the anesthetizing regimen of the new technological industries is transforming the Italian working class into neurotically obsessive automata. Within the office of *Il posto* the individuality of the workers whose home life we had glimpsed is reduced to a range of habits and ticks: the woman is often late (presumably because of troubles with her son); Carletto, the singer, wads papers and erringly tosses them at a basket; Don Luigi, the heir to the old magazines, cuts his cigarettes in half to economize, refusing the loan of one to a messenger; the fop continually combs his sideburns; the writer fiddles in frustration with a broken desk lamp. Later, his unanticipated death creates the opening for Domenico. For Olmi, as for Volponi, these are the frightening consequences of finding a fixed place in such a system. This interlude defines the working place as a zone of mutual indifference and even suggests that its schoolroomlike formality subjugates and intimidates the spirits of its temporary inhabitants from fully functioning in the world outside.

Il posto depicts the experience of an adolescent from the suburban town of Meda in the period from his first examinations for a job in a large corporation—its name and even its function are withheld from the viewer to generalize and to emphasize the alienation of the corporate experience—to his securing a position as a clerk. His mother stresses the idea that entry into such a corporation insures employment for life, even if at low wages, inscribing a fatefulness in this mundane passage.

Olmi's debts to neorealism are so uninhibitedly acknowledged here that Millicent Marcus could write convincingly: "It is as if we were to visit the Ricci household thirteen years after the events of *Bicycle Thief* to find Antonio not only comfortably employed, but the father to two upwardly mobile sons."[26] Marsha Kinder lists a number of the film's "images that are found in *Umberto D:* the cafeteria with its cheap food, the niggardly landlady who harasses the lonely bureaucrat, and the old man with a small dog riding on a streetcar."[27] Simultaneous with these touches from De Sica, there is throughout Olmi's early work a pervasive influence of Rossellini's attention to significant details. Although he has often acknowledged his debt to Rossellini, claiming, in fact, that seeing his postwar films made him a filmmaker, it would almost seem as though he encountered Rossellini secondhand, mediated through the films of Jacques Tati, and as though he saw in the alienated eccentricity of Tati's complex observations a latent potential for recovering a Rossellinian humanism. Therefore, instead of inventing an agent of the absurd and uncanny, as Tati does in Hulot, to be seen with wonder and comic incomprehension by the society around him, Olmi posits an innocent observer at the center of a society otherwise unconscious of its own absurdity. So in Domenico, Olmi gives us a witness to the oddities of Lombardian workers and pedestrians who is not yet stamped by his own peculiar habits. Yet the one glimpse the film-maker gives us of Domenico's adolescent abuse of his younger brother—whom he accuses of appropriating his no longer needed book strap—reinforces the assumption that he will eventually transfer his domestic aggression to the office, falling into a version of the petty patterns of the older clerks who mark their working spaces with idiosyncratic obsessions and jealously guard the insignificant signs of their seniority. In telling his brother to put the book strap back in its "place," Domenico utters the first of several senses of the film's title. In Italian "il posto" means the job, the place, the seat, and even a trumpet call. Domenico's employment entails finding a permanent place for himself, and even one of the rigidly hierarchical seats in a pattern of office desks, where his routine is punctuated by regulatory signals, from the morning alarm clock to the buzzers defining lunch and work shifts and even to the ceremonial clarion of the new year.

Even though *Il posto* outlines the passage from entry to maturity in a large corporation as a numbing accommodation to meaningless routine, it mounts a formidable resistance to its own pessimism. Its originality is largely a function of the dynamics of its contradictions: in the first place, the abbreviated story of the first job is also an even more tenuously suspended story of first love. The strongest counterforce to the bleakness of the representation of corporate life, however, is the bewildered interest of Domenico through whose perspective the details of urban street life, workplace idiosyncracies, and incipient romance become equally charged occasions of comedy, mystery, and wonder. His absorption with Magali, whom he met the day they took examinations for company positions, anesthetizes him to the immanent consequences of his job. By circumscribing the film's temporal span to the liminal period between the day of examinations and the moment Domenico takes over his first desk, the filmmaker can present the theater of routine as an excursion into an odd but unthreatening cityscape through the eyes of a fresh "suburban immigrant" for whom each moment offers a new curiosity. It is this youthful curiosity that distinguishes Olmi's vision of industrial life from the bleaker fictions of Volponi and Ottieri.

According to his collaborator and friend Tullio Kezich, who plays the psychological examiner in the film, the first cut ran twenty minutes longer, developing the romance until Domenico realized, with a shock that made him ill, that Magali also went out with other men. A final scene showed him wandering around Milan and ultimately encountering a vision of the "dolce vita" as he happened upon a group of models posing in a dump.

Furthermore, within the corporation Domenico encounters women who take a maternal interest in him. These women complement the role of his mother who mediates his quarrel with his brother, buys his clothes for him, pushes him toward the security of the corporate job, and negotiates permission from his father to attend the New Year's Eve party. Even Magali, herself an innocent, takes a slightly patronizing or more mature posture toward him, as when she tells him that his "old fashioned" name suits him or when she advises him on the style of a trench coat. The women at the New Year's Eve party continue and even raise to a carnival pitch the maieutic pressure of these female presences throughout the film. They assist in Domenico's conflation of corporation life with the symmetrically structured life of his lower-middle-class family, while all of the men he encounters at work, like the men at the party, are alienated monads.

By eliminating the first ending and concluding the film with Domenico's promotion to take the place of a clerk who died, Olmi puts a new emphasis on the displacement of eros into labor. In fact, the long romantic prelude charges the pivotal scene of the New Year's Eve party with significance: as his hope for the arrival of Magali evaporates, he gives himself over to the spirit of the event. The frustrated date becomes his initiation rite as a corporate employee.

A powerful and abrupt transition catapults the party into the occasion of Domenico's promotion. From a hand-held telephoto shot of the young man abandoning himself to a snake dance with the accelerating tempo of a festive tarantella, capped by the blowing of an absurd paper party horn, the image suddenly shifts to a slow pan of clerks surrounding the desk of the man who secretly wrote fiction at night. A series of dissolves of his now empty room symbolizes his death, perhaps even his suicide. This is the culminating moment of the film: through montage the parallel stories of first love and first job converge. To be precise, the disappointment of the erotic idyll was sufficiently indicated by Magali's absence from the party. The bitter confirmation of her independent love life would have been redundant, and it would have undermined the power of the transition from disappointment in spite of the festive socialization to the fundamental displacement of erotic aspiration onto the illusion of corporate "success."

That progress within the corporation is indeed an illusion is the message of the next and final scene. When the desk of the dead clerk is cleaned—and a chapter of his manuscript is thrown into a "dead" file surely never to be claimed—the desk is given to Domenico until one of the older clerks complains. Then they all scurry to move one desk closer to the front of the room, while Domenico assumes a post in the back with a flickering lamp already familiar to the viewers from the previous clerk's ill-tempered obsession with its unreliability.

I fidanzati

Each of Olmi's first three feature films orchestrates a similar transformation of the familiar contemporary Italian environment into an anthropological travelogue by the displacement of a young worker. The elaborate montage of *I fidanzati* responds to the fictive premise that Giovanni, a Milanese welder, can advance in his trade by working for a new plant in Sicily for eighteen months. His long-distance relationship with his fiancée Liliana constitutes one primary motive for montage, often evoked by Liliana's letters; another would be the trigger of memory set off by his loneliness in a strange environment.

The revitalization of psychological montage was widespread internationally in the early sixties from the radical achievements of Markopoulos, Brakhage, Hanoun, and Mekas to the banality of *The Pawnbroker* and *The Loneliness of the Long-Distance Runner*. The earlier successes of Kurosawa's *Ikiru* (1952) and Bergman's *Wild Strawberries* (1957) and the lively discussion of Resnais's *L'Année dernière à Marienbad* (1961) in Italian film journals provided a context for Olmi's departure from the aesthetics of the long take and complex mise-en-scène that had characterized until then the best Italian cinema.

I fidanzati begins in a Milanese dance hall with a scene evoking the New Year's Eve party of *Il posto*. After delineating a state of tension between Giovanni and Liliana, who refuses to dance with him and for a while turns down another partner when he dances with a stranger, Olmi sketches the cause of their conflict through an elliptical series of flashbacks. Throughout the opening eleven minutes the music of three dances can be heard continually, although frequently with diminished volume when the very sparse dialogue of the flashbacks occurs. Only with the takeoff and landing of the airplane that brings Giovanni to Sicily does the cessation of the music signal a change of matrices. Without developing a conventional narrative continuity, and leaving many questions suspended, the montage informs us that Liliana is upset by Giovanni's acceptance of a job that will keep him in Sicily for eighteen months. His situation is further complicated by his irresolution about placing his alcoholic father in an old-age home while he is away.

I discern four sections or movements to the film. The first, as I have already noted, centers on the Speranza dance hall in Milan; the second describes Giovanni's introduction to Sicily while staying at the company hotel; the third, his adjustment to Sicily during his stay in a *pensione*, slips into the fourth, his correspondence with Liliana. Throughout the opening movement the relationship of the couple remains at an impasse: the manner of their silence toward each other and the punishing way they have of dancing with other partners indicates, through what Kinder identified as the "pseudo-iterative mode," that they have succumbed to the habit of such standoffs.

Giovanni's introduction to Sicily is at once an invitation by his biased northern colleagues to share their attitude of superiority to the rustic traditions of the natives and at the same time a lapse into infantilism, brought about by homesickness and the exclusively male company. From the moment he is driven from the airport to the hotel, Giovanni suffers an alienation from his colleagues, who discuss the engineering schools they attended (which will ultimately spark his sympathy for the Sicilians they disdain); but initially the change of environment goads his memories. When the speeding driver, complaining about the sudden danger posed by a donkey cart entering the road, calls the Sicilian an "idiot" and an "animal," Giovanni remembers fragments of his departure and Liliana running away from him.

Olmi establishes a similarity between the factories in Milan and Sicily by filming both locations with moving camera shots, rhythmically assembled in the manner of the major Soviet films from the silent period which heroicized the dynamics of heavy industry. He is by no means single-mindedly critical of the national efforts of the Cassa per il Mezzogiorno to ameliorate the economy of the South. In fact, a beautiful montage of sparks cascading from the welders' work at night constitutes labor's equivalent to the fireworks at the festival of Acireale, the carnival that climaxes the second movement and marks the turning point of the film.[28]

Yet he acknowledges that the bigotry of the engineers and managers is shared in varying degrees of intensity by the northern foremen and skilled workers, and that it is bolstered by the sometimes comic maladjustments of the natives, such as the young woman whom a secretary has to keep from bringing her entire family with her on her first day of work. When an accident occurs, a co-worker tells Giovanni with sympathy that the Sicilians refuse to wear eye goggles, and hyperbolically, that at first they didn't come to work on rainy days. On the bus to the hotel, more northerners who have been longer in the South complain of the escalating costs and talk of the Sicilians' preference for strenuous agricultural work to the more profitable factory labor. Giovanni went to Sicily with the economic attitudes and aspirations of his fellow northern workers; in the flashbacks he repeats to Liliana the clichés of his class: that "this is the chance of a lifetime," and that "others will be eager to snatch the opportunity if he doesn't take it." However, the deeper pattern of his decision corresponds to the southern experience in the political literature of the late Fascist and postwar period: Vittorini's *Conversazione in Sicilia* (1937), Levi's *Cristo si è fermato a Eboli* (1945), and Pavese's *Il carcere* (*The Prison*, 1949), the latter two narratives of politically imposed exile describe the protagonists' geographical dislocations as spiritual encounters with enduring Italian values.

More directly than Ottieri's *Donnarumma all'assalto,* which preceded *I fidanzati* in transforming the political experience of the South into one of industrial alienation, Olmi's film recaptures from those founding narratives of anti-Fascist and post-Fascist fiction the spirit of personal regeneration in the face of the poverty and starkness of the South. Although the narrator of *Donnarumma,* a psychologist in charge of factory personnel, leaves his Campagna workplace with nostalgia, he described only a growing intensification of the atmosphere of misunderstanding, bordering on violence, caused by the fantasies of the local poor that the newly located company could employ virtually the whole town. However, Ottieri's wellmeaning psychologist demonstrates none of the humorous inanity of the company psychologist who reduced Domenico to giggles in *Il posto.*

The carnival of Acireale marks the turning point of *I fidanzati.* With a group of his co-workers, led by an older executive, whose looks and behavior invokes the great comic actor Totò, Giovanni encounters in the dense, mostly masked crowd first an old man whose intoxicated collapse reminds him of his father and then a seductive young woman who spontaneously sympathizes with him because he is so far from home: "poverino [poor little thing!]," she says, "si lontano [so far away]," offering him a kiss through her veil in compensation.

The reminder of his father occasions a brief montage that clarifies, in two or three elliptical strokes characteristic of the whole film, the situation in which Giovanni had left him. Olmi cuts from the falling drunkard in Acireale to Giovanni's father rising, alcoholically dazed, on his bed. In the next shot Giovanni hands over to a middle-aged woman (we never know more about her) documents which he said he signed so that she could put the old man in a home if necessary. She tells him his father has got drunk again and there is no hope for him, but a man, presumably her husband, interjects that if they put him in the home, they will not allow him wine. His commiserating language—"the only consolation for these poor old men [*questi poveri vecchi*]" points forward to the encounter at the carnival that immediately follows the flashback. Later, through one of Liliana's letters he will learn that the father has taken to watching television instead of drinking at night, which, from Olmi's perspective, might not be a wholly optimistic transference of consolations.

The spirit of the carnival persists that night, in a debased form, at the hotel. Arriving ahead of his companions, Giovanni recalls a New Year's Eve fête at the Speranza, with the habitués in party hats, including the woman with whom he danced and the swell who danced with Liliana. But the association of the two celebrations recalls the image of Liliana sitting alone as he dances with the other woman, from the opening scene of the film. Later, the links will be clarified when another flashback reveals him swimming with and kissing the other woman, followed by a scene with Liliana who has been told of the betrayal. Olmi's subtle art refrains from conjoining the innocent, passing flirtation at the carnival directly with the allusion to the affair. The acknowledgment of Giovanni's sexual presence, and the very possibility of an erotic relationship in the South—itself a development held in common by the novels of Vittorini, Pavese, and Levi—forces at this stage a reflection on the stagnation of his relationship with Liliana.[29] With exquisite timing Olmi holds off the images of the affair until Giovanni has received his first letter from Liliana.

On the night of the carnival his companions, loud and drunk, arrive at the hotel in a donkey cart much like the one insulted during the ride from the airport. They proceed to play clumsy practical jokes on Giovanni, rattling his blinds, and attempting to get into his locked door. But when he tries to revenge his disturbance, he suffers the embarrassment of a scolding from an awakened neighbor who catches him in the corridor with a douche filled with water. Thus what I take to be the second movement of the film ends with Giovanni's infantilization. Having separated from Liliana and his father, he tentatively establishes moral bonds with the alienated community of northern managers and workers. This regression is a necessary stage preliminary to the sentimental reeducation to be founded on his unmediated encounter with Sicily in the third movement and his new vision of Liliana in the fourth.

The Tatiesque humor of the film is quickened in what I take to be the third part, which begins as Giovanni moves from the hotel to a *pensione*. A number of vignettes are structured as gags. When Giovanni wanders into a church and stays to listen to an old priest solemnly sermonizing school-children, a stray dog upsets the lesson by barking in church. As a topos of north Italian estrangement from the South, this scene has its origin in *Cristo si è fermato a Eboli*, even though Olmi has claimed it reproduces an event he witnessed in Sicily. There is a running gag on the tendency of the *pensione*'s toilet door to get stuck, and another turning around the obsession of another roomer with his radio. The accumulation of whimsi-cal observations lends a picturesque quality to other, less comic details, such as a young Sicilian rolling a truck tire through the streets, or a car with a loudspeaker offering the finder of a lost wallet the five thousand lire in it as a reward for returning the lost papers it also contained. It is in this section that the visual poem of welding sparks aggrandizes Giovanni's nightlong labor.

His landlady gives him the first letter from Liliana when he returns in the morning to try unsuccessfully to get some sleep. Instead of giving us the text of the letter, as occurs throughout the fourth part, Giovanni's memories of swimming with and kissing the woman from the Speranza follow in his silent reading of it. The memory montage includes a scene with Liliana who has been told of the affair. More saddened than angry, she asks him if he still wants to marry her. That question remains sus-pended over the rest of the third movement as we see Giovanni wander in the Sicilian landscape and enter the church where the dog interrupts the priest. The sensitive placement of the memory of infidelity and the ques-tioning of the engagement frames Giovanni's explorations as a renuncia-tion of the erotic possibilities suggested in the carnival encounter, so that the act of writing to Liliana is simultaneously a repetition of their court-ship and a positive answer to her question.

In the final movement a duet of voices holds together the most elabo-rate interlacing of images in the film. The texts of six letters, alternately recited by Giovanni (in voice-over) and Liliana (speaking to the camera), flow almost uninterrupted, as the images freely alternate from writer to reader and often become illustrations of the text. In Liliana's last letter the pattern becomes even more complex; her evocation of the history of their relationship warrants the blending of new and already familiar images of their lives in Milan. Throughout the correspondence, dancing stands as a metonymy for their sexual fidelity: Giovanni tells her that he never goes dancing in Sicily and asks her if she still frequents the Speranza. Liliana answers that she avoids it because of the malicious innuendoes of the habitués.

Both the rhythm of the montage and the textual acknowledgment that the separation has rebuilt and strengthened their love climax with the film's most conventional moment, a kiss (presumably an illustration of the past) underscored by a musical flourish. Olmi is too sensitive to end his film so banally. Following the kiss, he shows Giovanni telephoning Liliana for the first time. Their awkward conversation—we hear only Giovanni—has none of the fluidity and sincerity of the letters. Liliana needs assurance that the call does not represent a crisis or an emergency; Giovanni says little more than that he is calling before taking the bus to work because the telephone rates are half-price on Sundays, but in the space of the very short conversation he talks himself into taking the day off.

During the phone call thunder can be heard in the background. The final images of the film describe a torrential storm in the Sicilian landscape. Olmi explained the origin of this scene to Charles Samuels in terms that recall the magic of *Miracolo a Milano*: since he needed an unseasonal storm for the conclusion, he prayed to his dead grandmother to intercede for him:

> I had this crazy dream: I was shooting my last scene in a downpour so terri-fic that it was actually painful; even the trees were bending under it. I went on filming, while my grandmother looked on, happy and satisfied. Imagine how I felt when I awoke from that vivid dream to see an utterly clear sky. Nevertheless, I told everyone to get ready for work because it would rain

that day. They looked at me as if I were crazy. We went to the salt flats and worked all day, without one drop. But by afternoon a storm came. . . . With machinery you can make rain, but not a storm like that.[30]

Within the film the sudden storm functions as a natural confirmation of Giovanni's renewed spirit. Walking in the rain, instead of going to work, he unintentionally adopts the Sicilian spirit previously mocked by the northerner who had told him at first the Sicilians did not come to the factory when it rained. In the same interview Olmi glossed the moment: "Now he no longer hides from her behind the excuse of money. He makes his most beautiful declaration of love; he says, 'Today I won't go to work.'"[31]

From the opening shots during the titles of musicians and cleaners entering the Speranza dance hall, Olmi's predilection for the carnivalesque representation of odd and distinctive types is evident. The two middle-aged women who initiate the first number by dancing with each other are odd but not grotesque (as in Fellini's version of the carnivalesque). Olmi told Samuels: "I wanted to communicate my love of the ordinary things in life. I began by taking pictures of objects and people sheerly for the love of them. Shooting these pictures was a way of coming closer to the world of work that I shared with my colleagues."[32]

His loving fascination with faces and gestures and with picturesque details had to be highly developed in *I fidanzati* to sustain the burden of associative editing and elliptical narrative. Aside from the two protagonists the camera does not dwell on anyone for long, but many of the minor figures are vividly delineated: in Milan the facial expressions of the self-assured habitué who dances with Liliana and the resigned pathos of Giovanni's father are particularly striking. In the latter case, the single candid speech of a sympathetic uniformed official at an old-age home where Giovanni considers leaving his father, intercut with images of melancholy old men, verbally and visually defines the danger immanent in his passivity; so that the sole subsequent image of the father watching a neighbor's television from his apartment balcony, inserted to illustrate a letter from Liliana, encapsulates his successful adjustment to his son's absence.

A great part of Olmi's peculiar and impressive achievement in *Il posto* and *I fidanzati* was the originality with which he contextualized otherwise conventional stories of amorous longing and maturing love within the dynamics of the industrial workplace. The clarity and precision with which he records the particulars of corporate labor contribute to the impression he convincingly renders that new rhythms and altered expectations have changed the character of daily life in Italy. These films maintain an openness to the possibility that this historical turn may be engendering a crisis in the arena of personal affections; but that openness also includes the suggestion that the traditional Catholic virtues may still be able to define a meaningful life.

Salvatore Giuliano

On 1 May 1947 the Sicilian bandit, Salvatore Giuliano, and his band opened fire on a political demonstration of fifteen hundred people at Portella della Ginestra, killing eleven and wounding sixty-five. For three years Giuliano successfully eluded a massive manhunt on the island. Six months after the shooting, Francesco Rosi, a Neapolitan film student, accompanied Luchino Visconti to Sicily as an assistant director on *La terra trema*. They lived on the other side of the island in Catania and shot in Acitrezza, while the manhunt was in its initial, intense phase. Giuliano was killed in June 1950 under circumstances never adequately explained. The romance of Giuliano and the Byzantine intrigues surrounding his career, his death, and its cover-up fascinated the Italian political imagination, with criminal suspicions directed even into De Gasperi's cabinet, nearly as much as the assassination of John Kennedy has fed American anxieties, in large part because of the suspicious deaths of principal witnesses in both cases.

Rosi's 1961 film, *Salvatore Giuliano*, isolating the main points in the life and death of Giuliano and the trial of his gang members, is the prototype of innumerable documentary dramas which reenacted scenes to direct attention to unresolved problems and contradictions. Yet none have equaled its intensity and authoritative power of imagery, including Rosi's own *Il caso Mattei* (*The Mattei Affair*, 1972), where he returned to the genre he invented to examine the implications of the suspicious death, in a private airplane, of the maverick petroleum czar.

The unanswered questions surrounding the Giuliano case become in Rosi's hands the foundations for an elaborate and ambiguous narrative structure that recalls Antonioni's *L'avventura* in both the mystery at the core of its subject and in the picture it gives us of contemporary Sicilian reality. Umberto Eco, in his contribution to *Menabò* 5, "Del modo di formare come impegno sulla realtà" (trans. "Form as Social Commitment" in

The Open Work), cites the then recent *L'eclisse* to show how "Antonioni lets his forms express the alienation he wants to communicate to his public."[33] In a lengthy footnote on recent cinema, eliminated from the reprinting of the essay in book form and therefore not included in the English translation, he contrasts the formal structure of *Rocco e i suoi fratelli* to that of *Salvatore Giuliano:*

> But [the resolution of all plot contradictions into a universal order] would not account for the substantial ambiguity of a film, otherwise meritorious, such as *Rocco e i suoi fratelli:* a very real problem, vividly accented in its contradictions (considering the entrance of southerners into northern industrial culture; the adaptation of their ethical schemes to those of an urban, industrial culture . . .) turned out to be practically exorcised by an "operatic" treatment that relocated the theme in the domain of nineteenth-century narrative. Beginning, crises and problems, cathartic finale: the audience left pacified and happy. But did the director want them to be happy about anything? I don't think so. Therefore the narrative structure took the author by the hand and forced him to make, in the guise of denunciation, a film for the psychological pacification of consumers. Now take the opposite example: *Salvatore Giuliano* by Rosi. Apparently in the old realistic school, but right away the viewer becomes aware of something disturbing in this sequence of "photographs" of reality and in the continual use of the *flashback:* there comes a point when he no longer can distinguish in which phase of the story he finds himself and he gets the impression that in order to understand the film perfectly he would have to have known all the facts from the beginning better than he knows them. But the truth is that in the story of Giuliano, in the very nature of his rapport with the mafia and with the police, or of the police with the carabinieri, or of Giuliano with Pisciotta, and so on, no one knows the facts exactly. In short, the particular narrative technique devolves from the actual "content" of the film and constitutes its most important statement: an unclear story is told to the viewer by an author who is the victim of the same obscurity and who does not want to cheat him by clarifying facts that are not clear, but wants to leave all doubts intact. So the director seems to let his film be organized by the situation rather than organizing the situation through his film.

Although the film has roots in what Eco called "the old realistic school" apparently to avoid the vagueness and potential misconstruction of "neorealism," Gianni Di Venanzo photographed it in a stylized, almost mannered, version of Aldo's depth compositions for *La terra trema*, with objects or persons in the near foreground to accentuate the depth. Rosi invests this strategy with a dramatic flair: a landscape in depth has only the barrel of a bandit's gun low in the frame to indicate the frontal plane; a lawyer in the right foreground, blocked by part of a wall, watches unseen the interaction between three figures in an open doorway in the middle distance, with the bright landscape through the open door contrasting the dark interior; a long row of carabinieri stretches from the camera to the horizon of a street in Montelepre. There is hardly a shot in the film that does not set up an extreme range between close and deep. Even in meticulously reproducing the courtroom of Viterbo, where Pisciotta, Giuliano's lieutenant, and the surviving band were tried, the bars of the enclosure (*gabbione*) for the accused provide convenient foreground markers.

In Rosi's first film, *La sfida* (*The Defiance*, 1958), Di Venanzo had shot an argument between neighbors situated on different levels of the interlocking roofs and staircases of densely compacted apartment buildings in Naples, making such dynamic use of foreground and depth figures that it looked like a mannered extrapolation from the carefully orchestrated scene outside the Valastros' house in *La terra trema* which I discussed in the third chapter. In *Salvatore Giuliano* Rosi and Di Venanzo extended that tour de force throughout the entire film.

The film evidences further stylization in its dynamics and editing patterns, although these, unlike the consistent foreground and background markers, shift as the film progresses so that they work through a morphology of organizational strategies, different in each of the eleven temporal zones as the film weaves backward and forward in telling the story of Giuliano's army. For instance, the opening episode in which the police photograph and take measurements of Giuliano's body the morning after his murder, and then let the press take photographs, is a static montage, with only one moving camera shot, slowly arching from the head and arm of the corpse to his feet and back. The stasis of the montage lays emphasis on the image of the dead body, familiar to many Italians from newspaper photographs in 1950; and it is also a foil to the following episode, set in Palermo in 1945, in which the camera moves or pans in almost every shot. But when the action suddenly returns to the morning after the shooting, the now fluid camera follows the reporters as they probe contradictions in the official report, retrospectively associated with the static montage.

The fourth section of *Salvatore Giuliano,* describing Giuliano's frustration of a massive military operation to capture him in 1946, begins and spectacularly concludes with baroquely complex moving camera shots of the arrival of the forces in Montelepre and their roundup of all the men in the town, while between these two poles can be seen a midday battle in the mountains and an embassy of mafiosi who establish an allegiance with Giuliano. The starkly lit scenes on the mountain are framed by the dense chiaroscuro of the interior shots in Montelepre.

The shift to the cemetery, where Giuliano's mother will formally identify her son's body, brings us back to the temporal progression of the first and the third zones, but now sound plays a distinctive role in counterpoint to the shifts between static and moving shots. The intense keening of the mother and another grieving woman actually continues in a new register the previous section's chorus of wails mounted by the women of Montelepre, who had swarmed into the town square where the men were assembled to be trucked to prison. When the mourners actually see Giuliano's body, laid out on a marble slab, initially cooled by two massive blocks of ice, the removal of which reveals the body posed like Mantegna's and Annibale Caracci's dead Christs, the women fall silent; the camera follows in closeup the mother's caresses and kisses over the exposed flesh of the corpse until she answers the local official that it is indeed her son. Then her subdued words rise into an aria of keening.

The sixth division of the film, representing Giuliano's recruitment of new troops in 1947, introduces shot-countershot to such an extent that the viewer becomes retrospectively aware of how rarely it was used up until now. And the seventh, comprising the capture and mostly the 1950 trial of Gaspare Pisciotta and the other survivors of Giuliano's band, formalizes shot-countershot into a rhythmically insistent matrix of long shots, in depth—either from behind Pisciotta in the enclosure of the accused, or from beside and behind the interrogating judge, or from the back of the courtroom. Within the sixth part, the massacre at Portella della Ginestra is the swiftest montage in the film, even containing fleeting allusions to the Odessa Steps scene from Eisenstein's *Battleship Potemkin.* The formalism of the long shots of the trial make occasional closeups of witnesses and the culminating slow dolly up to Pisciotta more resonant.

For the rest of the film the trial will remain the center of gravity, as the morning after Giuliano's death had been for the first half of the film. Thus, the eighth segment moves from the testimony of a carabinieri colonel to the events leading up to and including Pisciotta's murder of Giuliano, and the subsequent planting of the corpse in the courtyard where the police, in collusion, had claimed to have ambushed him. But when the scene returns to the courtroom for the ninth part, the shot-countershot is frontal and closer to the speakers, without the stylized framing from behind a head. Only during the reading of the verdict—life imprisonment for Pisciotta and those active at Portella della Ginestra, acquittal for several others—does the camera freely move isolating each of the accused and then following Pisciotta as he complains that he alone saved a carabinieri colonel from execution and that he should therefore be released.

The penultimate episode illustrates his death from poisoning in prison in a series of shots characterized by their low angle. The enigmatic finale is made up of merely two shots: a long shot of a Sicilian town with the date 1960 superimposed (with the sound of gunfire everyone scatters except one fallen man); and a medium shot of the dead body of the mafia liaison to Pisciotta, sprawled out like Giuliano had been in the courtyard. Throughout the film the separation of stylistic components is not so systemic that it undermines the quasi-documentary tone; gestures from one zone will appear with considerably less frequency or importance in another, modulating and perhaps even disguising the uniqueness of the film's internal design.

Similarly, a variety of strategies mark the transitions between these eleven zones of time in *Salvatore Giuliano*. A title card distinctly divides the opening from the part it labels "Palermo 1945." Furthermore, a voice-over narrator identifies the group on a balcony above a turbulent piazza as leaders of the Movement for an Independent Sicily (MIS). But this double imposition of narrative guidance only makes the unmarked return to the police and reporters on the morning of Giuliano's death all the more sudden and disorienting, since it follows an image of a carabinieri jeep under attack in 1945, without any cinematic punctuation to soften the transition.

Each subsequent return to the past again uses a voice-over to identify the place and time. Accompanying the voice during the second flashback (Montelepre in 1946), Rosi slowly and impressively probes the landscape with a flexible zoom lens for a minute and a half. Again, the return to the "present" occurs without punctuation, now to exploit the auditory echo of the keening women. He uses a fadeout to distinguish between blocks only once: after the third flashback, which includes the Portella della Ginestra massacre, he fades before introducing a photograph of Giuliano, which soon turns out to be part of his tomb, as the camera reveals the ministrations of his mother. The voice-over hesitates, prolonging the uncertainty of the time, before declaring that it is 1950 and thus setting up the story of the capture of Pisciotta. The capture itself culminates in a montage gesture unique to the film: the image of Pisciotta emerging from a trapdoor in an attic floor when the police have surrounded him cuts immediately to one of him rising in the defendant's enclosure to address the Viterbo court.

A more complex procedure introduces the flashback of the plot to kill Giuliano which divides the long courtroom scenes. Images of two newspapers announce the imminent testimony of General Luca (the head of the special carabinieri unit created to capture bandits) and his rival Chief Inspector Verdiani of the Palermo police. Two very long shots of Luca's testimony precede an unpunctuated shift to what turns out to be the corridor of a police station, but which could be taken for a part of the same Viterbo court building since the offscreen voice of the President of the Court can be heard over the image, talking of the difficulty of determining the role of the Mafia in the carabinieri attack. The sequences that follow are so elliptical, with unmarked leaps in time describing the trajectory of the conspiracy, that it is difficult to follow the narrative without outside information on the case. Rosi had earlier used this mode of ellipsis to distance us from the intensity of the quasi-military operations of the first flashback: in a series of three attacks on carabinieri—one in the night in a small town, another on an isolated barracks in the hills, and the third against a jeep on a mountain road—without voice-over to help us understand what to expect or even what is going on, and without cinematic punctuation to separate the attacks, he synopsized the successes of Giuliano's wing of the EVIS (Army of Volunteers for the Independence of Sicily). In both instances the elliptical and puzzling narration protects the film from lapsing into a conventional crime or suspense drama.

The concluding sequences are structured to suggest conspiracies that remain undefined. Pisciotta's final courtroom speech ends with his prediction that there will have to be another trial to determine how Giuliano died and that he will then tell what he has so far held back. With this tantalizing hint the scene cuts directly to the Ucciardone prison in Palermo. From a low angle the camera tracks through a barred gate following a guard. We assume that Terranova, one of those convicted for the Portella della Ginestra killings, poisoned Pisciotta, because we see him pocketing the bottle of medicine in Pisciotta's cabinet when the guards call him to help carry the convulsive convict to the infirmary, but there is no indication of what prompted him to do so. This is the only invention of Rosi's I can detect in an otherwise scrupulously researched scenario, although the powerful cemetery imagery of Giuliano's mother kissing his corpse may be a displacement of the reports that she demanded to be taken to the courtyard where his body was found and kissed the bloodstains on the ground.[34]

The finale is even more mysterious. A direct cut from the last shot in the prison—precisely reversing the opening gesture as Terranova, taking the visual position of the initial guard, shouts to the cells above him that "Gaspare is dead!"—brings us a Sicilian town as the date 1960 in white letters dramatically flares out from the distance, as if the underweb of the conspiracies is about to be revealed. But we only hear gunfire and, in the next and final shot of the film, see a body lying prone which may be that of the unnamed Mafia liaison between Luca and Giuliano's gang, although the shot deliberately hedges a clear identification. Many Italian viewers in 1962 would remember that Benedetto Minasola, who indeed was Luca's Mafia connection, was assassinated in 1960 in San Giuseppe Jato.

A quest for accuracy of detail, which Rosi may have learned from working with Visconti, counterbalances the film's stylistic peculiarities. Rosi shot in the very houses and courtyards where Giuliano's drama occurred.[35] Many compositions re-create news photographs of the events. The actor, Frank Wolff, looks very much like the handsome Pisciotta. Many of the cast were taken from the Sicilian towns where Rosi filmed. Even fleeting background images reflect Rosi's visual research: the wall poster Giuliano made showing a chain that held Sicily to Italy severed while another chain totes Sicily to the United States, or the naive mural of a lion, symbolizing "the king of Montelepre," over his bed in his mother's house—his major concession to the fictive texture of cinema was his decision to use standard Italian, with a few Sicilian lines for inessential greetings and cries; in this too he learned from Visconti, but negatively.

He enlarged upon the *coralità* that Spitzer identified in Verga's *I Malavoglia* and which Visconti incorporated in *La terra trema* by dispersing choral effects among the reporters in the first and third parts, the women of Montelepre in the fourth, and the codefendants of Pisciotta in the trial scenes. Like Antonioni who depicted a mass reaction to Claudia's unescorted stroll in Noto, Rosi represents the otherness of Sicily through group reactions, while Olmi prefers the isolate, uncanny detail.

In contrast to this there is an unrealistic, yet nevertheless moving moment early in the film, when an elderly separatist, in a baroquely elaborate shot, incites some of Giuliano's band to fight for the freedom of Sicily, and then, as the camera follows him closely, pauses and, speaking to himself, apostrophizes the very landscape: "Sicily awake! Too long is this shameful and this sad dream in which you have lost even your honor. Now the trumpets loudly sound and you can no longer sleep, because dreaming would be death." The camera, in this long, complex shot, finally pans away from him to the mountainous landscape as he melancholically alters his rhetoric: "Roses, roses, white roses of Sicily, turn red with our red blood. But the sons, and the sons of sons will live free in a free land and they will lift their brows to the sky and smile on the future." Although Rosi shot the film with direct sound, an unusual practice in Italy, he called a few of the actors to Rome to dub some speeches, including an aged separatist especially engaged for this minor role because of the emotion he expressed every time he recited this traditional separatist hymn before the landscape. But even in the studio he could not repeat it without sobbing. Rosi gets as much of the strange power of this moment from the quaking voice as from the hymn. Then he immediately punctures its sincere emotionalism with the three violent scenes of Giuliano's campaign against the carabinieri.

Salvatore Giuliano has none of the heroic epic elegance of *La terra trema*. Visconti retarded the pace of his film to imbue it with the rhythms of Vergan fatalism, against which he slowly inscribes his own version of Gramscian meliorism. Rosi's film is antiheroic. He astutely avoided censorship by quoting court documents whenever the corruption of the state was in question.[36] There is no mention of Scelba, who was the interior minister during the search for Giuliano and who, as prime minister in 1954 (when Pisciotta was poisoned), might have had the most to lose from a scandal. Nevertheless, the film implicitly indicts Scelba and all of his allies in the right wing of the DC, at the very moment when they were making their last stand against the opening to the Left. In fact, Scelba himself would soon turn down another ministerial portfolio in Fanfani's coalition with the moderate Left. Rosi's film suggests, as no other Italian film had done, that the long hegemony of the DC was predicated upon and continually reinforced by terrorist manipulation and collaboration with organized crime.

CHAPTER 9

Conclusion

By 1963 the economic miracle had turned into a recession. In the elections that year for the National Assembly the support for the dominant DC was somewhat eroded—a fall from 42.4 percent of the vote in 1958 to 38.3 percent—with parallel gains by the Communists and the parties of the far Right. From February 1962 until May of the next year Amintore Fanfani led a cabinet including Social Democrats (PSDI), and after December 1963 Aldo Moro put together three consecutive cabinets with both Socialist and Social Democratic ministers (until the summer of 1968). Their program of reform was attended by serious inflation, frequent and crippling labor strikes, and secret contingency plans for using the carabinieri against leaders of the Left. The consequences of the spectacular and reckless building boom from 1958 to 1963 were evident both in the radical transformation of the landscape around the cities and in pollution everywhere. Moro himself undermined the reformist attempt, led by the DC minister of public works, Fiorentino Sullo, in 1962 and 1963 to curb the sprawl by ending the laissez-faire speculation in land and construction.

In 1963, for the first time, only half the population attended church. And by the early 1960s there was a television in half of all Italian homes. Both the Left and the Right decried what Paul Ginsborg called the "increased . . . tendency towards passive and familial use of leisure time, and [the decline of] . . . other more participatory and collective pastimes."[1] In a similar spirit of atomization or isolation the major Italian filmmakers were turning toward the elaboration of private fantasies and other expressions of subjective psychology. Fellini's *Otto e mezzo* (1963) was both the precursor and the most extravagant example of this tendency. Bertolucci's first two films, *La commare secca* (*The Grim Reaper*, 1962) and *Prima della rivoluzione* (*Before the Revolution*, 1964), point toward the exploration of madness and creativity that would become an obsession of Italian films. Soon after, Bellocchio would make his first film, *I pugni in tasca* (*Fists in the Pockets*, 1965). The Tavianis' first feature film, in collaboration with Valentino Orsini, *Un uomo da bruciare* (*A Man for Burning*, 1962), focused on the southern question, depicting the work and death of Salvatore Carnevale, a syndicalist murdered by the Mafia. As such, the subject would seem in a direct line with the Sicilian works of Visconti and Rosi. However, the Tavianis and Orsini freely mixed their hero's sexual and egoistic fantasies with his struggle to organize workers, making the film as much a subjectivist critique of the cult of personality as an argument for unionization—so much so, in fact, that the PCI initially repudiated it. This tendency is all the more evident with the transition to color: Fellini's *Giulietta degli spiriti* (*Juliet of the Spirits*, 1965), Antonioni's *Blow Up* (1966), Pasolini's *Teorema* (1968), and Bertolucci's *Partner* (1968) use color to intensify expressionistic portraits of psychological crises.

With characteristic prescience and speculative vitality, Pasolini theorized this tendency in his 1965 essay "The 'Cinema of Poetry.'" The thrust of Pasolini's article was historical and critical, as befitted the occasion of its initial delivery at the Pesaro Film Festival of 1964. He argued that there was a growing tendency, internationally, toward a "cinema of poetry" in which obsessive emphasis on self-conscious technical gestures indirectly represented the subjectivity of neurotic characters. He further speculates that contemporary technological jargon forces workers into using the discourse of the capitalists who own the factories where they work. He drew his main examples from Antonioni's *Il deserto rosso,* Bertolucci's *Prima della rivoluzione,* and the early films of Godard. In his analysis, Pasolini wavered between praise for the formal achievements of these works and criticism of their bourgeois themes. But this criticism was not the controversial aspect of his paper. Rather, it was the theoretical underpinnings of his critique which attracted attention.

Pasolini was an eccentric, unsystematic theoretician of the cinema, fond of speculation and at times naive in his adaptation of terms from other theoreticians or from the philosophical tradition. From the very beginning of his project, he conceived his theory as an adaptation of linguistics to cinema, and subsequently, he often found himself in polemical confrontations with the French, and especially Christian Metz. Yet we will understand Pasolini's film-historical concerns more fully if we put aside his relationship to other film theoreticians and examine the intellectual sources of his essays on the subject.

His "Comments on Free Indirect Discourse" illuminates a number of issues touched upon in "The 'Cinema of Poetry.'" Pasolini makes it clear that he wrote this essay in response to Giulio Herczeg's *Lo stile indiretto libero in italiano* (*The Free, Indirect Style in Italian*, 1963), a book on the use of indirect speech in Italian poetry and fiction which draws heavily on Spitzer's impressive essay "L'originalità della narrazione nei 'Malavoglia'" (*Belfagor,* 1956) and on the work of several Italian literary historians well known to Pasolini. What Pasolini never acknowledges is that Herczeg concludes his short volume with a series of observations on Pasolini's own novel, *Una vita violenta* (1959). Furthermore, in 1965 Franco Fortini published his collection, *Verifica dei poteri: Scritti di critica e di istituzioni letterarie* (*Inspection of the Powers: Writings in Criticism and on Literary Institutions*), which contained an ideological analysis of Spitzer's writings. Pasolini extends and elaborates his version of Fortini's critique of Spitzer in his response to Herczeg: he wants to argue that the Spitzerian position of the book (and implicitly the Spitzerian approach to his own prose) must be recast in political terms, with a linguistic sensitivity to class distinctions. Thus, he argues that free indirect discourse marks the alienation of literary Italian (the instrument of the bourgeoisie and the bourgeois writer) from the spoken dialects it tries to repress.

In the concluding pages of the essay Pasolini makes a number of daring leaps. In stressing the centrality of free indirect discourse for contemporary Italian fiction—his examples are works of Gadda, Moravia, and Morante—he stretches the term to include first-person narration: thus, *La noia* "is also a single free indirect discourse from beginning to end: and the *I* here is no more than a *he* who, in order to reanimate his thoughts better for the author, becomes *I.*"[2] Ultimately Pasolini's argument becomes political; having blurred the rhetorical distinction between free indirect discourse and first-person narration in order to assert that most of the best contemporary fiction is the free indirect discourse of an author speaking through his book, he finds that an author cannot ventriloquize outside of his own social class.

From this point the intellectual leaps become vertiginous: pop art becomes the free indirect discourse of painting; and the Italian literary avantgarde (by which he means largely the authors of *Il Verri*) have mythologized a free indirect discourse of technology, while the genuine linguistic transformation—in full gear, he claims, in the mid-1960s—escapes all linguists and literary practitioners: "the technological language of the new type of workers and bosses." Thus he bends the discussion of free indirect discourse into an essay on the problems of literary language and industrialization confronted in the *Menabò* debates I discussed in the previous chapter. But they are less our concern now than the way in which he positions his argument for an extension into film theory.[3]

Seeing pop art as the free indirect discourse of painting is the transitional step between the stylistic and rhetorical analysis of fiction and the postulations of "The 'Cinema of Poetry.'" So, he affirms that the new "free indirect subjective" tendency he observed in most of the films at the Pesaro Festival was the result of stylistic rather than linguistic developments in cinema. (Here he freely adapted Spitzer's rejection of Devoto in the Verga debate of a decade earlier, under the influence of Herczeg's revival of the issue.) The first, and most elaborate, example he gives is Antonioni's *Il deserto rosso*. When he saw the film in Paris the previous year, he reversed his judgment of Antonioni and, apparently at the same time, formulated the thesis of "The 'Cinema of Poetry'" *in nuce;* for he outlined it simply and directly in his column in *Vie nuove* on 7 January 1965:

> [Antonioni's] "liberation" . . . became possible by creating the "stylistic condition" the novels call "free indirect discourse," and which would have to be called "free indirect vision" in cinema by analogy. Thereby the author sees the world through the eyes of his character.
>
> In *Deserto rosso* Antonioni no longer hangs his vision of the world, as he had done in his previous films, on a vaguely sociological content (the neurosis of alienation): rather he looks at the world through the eyes of a sick woman. . . . By means of this stylistic mechanism Antonioni freed himself: he can finally see the world through *his* eyes, because he has identified his own delirious vision of aestheticism with the vision of a neurotic.[4]

In both the *Vie nuove* text and the more elaborately theoretical essay Pasolini specifies two traits as characteristic of Antonioni's "free indirect" style: the reframing of an object from different angles and/or at different depths, and the "abstract" composition of landscapes which characters enter and exit. The former "leads to an insistence that becomes obsessive, as it becomes the myth of the actual, distressing, autonomous beauty of things"; and the latter gives us a landscape "as if regulated by a myth of pure pictorial beauty that the personages invade, it is true, but adapting themselves to the rules of that beauty instead of profaning them with their presence."[5]

The issues animating many of Pasolini's essays of the early sixties are also at stake in *Il deserto rosso*: the centrality of factory work and its language within Italian culture of the sixties, the new class of neocapitalist managers, and the rape of the landscape.[6] Italo Calvino had addressed these issues with his stories *La speculazione edilizia* (*Speculation in Construction*) and *La nuvola di smog* (*Smog*) as early as 1957 and 1958, respectively. The former concerns the moral consequences of the largely illegal building boom, and the latter, pollution. (After *Salvatore Giuliano*, Rosi focused on the first of these topics: political corruption in the construction business in Naples is the subject of *Le mani sulla città* [*Hands over the City*, 1963].)

The narrator of *La nuvola di smog*, the alienated editor of a journal devoted to ecology (a front for the same capitalists who were polluting the environment), becomes obsessed with contamination:

> Those blackened façades of the houses, those dulled panes of glass, those human faces almost erased, that haze which now, as autumn advanced, lost its humid bad-weather stink and became a kind of quality of all objects, as if each person and each thing had less shape every day, less meaning or value. Everything that was, for me, the substance of a general wretchedness, for men like [his publisher] was surely a sign of wealth, supremacy, power, and also of danger, destruction, and tragedy, a way of feeling filled—suspended there—with a heroic grandeur.[7]

It turns to grotesque comedy when it undermines his erotic life:

> I was looking at her breasts, still those of a young girl, the pink, pointed tips, and I was seized with torment at the thought that some dust from the book's pages might have fallen on them, and I extended my hand to touch them lightly in a gesture resembling a caress but intended, really, to remove from them a bit of dust I thought had settled there.

Instead, her skin was smooth, cool, undefiled; and as I saw in the lamp's cone of light a little shower of dust specks floating in the air, soon to be deposited also on Claudia, I threw myself upon her in an embrace that was chiefly a way of covering her, of taking all the dust upon myself so that she would be safe from it.[8]

Giuliana, the protagonist of *Il deserto rosso,* has none of the ironic detachment of Calvino's journalist. The pollution and disease she continually encounters, or perhaps sometimes imagines, fills her with fear and an occasionally sexual paralysis. As Pasolini so astutely noted, Antonioni never takes us completely outside of her vision to be able to ascertain the objectivity of her observations; for even when she is not on the screen the "delirious vision of aestheticism" determines the eccentric color patterns and camera strategies. As the wife of a factory manager in Ravenna, she even lives in a modernistic apartment whose details are consonant with the factory's architecture, design, and bold color patterns. Thus the stylistic system of the film justifies Pasolini's "leap" of identifying the filmmaker's vision with the protagonist's: when Antonioni hit upon the nexus of hallucinatory neurosis and pollution, he had the vehicle for giving free range to his first color experiments, and for making gorgeous cinema of industrial ugliness.

Il deserto rosso situates itself in this milieu of strikes, economic uncertainty, and political pessimism: just as the shooting of the film was ending, Aldo Moro formed his first Center-Left government and instituted an austerity plan to deal with the shrinking economic growth rate. But more importantly, it reflects the increased role of psychoanalytic discourse in Italian intellectual life since the late fifties. Michel David's very useful book *La psicoanalisi nella cultura italiana* (1966) chronicled the increased attention to psychoanalytic issues in such journals as *Aut-Aut, Il Menabò,* and *Il Verri,* pointing out as well that Chiarini, the director of the Venice Film Festival, in which *Il deserto rosso* won the Golden Lion for 1964, described the tendency of the 1964 festival as a year of "cinema post-psicoanalitico."[9]

The plot of *Il deserto rosso* falls neatly within the pyschoanalytic parameters we have already encountered in Antonioni's work: a sexually acquisitive male (Corrado, an engineer and factory owner) encounters a woman, the center of interest, at a critical moment in her psychic life. As in *La notte,* her husband (Ugo) is tacitly complicit in her flirtation. But unlike all the previous films, the heroine is clinically neurotic.[10] Her reaction to pollution and disease is interwoven with her psychosexual fantasies and delusions.

Still, the pollution of the Po delta is a genuine ecological problem. In 1950 major discoveries of natural gas and oil in the Po region began the transformation of the Italian economy that culminated in the economic miracle of the late fifties and early sixties. The director of the natural resources trust, ENI, Enrico Mattei, gradually became one of the most powerful and independent men in Italy, publishing his own newspaper and virtually negotiating his own foreign policy. Until his suspicious death in an airplane accident in 1962, he was the most autonomous power of the left wing of the DC. He gathered a new class of professional managers, like Ugo in the film, many of them with international business degrees, to run ENI enterprises. Under his reign the Adriatic coast around Ravenna became a jungle of petrochemical refineries. Antonioni situated *Il deserto rosso* in this environment; its characters include private capitalists, ENI managers, undefined members of the managerial class, skilled workers, and their wives. Furthermore, he intensified and psychologized the chromatic distortions of the pollution in his first use of color: he had the ground spray-painted; turned the vegetables and fruit on a stand gray; shot with short focus lenses in mist, fog, and through fumes, so that actual discolorations bled into hallucinations.

From the very opening of *Il deserto rosso* we are in an infernal landscape: yellow fumes belching from a smokestack—"obsessively" reframed according to the first of the two filmic tropes Pasolini noted; striking workers enveloped in Bosch-like plastic rainwear; a dumping ground bleached gray and belching smoke, in which Giuliana devours a sandwich she purchased, compulsively, from a worker even as he was eating it.

A sophisticated chain of Dantean allusions (yet again!) connect the violated landscape to the sexual predator; the former by topological irony, the latter through an allegorical parallel. Dante wrote much of his *Commedia* in Ravenna, where he lived in exile from Florence and where he is buried. His image for the earthly paradise, Eden at the summit of the mount of Purgatory, turns on a simile to the once beautiful harbor of Ravenna. Dante described the pine forest in *Purgatorio* 28 (l.7–21) thus:

Un'aura dolce, sanza mutamento
avere in sé, mi feria per la fronte

non di più colpo che soave vento;
per cui le fronde, tremolando, pronte
tutte quante piegavano a la parte
u' la prim' ombra gitta il santo monte;
non però dal loro esser dritto sparte
tanto, che li augelletti per le cime
lasciasser d'operare ogne lor arte;
ma con piena letizia l'ore prime,
cantando, ricevieno intra le foglie,
che tenevan bordone a le sue rime
tal qual di ramo in ramo si raccoglie
per la pineta in su 'l lito di Chiassi,
quand' Eolo scilocco fuor discioglie.

[A sweet breeze that had no variation in itself was striking on my brow with
the force only of a gentle wind, by which the fluttering boughs all bent freely
towards the quarter where the holy mountain casts its first shadow; yet were
they not so deflected from their upright state that the little birds among the
tops ceased practicing all their arts, but singing they greeted the morning
hours with full joy among the leaves, which kept such burden to their rhymes
as gather from branch to branch through the pine forest on Chiassi's shore
when Aeolus lets forth Sirocco.]

Chiassi was the port of Ravenna. This Edenic locus has become the center
of the oil refineries at the mouth of the Po. The very factory Ugo directs is
surrounded by pines, but the film makes it abundantly clear that Dante's
arcadian site has become a fantasyscape of foul pollution.

I wish to bring forward the suggestion that into this inferno on the
ruins of earthly paradise, Antonioni has introduced a version of Ulysses as
he appears in canto 26 of *The Inferno*. Unlike the hero of *The Odyssey*,
Dante's Ulysses does not remain at home after his wanderings; he is instead
a false counselor who leads his men to destruction because:

vincer poter dentro da me l'ardore
ch'i' ebbi a divenir del mondo esperto,
e delli vizi umani e del valore [l.98–100]

[love could not conquer in me the longing I had to gain experience of the
world, and of human vice and worth]

He sailed beyond Gibraltar, south through the Atlantic until, within sight of a great mountain, a whirlwind drowned the ship. The mountain, of course, was Purgatory, and Ulysses' sinfulness, according to Dante, included the arrogant quest to conquer the pinnacle to which only death and spiritual grace gives access. But Antonioni, unlike Fellini, has little use for this theology. His Dante is a poet of the Italian landscape and the keen observer of psychological types. Antonioni's Corrado is the erotic adventurer of Ulysses' wanderings and the persuader who lures men to help him on his reckless quest for experience. He reveals his Odyssean lineage in a speech in Giuliana's unfinished shop, perhaps significantly on the Via Alighieri (although dialogue does not reveal that it is not named for the poet). After describing his wanderings in Italy—from birth in Trieste, to Bologna, Milan, and Bologna again—he admits: "The truth is that I don't want to stay here or there. So I've decided to leave." He avoids answering her question, "where?" Instead, he takes her on a recruiting mission where they find only the frightened wife of a worker he wants to join him. Later we discover that like Dante's Ulysses he wants to take men south to Patagonia, to the very place the whirlpool struck down Ulysses' ship, where Corrado proposes to build a factory.

He learns to take advantage of Giuliana's neurosis in seducing her. In the space where she would have her shop, he plays along with her troubled uncertainty about choosing a color for the walls, or even what to sell. He displays knowledge of exotic situations and phenomena which excite both her anxiety and her fascination: at one point he unintentionally frightens her with his knowledge of strange underwater fish. She also expresses her fear of infinity when he takes her to the radio telescope of the University of Bologna, itself a strange construction of towers filling the landscape, where he tries to lure away a worker. Yet when Corrado declares his credo to her (avoiding her direct question of whether he subscribes to the Left or to the Right)—tentative belief in humanity, less in justice, more in progress—she can temporarily repel the seduction behind it as merely "nice words." In the light of the subsequent action of the film, his bragging about his clear conscience and sense of fair play must be read as deceptive rhetoric, the language of seduction, which Giuseppe Mazzotta takes to be the characteristic of Dante's Ulysses.[11]

All around Giuliana are the visible scars of pollution and the signs of disease. A ship bearing a flag of quarantine enters the harbor; her son pretends to have contracted polio, to her panic. Giuliana's own mode of rhetoric fuses fantasy with self-revelation as she tells her son a story, illustrated by a brilliant shift of color tones. Thus, into this film of murky colors in short focus, Antonioni introduces an episode in the conventional color of a travelogue (or today, a television advertisement), with depth of focus, made striking by contrast to the rest of the film. The story Giuliana tells her son is evidently a fantasy of her own preadolescence, in an environment with none of the hellish impurities and disease she perceives around her. Yet it is also a story of the awakening of her sexuality, implicitly collapsing the oncoming of menstruation with the loss of cleanliness and clarity.

The bedside story deserves close attention in itself and for its placement in the film. The sexuality of the fictive girl, always alone on the island, is emphasized by the narrative—that she does not like boys or adults—and by the uncommented visual detail of her taking off the top of her two-piece bathing suit as she leaves the beach. In a way she too is a child Matelda, or perhaps a fusion of Matelda and Diana, in an enchanted paradise with birds and wild rabbits. But her serenity is disturbed by the arrival of a phantom ship and the subsequent disembodied female voice that lures her to explore a cove where she suddenly realizes that the rocks resemble flesh.

Thus interwoven in her story are elements of the Flying Dutchman and Ulysses' encounter with the Sirens. Like Senta in Wagner's opera and Odysseus, she is attracted by forces that would lead her to destruction. We already know that Giuliana is recovering from an automobile accident, and it seems likely, from one of her stories to Corrado, that she had attempted suicide. Thus, in her story, sexual awakening is confused with the magical ideas of erotic self-sacrifice and the quest for hidden experience and knowledge.

From early in the film we know that her "accident" has left many traces, among them her refusal of her husband's sexual overtures. In the chain of associations of this "postpsicoanalitico" film, pollution and sexuality are confused. Her fantasies of the prepubescent moment evoke a clean, ecologically harmonious landscape, but that very evocation ineluctably contains the excitement and fascination of an eroticized world of mystery, desire, and flesh.

The story seems to have a therapeutic effect on her son, who "regains" the use of his legs after hearing it. But this magical effect is actually just another indication that his illness is Giuliana's imaginative projection, and that by recounting the fantasy she has overcome the compulsion to project the image of disease and arrested growth on her son. But unlike the healthy psychological use of fairy tales Bruno Bettleheim describes in *The Uses of Enchantment,* Giuliana's story merely shifts her compulsive behavior; for the story apparently reawakens her need for erotic sacrifice, propelling her in a panic to Corrado's hotel room, where he falsely argues in order to have sex with her that he and she have similar fears and experiences. The story is further linked to the culmination of the seduction by a verbal parallel. In answer to Valerio's question "who was singing?" she said "tutti"—everyone and everything. When Corrado asks what she fears, she concludes her catalogue with "everything: the streets . . . the factories . . . the colors . . . the sky . . . the people . . . everything." Leaving Corrado in the morning she continues the pattern of the fantasy by distractedly trying to go aboard a Turkish ship.

During the seduction, the intercourse, and its aftermath, Antonioni lavished on the objects and walls of Corrado's hotel room the uncanny color effects which he had previously directed to the landscape and to fruit. This sequencing is typical of the whole film: the identification of the color effects with Giuliana's psychosexual neurosis comes *after* those effects had been posited more ambiguously in the natural world. Similarly, we see a magazine article about polio, which may have been the cause of Giuliana's panic about her son, or even her son's misguided game of simulation, *after* the event. The purpose of such hysteron proteron, of course, is to establish the identification with Giuliana's aberrant perspective before providing us with hints at its proximate causes.

The film ends with Giuliana catechizing her son, in a terminal allusion to the opening of *Purgatorio* 28 which portrayed the Edenic beauty of Chiassi as the site where little birds ("augelletti") happily sang to the dawn; the yellow fumes with which the film opened frame its closure:

Valerio: Why is the smoke yellow?
Giuliana: Because it is poison.
Valerio: Then if a bird flies into it, he dies.
Giuliana: Yes, but the birds have learned not to fly through there any more.

The opening sounds of the film had not been bird songs but the blasts of factory exhaust and the loudspeaker of a striker accosting disloyal workers within. Antonioni subtly mixed bird sounds into the industrial cacophony just as the scene was ending to make the transition to the noises within Ugo's factory more acute. The fantasy story of the enchanted island was indeed a visual and auditory "island" within the film, where the sounds of birds and the ripple of waves precede the wind driving the phantom ship and ultimately the wordless soprano voice of the Siren. Here at the end Giuliana seems to make the self-protecting birds allegorical figures for her own experience with Corrado.

Il deserto rosso is, indeed, a crucial work of the transitional moment when the works marked by the economic miracle turn toward what Pasolini identified with the "cinema of poetry." With the advantage of hindsight and the knowledge of Antonioni's other films of the sixties, we might say that on some level the filmmaker recognized that the vital crisis in Italian culture which inspired his films with Monica Vitti had passed, and in making *Blow Up* (1966) in London and *Zabriskie Point* (1970) in California he was in quest of relocating that vitality.

Nearly fifty years have passed since the earliest film in our sequence, *Roma, città aperta*. It stands virtually at the halfway point in the history of the cinema since 1895. Its concluding images of a confraternity of boys, educated by the brutalities and losses of the war and heroics of the Resistance, headed toward the historic center of Rome, once constituted an optimistic icon for the new Italian state. The "vital crisis" molded by the tensions between embedded institutions, such as the Church and the Fascist infrastructure of government and law, helped to shape a number of major films that modified, in their terminal images, that optimistic icon: the tragic destruction of the boys' alliance in *Sciuscià*, the determination of the humiliated brothers in *La terra trema,* and the humiliation of father and son in *Ladri di biciclette.* The culmination of this progressively more pessimistic iconography was the collective flight of the poor at the end of *Miracolo a Milano.*

The children of that first "vital crisis" in Italian cinema grew into the young protagonists of the second. But at the end of many of the great films by the older generation of filmmakers of the economic miracle, desperate or emotionally exhausted couples tend to replace the representatives of Italy's future. Visconti, however, seems to have chosen to reaffirm the concluding note of his earlier film, by showing Luca optimistically poised in front of posters of his brother, Rocco. All the films I have discussed of the younger generation of filmmakers, the new wave, are interesting exceptions to those alternatives: Pasolini's and Rosi's films end in death; Olmi leaves his two protagonists adjusting to the new conditions of corporate work.

Thirty years have passed since Giuliana told Valerio the myth of the precautionary birds. The Italian cinema has certainly had its share of major films since then, but no "vital crisis" has precipitated a comparable concentration of imaginative energy. During that period a number of older Valerios have acted out in films the psychic consequences of the childhood Antonioni sketched out for him. So the ending of *Il deserto rosso*, which I have selected as one postmortem to the second vital crisis—the other, *Uccellacci e uccellini*, ends my Introduction—has emblematic import in this catalogue: for once the final image is mother and son, an Oedipal rather than a religious configuration now; but the mother is a neurotic, and desperately confused, and the young icon of the future Italy has already shown his skill at making her crazier.

Notes

1. INTRODUCTION

1. Federico Fellini, *Le notti di Cabiria* (Modena: Cappelli, 1965), p. 231.

2. Gian Piero Brunetta, *Storia del cinema italiano dal 1945 agli anni ottanta* (Rome: Editori Riuniti, 1982), pp. 523 ff. Brunetta begins his discussion of the "boom" years by citing an open letter drafted by Rossellini to Umberto Tupini, the minister of entertainment, in *Italia domani* (13 September 1959) announcing the signs of revitalization and calling for support for artistic development.

3. Italo Calvino, *The Uses of Literature,* trans. Patrick Creagh (New York: Harcourt, Brace, Jovanovich, 1986), pp. 82–83, 85, 87.

4. Angus Fletcher, *Colors of the Mind: Conjectures on Thinking in Literature* (Cambridge: Harvard University Press, 1991), p. 96.

5. Erwin Panofsky, *Meaning in the Visual Arts* (Garden City, N.Y.: Doubleday, 1955), pp. 30–31.

6. René Wellek, *Discriminations* (New Haven: Yale University Press, 1970), p. 188.

7. Leo Spitzer, *Classical and Christian Ideas of World Harmony: Prolegomena to an Interpretation of the Word "Stimmung,"* ed. Anna Granville Hatcher (Baltimore: Johns Hopkins University Press, 1963), p. 24.

8. Spitzer, *Classical and Christian Ideas,* pp. 23–63, in which the discussion of birds as teachers and emblems of divine consonance is subsumed.

9. Spitzer, *Classical and Christian Ideas,* p. 28.

10. Leo Spitzer, "*Explication de Texte* Applied to Walt Whitman's Poem 'Out of the Cradle Endlessly Rocking,'" in *Essays on English and American Literature* (Princeton: Princeton University Press, 1962), p. 16.

11. See Barth David Schwartz, *Pasolini Requiem* (New York: Pantheon, 1992), pp. 486–487.

12. Schwartz, *Pasolini Requiem*, p. 488. Schwartz's translation; second ellipsis in original.

13. Naomi Greene, *Pier Paolo Pasolini: Cinema as Heresy* (Princeton: Princeton University Press, 1990), pp. 86–87.

14. Pier Paolo Pasolini, *Uccellacci e uccellini* (Milan: Garzanti, 1965), p. 210.

15. Franca Faldini and Goffredo Fofi, eds., *L'avventurosa storia del cinema italiano: Raccontata dai suoi protagonisti, 1960–1969* (Milan: Feltrinelli, 1981), pp. 404–405.

16. Pier Marco De Santi, *I film di Paolo e Vittorio Taviani*, Effetto Cinema 16 (Rome: Gremese, 1988), p. 64.

2. ROSSELLINI'S RESISTANCE

1. Nedo Ivaldi, ed., *Convegno di studi: La Resistenza nel cinema italiano del dopoguerra* (La Biennale di Venezia, XXXI Mostra Internazionale d'Arte Cinematografica, 1970), p. 9.

2. Ivaldi, ed., *La Resistenza*, p. 10.

3. See Peter Brunette, *Roberto Rossellini* (New York: Oxford University Press, 1987), pp. 28, 50.

4. Ivaldi, ed., *La Resistenza*, pp. 10–11.

5. James T. Farrell, *Literature and Morality* (New York: Vanguard Press, 1946), pp. 120–121. Reprinted with extensive revisions, including the passage quoted, from *New International* (August 1946).

6. *New International* (August 1946), p. 187.

7. Meyer Schapiro, "A Note on 'The Open City,'" *New International* (December 1946), pp. 312–313.

8. Enzo Piscitelli, *Storia della resistenza romana* (Bari: Laterza, 1965), pp. 285–286.

9. Gianni Rondolino, *Roberto Rossellini* (Turin: UTET, 1989), pp. 69, 75; Piscitelli, *Storia della resistenza romana*, pp. 286–287.

10. Rondolino, *Rossellini*, p. 76.

11. *Enciclopedia dell'antifascismo e della resistenza* (Milan: La Pietra, 1976), 3:826. See also Brunette, *Rossellini*, p. 364, note 5.

12. Roy Armes, *Patterns of Realism* (South Brunswick, N.J., and New York: Barnes, 1971), p. 68.

13. Franco Andreucci and Tomasso Detti, *Movimento operaio italiano: Dizionario biografico, 1853–1943* (Rome: Editori Riuniti, 1977), 3:656–658.

14. See Brunette, *Rossellini*, p. 44, for a summary of Amidei's criticism of the "utter conventionality" of the film's "elements of popular narrative."

15. Giorgio Amendola, *Lettere a Milano: Ricordi e documenti, 1939–1945* (Rome: Editori Riuniti, 1974), p. 185. Amendola records that the partisan struggle

in occupied Rome often took the form of such spontaneous seizures of scarce staples. He mentions the scene in Rossellini's film as illustrative of his point.

16. Angela Dalle Vacche, *The Body in the Mirror: Shapes of History in Italian Cinema* (Princeton: Princeton University Press, 1992), pp. 180–181.

17. Ivaldi, ed., *La Resistenza*, p. 11.

18. Donald Heiney, *America in Modern Italian Literature* (New Brunswick, N.J.: Rutgers University Press, 1964).

19. Gianni Puccini: "We cannot name a single film to compare to it. If you want an improbable literary comparison, think of a Hemingway born in Rome" (*Film Rivista*, 31 July 1946). Remo Borsatti: "I would not know of any film to compare with it. If you want an improbable literary comparison, imagine Hemingway born under a Roman sky" (*Fronte Democratico* [Cremona], 19 September 1943). Quoted, without comment on the nearly identical words, in *Rosselliniana: Bibliografia internazionale Dossier "Paisà,"* ed. Adriano Aprà (Pesaro: Di Giacomo, 1987), pp. 147, 157.

20. André Bazin, *What Is Cinema?*, trans. Hugh Gray (Berkeley: University of California Press, 1971), 2:34.

21. Robert Warshow, *The Immediate Experience* (Garden City, N.Y.: Doubleday and Co., 1962), p. 252; originally published in *The Partisan Review* (July 1948).

22. JoAnn Cannon, *Italo Calvino: Writer and Critic* (Ravenna: Longo, 1981), p. 22.

23. Apparently the original scenarios for Rossellini's early films only exist in fragments. The *soggetto* of *Paisà* and other surviving scenarios from the time of production were published in *Rosselliniana: Bibliografia internazionale Dossier "Paisà."* Amidei's *soggetto* had six episodes of which three—the first, the second, and the fifth—correspond to the opening three sections of the finished film. The third episode (of the outline) takes place in a makeshift hospital in Naples: a rich American nurse rededicates herself to the dying after the death of a nun, her double. The fourth episode of the finished *Paisà* has a very tenuous relationship to this story. The fifth retains only the protagonist, a Catholic army chaplain, from the outline's fourth episode, which describes the agony of conscience of a priest who killed a vicious Nazi. (The published *La Trilogia della Guerra* was made from available prints on an editing table more than twenty-five years after the films were finished.)

24. Peter Bondanella makes the interesting suggestion that this episode is a version of the third story, told the first day of Boccaccio's *Decameron* (in which the Jewish usurer Melchizedek shrewdly avoids a trap by inventing a parable in which Islam, Judaism, and Christianity are coequal heirs of a single fatherly God). His *Films of Roberto Rossellini* (New York: Cambridge University Press, 1993) was published as this book was going to press; see p. 78.

25. Aprà, ed., *Rosselliniana*, p. 152.

26. Roy Armes, *Patterns of Realism*, p. 77.

27. Brunette repeatedly contests it (*Rossellini*, pp. 67–69, 72, 369, note 8);

Dalle Vacche recognizes its precedence in foreshadowing her analysis of the body in *Paisà* (*Body in the Mirror*, pp. 184–185).

28. Warshow, *Immediate Experience*, pp. 256–257.

29. Dalle Vacche, *Body in the Mirror*, pp. 186–187.

30. Roberto Rossellini, *Il mio metodo: Scritti e interviste*, ed. Adriano Aprà (Venice: Marsilio, 1987), p. 37.

3. VISCONTI: THE NATIONAL LANGUAGE, DIALECT, AND THE SOUTHERN QUESTION

1. Janet Flanner, *Janet Flanner's World: Uncollected Writings 1932–1975*, ed. Irving Drutman (New York: Harcourt, Brace, Jovanovich, 1979), p. 249.

2. Geoffrey Nowell-Smith, *Luchino Visconti* (Garden City, N.Y.: Doubleday, 1968), pp. 51, 53.

3. Antonio Gramsci, *Selections from Cultural Writings*, ed. David Forgacs and Geoffrey Nowell-Smith, trans. William Boelhower (Cambridge: Harvard University Press, 1985), pp. 377–378.

4. Millicent Marcus aptly describes the relationship of the film to the original text as "typological" in the first chapter of her *Filmmaking by the Book: Italian Cinema and Literary Adaptation* (Baltimore: The Johns Hopkins University Press, 1993). This study, which appeared as mine was in its final stages, anticipates several points developed here. Furthermore, her emphasis on the scenes of 'Ntoni throwing the scales into the sea, the Valastro women keeping vigil during the storm, and the gossips taunting 'Ntoni after he visits the bank corresponds to my intuition of the iconographic significance of these scenes. In the first two of them there are visual echoes of traditional representations of Christ throwing the money changers from the Temple and of the Marys mourning His death, although I doubt Visconti deliberately invoked them.

5. See Lino Miccichè, *Visconti e il neorealismo* (Venice: Marsilio, 1990), for an exhaustive account of the relationship of the film to the novel and for a shot-by-shot analysis of its filmic style.

6. Nowell-Smith, *Visconti*, pp. 40, 49.

7. Visconti, "Anthropological Cinema," in *Springtime in Italy: A Reader in Neorealism*, ed. David Overbey (Hamden, Conn.: Archon, 1979), pp. 84–85.

8. The translations of the commentary are based on Luchino Visconti, *La terra trema*, transcription by Enzo Ungari, with Claudio Battistini and G. B. Cavallaro (Bologna: Capelli, 1977). The ellipses are in the text.

9. Miccichè, *Visconti e il neorealismo*, pp. 180–181.

4. DE SICA'S AND ZAVATTINI'S NEOPOPULISM

1. Charles Samuels, *Encountering Directors* (New York: Da Capo, 1987), pp. 149–150.

2. Brunetta, *Storia del cinema italiano,* p. 386.

3. Paul Ginsborg, *A History of Contemporary Italy: Society and Politics, 1943–1988* (London: Penguin, 1990), pp. 91–92. Ginsborg's splendid book appeared, first in an Italian translation, then in English, while I was working on this book. I have used it massively. Any reader without a grounding in contemporary Italian history would benefit from reading it along with this book.

4. Ginsborg, *History,* p. 149.

5. The Bersaglieri were the most noted Italian army corps.

6. Samuels, *Encountering Directors,* p. 151.

7. Monsignor Eduardo Prettner Cippico was arrested at the time of the 1948 elections for theft of jewels and documents and illegal usury. The Communist press made much of the scandal. See *Time* (22 March 1948). Amidei identifies Cippico as the secret adviser to the producer Tamburella in Franco Faldini and Goffredo Fofi's (eds.) *L'avventurosa storia del cinema italiano: Raccontata dai suoi protagonisti, 1935–1959* (Milan: Feltrinelli, 1979), p. 114.

8. Peter Bondanella, *Italian Cinema from Neorealism to the Present* (New York: Continuum, 1990), pp. 55–56.

9. Faldini and Fofi, *L'avventurosa storia del cinema italiano, 1935–1959,* p. 113.

10. Cesare Zavattini, *Sequences from a Cinematic Life,* trans. William Weaver (Englewood Cliffs, N.J.: Prentice-Hall, 1970), pp. 24–25. Buñuel parodied the idealism of the casting of *Sciuscià* four years later in *Los Olvidados,* where the cruelties and sexual tensions among street urchins confound the idealism of liberal penologists. Pasolini would reintroduce Buñuel's ugly characters and the cinematic access to their dreams in his portrait of Roman subproletarian youth, *Accattone* (1960, released 1961).

11. Samuels, *Encountering Directors,* p. 151.

12. Samuels, *Encountering Directors,* p. 162.

13. Faldini and Fofi, *L'avventurosa storia del cinema italiano, 1935–1959,* p. 113. Also quoted in Stephen Harvey's "Vittorio d.: De Sica behind the camera and on the screen," in *I Quaderni di cinecittà: De Sica* (Rome: Ministero del turismo e dello spettacolo, 1992), p. 26.

14. Cesare Zavattini, *Una, cento, mille lettere,* ed. Silvana Cirillo (Milan: Bompiani, 1988), p. 99.

15. Faldini and Fofi, *L'avventurosa storia del cinema italiano, 1935–1959,* p. 134.

16. Luigi Bartolini, *Bicycle Thieves,* trans. C. J. Richards (New York: Macmillan, 1950), p. 9.

17. Bartolini, *Bicycle Thieves,* pp. 8–9.

18. Bartolini, *Bicycle Thieves,* p. 135.

19. Pierre Sorlin, *European Cinemas, European Societies, 1939–1990* (New York: Routledge, 1991).

20. Kristin Thompson, *Breaking the Glass Armor: Neoformalist Film Analysis* (Princeton: Princeton University Press, 1988), p. 210.

21. Pio Baldelli, *Cinema dell' ambiguità: Rossellini–De Sica e Zavattini–Fellini* (Rome: Samonà e Savelli, 1971), p. 219.

22. Faldini and Fofi, *L'avventurosa storia del cinema italiano, 1935–1959*, p. 135.

23. Franco Fortini, *Dieci inverni, 1947–1957* (Milan: Feltrinelli, 1957), pp. 152–153.

24. Fortini, *Dieci inverni*, pp. 154–155.

25. Fortini, *Dieci inverni*, pp. 155–156.

26. *Cinema nuovo* 13 (15 June 1953): 362–363.

27. *Cinema nuovo* 13 (15 June 1953): 363.

28. Ginsborg, *History*, pp. 163–164. After 1953 the dynamic Mattei served as director of ENI, the state's natural resources conglomerate; he would develop and exploit Italy's oil such that he became a controversial, independent force in Italy's economy and even its international policy. (The Ravenna of Antonioni's *Il deserto rosso* gives cinematic evidence of the petrochemical industry Mattei developed. His fatal airplane crash in 1962 became the basis for Francesco Rosi's investigative film *Il caso Mattei* [1971]).

29. Ginsborg, *History*, p. 472, note 16.

30. Zavattini, *Sequences*, pp. 26–27.

5. BETWEEN THE VITAL CRISES

1. Ginsborg, *History*, p. 214.

2. See Peter Bondanella, *Italian Cinema from Neorealism to the Present*; Myra Liehm, *Passion and Defiance: Film in Italy from 1942 to the Present* (Berkeley: University of California Press, 1984); Gian Piero Brunetta, *Storia del cinema italiano dal 1945 agli anni ottanta*; Vittorio Spinazzola, *Cinema e pubblico: Lo spettacolo filmico in Italia, 1945–1965* (Milan: Bompiani, 1974).

3. Censorship prohibited the filming of the original Italian story in the three-part *I vinti* (1952) in which an MSI terrorist kills himself in a deluded act of political courage.

4. Federico Fellini, *Fellini on Fellini*, ed. Anna Keel and Christian Strich, trans. Isabel Quigley (New York: Delta, 1974), p. 63.

5. Guido Aristarco, *Neorealismo e nuova critica cinematografica: Cinematografia e vita nazionale negli anni quaranta e cinquanta: Tra rotture e tradizioni* (Florence: Nuova Guaraldi, 1980), pp. 7 ff.

6. Vittorio De Sica, "Analyzing *Umberto D*," *New York Times*, 30 October 1955, Sec. 10, p. 5. Cited in Millicent Marcus, *Italian Film in the Light of Neorealism* (Princeton: Princeton University Press, 1986), pp. 99–100.

6. ANNUS MIRABILIS

1. Peter Bondanella, *The Cinema of Federico Fellini* (Princeton: Princeton University Press, 1992), pp. 137–138. These sources are further elaborated in Tul-

lio Kezich, *Fellini* (Milan: Rizzoli, 1988), pp. 272–280, and in Federico Fellini, *Fellini on Fellini*, pp. 67–83.

2. Angelo Solmi, *Fellini*, trans. Elizabeth Greenwood (London: Merlin, 1967), pp. 154–155.

3. Elio Vittorini, "Lo sberleffo del clown," *Schermi*, no. 21 (March 1960). Quoted in Federico Fellini, *La dolce vita* (Bologna: Garzanti, 1981), pp. 192–193.

4. John Simon, *Acid Test* (New York: Stein and Day, 1963), p. 19.

5. John P. Welle, "Fellini's Use of Dante in *La Dolce Vita*," *Studies in Medievalism* 2, no. 3 (Summer 1983): 53–65.

6. Barbara K. Lewalski, "Federico Fellini's *Purgatorio*," in Peter Bondanella, ed., *Federico Fellini: Essays in Criticism* (New York: Oxford University Press, 1978), p. 114. Originally published in *Massachusetts Review* 5, no. 3 (Summer 1964).

7. Anne Paolucci, "Italian Film: Antonioni, Fellini, Bolognini," *Massachusetts Review* 7, no. 3 (Summer 1966).

8. I have used Charles S. Singleton's translation of Dante throughout from *The Divine Comedy* (Princeton: Princeton University Press, 1970, 1973, 1975, 1977).

9. Pier Paolo Pasolini, *Passione e ideologia* (Milan: Garzanti, 1973), p. 323.

10. Pier Paolo Pasolini, "The Catholic Irrationalism of Fellini," trans. Frank and Pina Demers, *Film Criticism* 9, no. 1 (Fall 1984): 68–69.

11. Pasolini, "Catholic Irrationalism," p. 71.

12. Quoted by Aristarco, *Neorealismo e nuova critica cinematografica*, p. 84. First ellipsis is Aristarco's. Aristarco footnotes Franco Fortini, *Verifica dei poteri* (Milan: Il Saggiatore, 1965; Garzanti 1974), without citing a page. I have been unable to find the passage in the 1974 edition.

13. Faldini and Fofi, *L'avventurosa storia del cinema italiano, 1960–1969*, p. 31.

14. Peter Brooks, *The Melodramatic Imagination: Balzac, Henry James, Melodrama, and the Mode of Excess* (New York: Columbia University Press, 1985), p. 5.

15. Joseph Lopreato, *Peasants No More: Social Class and Social Change in an Underdeveloped Society* (San Francisco: Chandler, 1967), pp. 75–76.

16. Brunetta, *Storia del cinema italiano*, pp. 753–755.

17. Rondolino, *Visconti*, p. 402.

18. Rondolino, *Visconti*, p. 334.

19. "Quattro domande sul cinema italiano," *Cinema nuovo*, no. 150 (March–April 1961): 135.

20. Umberto Eco, *The Open Work*, trans. Anna Cancogni (Cambridge: Harvard University Press, 1989).

21. Umberto Eco, *Opera aperta* (Milan: Bompiani, 1976), p. 228.

22. Lorenzo Cuccu, *La visione come problema* (Rome: Bluzoni, 1973), p. 23.

23. Brooks, *Melodramatic Imagination*, p. 198.

24. Seymour Chatman, *Antonioni; or, The Surface of the World* (Berkeley: University of California Press, 1985), pp. 100–101.

25. Identified in Seymour Chatman and Guido Fink, eds., *L'avventura—Michelangelo Antonioni, Director* (New Brunswick, N.J.: Rutgers University Press, 1989). Wendy Roworth had helped me to identify the subject of the painting before I had access to the Chatman and Fink annotated script.

26. Spinazzola, *Cinema e pubblico*, p. 264.

27. See Christopher Orr, "Oedipus on the Po: Antonioni's *Il Grido*," *Film Criticism* 9, no. 1 (Fall 1984): 8–16, and Jacob Arlow, "The Revenge Motive in the Primal Scene, *Journal of American Psychoanalytical Association* 28, no. 3 (1980): 519–541, for a discussion of *Blow Up*.

28. Much of this is noted by Simon O. Lesser in his psychoanalytic study of the film, "*L'avventura*: A Closer Look," *Yale Review* 54, no. 1 (Autumn 1964): 41–50.

29. See Sam Rohdie, *Antonioni* (London: BFI, 1990), pp. 65–67. There are discussions of De Chirico and Antonioni in both Cuccu and Chatman as well.

30. Stanley Cavell, *The World Viewed* (Cambridge: Harvard University Press, 1979), pp. 95–96.

31. Chatman and Fink, *L'avventura*, p. 197.

32. Pier Paolo Pasolini, *Le belle bandiere: Dialoghi, 1960–1965*, ed. Gian Carlo Ferretti (Rome: Editori Riuniti, 1977), pp. 120–121.

33. *Film selezione* (March–April 1962), pp. 10–13.

34. Alberto Moravia, *The Empty Canvas*, trans. Angus Davidson (New York: Farrar, Straus, Cudahy, 1961), p. 6.

35. *Either/Or* 1, trans. Howard V. Hong and Edna H. Hong (Princeton: Princeton University Press, 1987), p. 286.

36. Franco Valobra, "Antonioni e Godard," *Il Verri* 6 (December 1960): 143.

37. Michelangelo Antonioni, "La malattia dei sentimenti," *Bianco e nero* 22, nos. 2–3 (February–March 1961), trans. Louis Brigante, *Film Culture*, no. 24 (Spring 1962). He argues that whereas it was once valid to make a film about a man who needed and stole a bicycle, now it is important to examine "what of all the things that have happened . . . [to one's characters] have remained inside them, not so much the transformations in their psychology or their feelings, but the symptoms of these changes that occurred within their psychology and feelings and perhaps also in their morality." Quoted in Rohdie, *Antonioni*, p. 71.

7. ANTONIONI'S PSYCHOANALYSIS OF THE "BOOM"

1. Rohdie, *Antonioni*, pp. 149–150.

2. Faldini and Fofi, *L'avventurosa storia del cinema italiano, 1960–1969*, p. 267.

3. See Nöel Burch, *Theory of Film Practice*, trans. Helen R. Lane (Princeton:

Princeton University Press, 1981), pp. 45–46, for a discussion of the editing of the nymphomaniac sequence.

4. Chatman, *Antonioni,* pp. 67–68. He does not indicate whose Freudian interpretation of the film he rejects.

5. Samuels, *Encountering Directors,* p. 19.

6. "Uomini, scimmie e cose," ed. Roberto Leydi, *L'Europeo* (Milan), 22 April 1962. Carlo di Carlo published the entire transcript, "Dibattito su *L'eclisse,*" in *Michelangelo Antonioni* (Rome: Edizioni di Bianco e Nero, 1964), pp. 87–118.

7. Translation by Joan Esposito. Unpublished.

8. "Le idee e il linguaggio di Antonioni: Un dibattito sull'*Eclisse,*" *Il Contemporaneo* 47 (June 1962): 17–18.

9. Although the film seems to take place in a few days, possibly from dawn on a Thursday to dusk the following Monday, the issue of *L'Espresso* seen in the final montage appeared about seven weeks after 21 July, the date on the Borsa clock. Antonioni has telescoped the time of the film.

10. Parts of *La signora senza camelie* and *L'avventura* were shot in Rome, as were some of his short and episodic films.

11. Irving R. Levine, *Main Street Italy* (Garden City, N.Y.: Doubleday, 1963), p. 418.

12. Gilberto Perez, "The Point of View of a Stranger: An Essay on Antonioni's *Eclipse,*" *Hudson Review* 44, no. 2 (Summer 1991): 236–237.

13. Rohdie, *Antonioni,* p. 3.

14. Joan Esposito has written on the relationship of *L'eclisse* to Walter Benjamin's "dialectical images" with great insight. Although she does not make the claim, Antonioni was probably familiar with the Frankfurt school, which attracted much attention in Italy in the early sixties. The allusion to Adorno at the opening of *La notte* is evidence of this. See Joan Esposito, "Antonioni and Benjamin: Dialectic Imagery in *Eclipse,*" *Film Criticism* 9, no. 1 (Fall 1984): 35–46.

8. NEW WAVE NEOREALISM: PASOLINI, OLMI, ROSI

1. Bondanella makes a similar point: *Italian Cinema,* p. 173.

2. Pier Paolo Pasolini, in Federico Fellini, *Le notti de Cabiria,* p. 231.

3. Aldo Vergano's *Il sole sorge ancora* begins in a brothel from which the protagonist makes an escape when Nazi-Fascist soldiers enter in an initial scene similar to that of *Roma, città aperta.*

4. See Christopher Orr, "Oedipus on the Po: Antonioni's *Il grido,*" for a psychoanalytic reading; Luciana Bohne, "The Discourse of Narcissism in *L'avventura,*" for an extension of that psychoanalytic reading to Antonioni's next film; Allison Graham, "The Phantom Self: James M. Cain's Haunted American in the Early Neorealism of Visconti and Antonioni," for a discussion of the relationship of *Ossessione* to *Il grido;* and finally, John Martin, *Foutre le camp au Venezuela:*

The *Il grido* French Connection," for an alternate reading of Antonioni's film; all in *Film Criticism* 9, no. 1 (Fall 1984).

5. Cesare Pavese had translated *Moll Flanders* in 1938.

6. Alberto Moravia, *The Woman of Rome*, trans. Lydia Holland (New York: Farrar, Straus, 1950), p. 180.

7. Spinazzola, *Cinema e pubblico*, p. 279.

8. Pier Paolo Pasolini, *Heretical Empiricism*, ed. Louise K. Barnett, trans. Ben Lawton and Louise K. Barnett (Bloomington: Indiana University Press, 1988), pp. 236–237.

9. Rinaldo Rinaldi, *Pier Paolo Pasolini* (Milan: Mursia, 1982), pp. 228–232.

10. Gian Piero Brunetta, *Forma e parola nel cinema* (Padua: Liviana, 1970). Brunetta writes convincingly of the alternative goals of women and food in this film. At one point he identifies "Stella-Beatrice."

11. Pier Paolo Pasolini, *Lutheran Letters*, trans. Stuart Hood (Manchester, England: Carcanet, 1983), p. 100.

12. Faldini and Fofi, *L'avventurosa storia del cinema italiano, 1960–1969*, p. 39.

13. *Pier Paolo Pasolini: A Future Life*, ed. Laura Betti et al., trans. unspecified (Rome: Fondo Pier Paolo Pasolini, 1989), p. 19.

14. Faldini and Fofi, *L'avventurosa storia del cinema italiano, 1960–1969*, p. 46.

15. Faldini and Fofi, *L'avventurosa storia del cinema italiano, 1960–1969*, p. 40.

16. Pio Baldelli, *Film e opera letteraria* (Padua: Marsilio, 1964), and Naomi Greene, *Pasolini*, have written about the Dantean allusions and the religious theme of the film.

17. Brunetta, *Forma*, p. 108.

18. To this catalogue one could add the exploitation of migrant workers in De Santis's *Riso amaro* (*Bitter Rice*, 1949).

19. *Il Menabò* 4:13.

20. *Il Menabò* 5:85.

21. *Il Menabò* 4:21.

22. *Il Menabò* 4:19–20.

23. Paolo Volponi, *My Troubles Began*, trans. Belén Severeid (New York: Grossman, 1964), p. 16.

24. If it is his mistress, as Bondanella reads the scene (*Italian Cinema*, p. 174), it may be the affair, not his homemade haircut, he tries to hide.

25. Jeanne Dillon, *Olmi*, Il Castoro Cinema 116 (March–April 1985): 25.

26. Marcus, *Italian Film*, p. 214.

27. Marsha Kinder, "The Subversive Potential of the Pseudo-Iterative," *Film Quarterly* 43, no. 2 (Winter 1989–90): 11.

28. Samuels, *Encountering Directors*, p. 112.

29. The montage is so subtle and ambiguous that as careful an observer as

Jeanne Dillon misreads it as an affair with the Sicilian woman. *Olmi*, pp. 29, 31–32.

30. Samuels, *Encountering Directors*, p. 110.

31. Samuels, *Encountering Directors*, p. 106.

32. Samuels, *Encountering Directors*, p. 100.

33. Umberto Eco, *The Open Work*, p. 149.

34. Billy Jaynes Chandler's *King of the Mountain: The Life and Death of Giuliano the Bandit* (De Kalb: Northern Illinois University Press, 1988) provides detailed corroboration of Rosi's narrative and illuminates many things he elides. He does not comment on the accuracy of the film but judges it "too celluloid, too detached. It did not portray adequately the drama and the passion of its subject's life." Of course, Giuliano was not the film's subject; it was the political culture in which Giuliano was an instrument.

35. News photographs of the trial reveal that Rosi's Viterbo courtroom is a set, but a very accurate one. I have not been able to determine the authenticity of the prison of Palermo. The film historian Lino Micciché assures me that it is a set.

36. He had to cut only some images of Giuliano's naked corpse and a shot of a carabiniere hitting a woman with the butt of his rifle.

9. CONCLUSION

1. Ginsborg, *History*, p. 242.

2. Pasolini, *Heretical Empiricism*, p. 90.

3. See Greene, *Pasolini*, pp. 115 ff., for an illuminating discussion of the relationship of this essay to Bakhtin and Deleuze.

4. Pier Paolo Pasolini, *La belle bandiere*, p. 284.

5. Pasolini, *Heretical Empiricism*, p. 179. The same words are to be found in the *Vie nuove* letter.

6. Significantly, Paul Ginsborg turns to Pasolini for a concise image of the pollution problem: "It was Pasolini . . . who provided the strongest image of an Italy that was changing for the worse, an Italy where the old values, dialects, and traditions were being destroyed for ever. The fireflies, wrote Pasolini, had disappeared: 'In the early 60s, with the pollution of the air, and above all in the countryside with the pollution of the water . . . the fireflies began to disappear. The phenomenon was as rapid as lightning. After a few years they were not there anymore.'" (*History*, p. 249).

7. Italo Calvino, "Smog," trans. William Weaver, in *The Watcher and Other Stories* (New York: Harcourt, Brace, Jovanovich, 1971), p. 95.

8. Calvino, "Smog," p. 112.

9. Michel David, *La psicoanalisi nella cultura italiana* (Turin: Borighieri, 1970), p. 589.

10. William Arrowsmith insists that the film "is not a story of neurosis, but an account of individuation," in "Antonioni's 'Red Desert': Myth and Fantasy," in

The Binding of Proteus: Perspectives on Myth and the Literary Process, ed. Marjorie W. McCune, Tucker Orbison, and Philip M. Withim (Lewisburg, Pa.: Bucknell University Press, 1980), p. 313.

11. Giuseppe Mazzotta, *Dante, Poet of the Desert: History and Allegory in "The Divine Comedy"* (Princeton: Princeton University Press, 1979).

Index

Gramsci, Antonio, 61–63, 130–131, 206
Grant, Cary, 93
Greene, Naomi, 10, 24
Guerra, Tonino, 146
Gullace, Maria Teresa, 34–35, 43

Hay, James, 37
Hemingway, Ernest, 44, 223n
Herczeg, Giulio, 209–210

Ingrao, Pietro, 3, 30
Interlenghi, Franco, 87

John XXIII (Pope), 7
Joyce, James, 122, 133

Kafka, Franz, 122
Kenjatta, Jomo, 166
Kezich, Tullio, 190
Khrushchev, Nikita, 3, 158
Kierkegaard, Søren, 121, 141–142
Kinder, Marsha, 189, 193
Koch, Piero, 34

La Pira, Girogio, 110
Lampedusa, Giuseppe Tomasso de, 172
Levi, Carlo, 155, 195; *Christo si é fermato a Eboli*, 44, 123, 194, 196; *L'orologio*, 45
Lewalski, Barbara, 112–113
Liehm, Mira, 10
Lizzani, Carlo, 90
Longhi, Roberto, 10, 180
Lopreato, Joseph, 128
Lukács, Georg, 122, 155

Mafia, 59–61, 65, 204–205
Magnani, Anna, 4, 39, 105, 108

Magnano, Silvana, 103, 108
Malaparte, Curzio, 55
Mann, Klaus, 48
Mann, Thomas, 122
Mantegna, Andrea, 202
Manzoni, Alessandro, 63
Maraini, Dacia, 56
Marcus, Millicent, 10, 189, 224n
Martelli, Otello, 113
Marx, Karl, 19–21, 66, 105, 168
Massina, Giulietta, 144, 146
Mastroianni, Marcello, 146, 153, 162
Mattei, Enrico, 98–99, 103, 213, 226n
Mazzotta, Giuseppe, 215
Méliés, Georges, 100–101
Menabó, Il, 158, 185–187, 199–200, 210, 212
Metz, Christian, 209
Micciché, Lino, 10, 76–77
Michi, Maria, 34, 103
Michietti, Francesco Paolo, 71
Mida [Puccini], Massimo, 3, 105
Minasola, Benedetto, 205
Montale, Eugenio, 42
Morandi, Giorgio, 115
Morante, Elsa, 209
Moravia, Alberto, 30, 43, 168, 209; *La noia*, 90, 133, 140–142, 209; *La romana*, 175
Moreau, Jeanne, 145–146, 162
Moro, Aldo, 207, 212
Morosini, Giuseppe, 30, 34, 43
MSI (Movimento Sociale Italiano), 59, 105, 110, 160, 179, 226n
Musati, Cesare, 168
Mussolini, Benito, 14, 28, 59, 77, 102, 106, 159, 176
Mussolini, Vittorio, 3

Napoli, Tomasso Maria, 138
Negarville, Celeste, 34–35, 43
Ninchi, Annibale, 120

Vittorini, Elio, 29, 43–45, 102, 111, 157, 185–187, 194
Vizzini, Don Calogero, 60
Volpone, Paolo, 186, *Memoriale*, 188, 190

Wagner, Richard, 216
Warshow, Robert, 45, 55–56
Weill, Kurt, 14
Welle, John P., 112

Wellek, René, 16
Whitman, Walt, 16, 19
Wolff, Frank, 205

Zampa, Luigi, 29
Zavattini, Cesare, 4, 9, 11, 26, 57, 79–81, 85–89, 91, 96–98, 100–101, 105–107, 173; *Amore in cittá*, 107
Zolla, Elémire, 168